Murder and
Politics
in Colonial Ghana

Murder and Politics
in Colonial Ghana

Richard Rathbone

Yale University Press
New Haven & London 1993

Set in Baskerville by Best-set Typesetter Ltd., Hong Kong,
and printed and bound in Great Britain
by St Edmundsbury Press

Library of Congress Cataloging-in-Publication Data
Rathbone, Richard
Murder and politics in colonial Ghana / by Richard Rathbone
p. cm.
Includes bibliographical references and index.
ISBN 0-300-05504-8 (alk. paper)
1. Murder—Ghana—Kibi. 2. Trials (Murder)—Ghana—
Kibi. 3. Mensah, Akyes, d. 1944. 4. Akan (African
people)—Ghana—Kibi—Funeral customs and rites.
5. Kibi (Ghana)—Politics and government. I. Title.
HV8535.G343.K527 1993
384.1′523′09667—dc20   92-44866
                                                                                   CIP

A catalogue record for this book is available from the
British Library.

'Although it is not always nice to repeat history, it must be remembered that any Stool or family without tradition loses its intrinsic value. It is utmost essential that Akyem Abuakwa shall have its history retained in print for the benefit of the present and future generations.'

– Okyenhene Nana Sir Ofori Atta I to all
Akyem Abuakwa chiefs, 19 December 1925
(Akyem Abuakwa State Archives, 3/266)

Contents

List of Illustrations

Preface

At the heart of this book are several interwoven stories about the disgrace of an African royal family, the decline of a great African state and then the dismal twilight of the career of one of Britain's most progressive colonial governors. These accounts attracted me long ago. Then, as now, I was working on the interplay of African nationalism and colonialism in what became the independent state of Ghana. What emerged was a straightforward if complex narrative. But beneath that formally documented exterior lay an unwritten-up but intriguing cat's cradle of histories which hinted at personal feuds, sectional ambitions, scandals and secrets. However good these stories were, their wider significance could only be guessed at by a young research student, even if many of my oral informants insisted that their inside information was a better explanation of this or that event than the documents provided.

The intellectual environment of the mid-1960s was very receptive to conspiracy theories; but the 'rules' of historical evidence, which students must respect, controlled my tendency to wild speculation and insisted, very properly, on the full documentation of argument. But like many research students, I 'knew' more than I set down in the eventual thesis.[1]

One of the most persistent stories I heard was that of the 'Kibi murder'. The secondary material suggested that it was important. For reasons which will become obvious, the Gold Coast's Governor from 1941 to 1947, Sir Alan Burns, devoted many pages to this in his valuable memoirs.[2] Interviewing him twenty years after the events and in an atmosphere far removed from the bustle of Ghana,[3] that obsessional concern was repeated, making it hard for me to steer our conversations back to issues such as constitutional reform.

In his autobiography[4] Kwame Nkrumah, the Gold Coast's first Prince Minister and Ghana's first President, described the case and his

---

1 'The Transfer of Power in Ghana', unpublished Ph.D thesis (University of London, 1968).
2 *Colonial Civil Servant* (London, 1949).
3 In the library of the Athenaeum Club.
4 *Ghana; an Autobiography* (London, 1957).

view of its importance to the motivation of a group of politicians he had come to dislike greatly. On the only occasion I ever spoke to him, he gave the case prominence in his analysis of why older and more moderate nationalists had become more radical after 1946. Dennis Austin's magisterial *Politics in Ghana*,[5] which remains the major source on Ghanaian political history in the 1940s and 1950s, also touches on it, although it is tucked away in a long footnote.

At that time I had no access to the unpublished official documentation in London;[6] like other researchers I used newspapers to fill some of this gap. The Gold Coast press from 1944 to 1950 was haunted by the case. To my surprise it also commanded many column inches in the British press at a time when colonial matters were rarely touched upon. In Ghana, a more permissive regime at the National Archives than that of the British Public Record Office allowed me to get closer to the case, which was frequently discussed in the country's ruling Executive Council, whose minutes I could consult. The salience of the case was, moreover, pressed upon me again and again by the many veteran Ghanaian politicians who have been kind enough to share their memories during my research periods in Ghana.

In the event my final coverage of the case in the thesis was both short – only five pages – and limited to its implications for the relationship between some of the Gold Coast's nationalists and the Governor. I knew too little to be able to address the more complex questions about what the case might have meant. And there it rested. But in 1987 I began research on a project intended to document the last years of colonial rule in Ghana.[7] This involved close reading of thousands of the recently opened files covering that period of Ghana's recent history in the British Public Record Office at Kew.[8] My memory was jogged by coming up against material on the case including one of the transcripts of the murder trial itself.

Encountering the case in the PRO re-awakened my interest. That might have gone nowhere had it not coincided with my first sight of *An Account of the Kibi Ritual Murder Case* by H.A. Nuamah.[9] This is a fascinating memoir by one of the most important detectives in the case who went on to very senior positions in the post-Independence

5   London, 1964.
6   The closure period for official records was still fifty years.
7   *Ghana*, 'British Documents on the End of Empire' series, 2 vols. (London, 1992).
8   Under a more liberal thirty-year closure rule which meant that from 1988 I could consult all of the released material up to Ghana's independence on 6 March 1957.
9   Accra, 1985.

Ghanaian police force. The PRO material and Nuamah's account[10] provided a dense, complex body of material to which I have tried to add the fruits of three years' research in Ghana, the United Kingdom and the United States of America.

In the course of that research I signalled my initial conclusions in two coat-trailing pieces: one appears in the *Journal of African History*; the other in a Boston University African Studies Center working paper.[11] A number of friends and colleagues usefully criticised these articles and made valuable suggestions about the direction of further work. Amongst these, David Cohen's astute comment that the journal article began in one voice and ended in another was the most unnerving. I knew I had a pretty full picture of the meanings and implications of this case for the colonial presence in the Gold Coast because of the richness of the documentation. But that merely threw into sharp relief my much slighter understanding of its implications in Ghana. Since that time my research, and especially that in Ghana, has tried to fill at least some of the gaps Cohen pointed out.

My other debts are numerous. In Britain my colleague and friend David Anderson's intellectual and personal energy encouraged me by example. I should also like to thank those who heard or read and then commented on parts of this work: Anthony Allott, Michael Anderson, Augustus Casely-Hayford, the late Michael Crowder, Donal Cruise O'Brien, John Dunn, Richard Jeffries, John Lonsdale, Shula Marks, David Parkin, John Peel and Andrew Roberts. P.D. James generously helped me to understand the grim forensic evidence with which I had to grapple. A particular debt is owed to John Parker, from whom I have learnt more than I have taught him and whose company in Ghana in 1991 is a good memory. I got further ideas from the African history research seminars at the School of Oriental and African Studies, Cambridge and Oxford Universities. Harriet Rathbone did some valued research for me in the British Library newspaper collection.

More formally I must record my gratitude to the School of Oriental and African Studies for allowing me study leave in 1990–91. I also

10 Drawn very largely from the account in the National Archives of Ghana (NAG), CSO 15/3.0170 SF73 file sequence. I am certain that Nuamah had his own copy of this file as he did not consult it in the NAG. This same material also informed the account of one of the British police officers in the case, E.M. Berkley-Barton: 'The Case and Attendant Circumstances relating to the Trial Rex *v.* Abontendomhene Asare Apietu & 7 Others'. This is undated but written in 1947 and is in Rhodes House Library, Oxford: Mss Afr S 579.

11 'A Murder in the Colonial Gold Coast; Law and Politics in the 1940s' vol. 30, no. 3, 1989. *Politics and Murder; a West African Case*, Boston University African Studies Center working papers no. 164 (Boston, 1992), p. 30. The latter was written in early 1991.

warmly thank both the British Academy and the Nuffield Foundation who jointly funded my research in Ghana in 1991, without which I should have been unable to finish the book.

In North America, the Shelby Cullom Davis Center at Princeton offered me a fellowship and in that peaceful atmosphere I was able to draft half of the manuscript during the first semester of 1990–91. I should like to thank particularly the Center's then Director, Natalie Zemon Davis, whose vivid, dauntingly broad historical imagination was constantly helpful. At Princeton I enjoyed 'shop-talk' and stole ideas from Peter Brown, Sarah Brett Smith, Michael Cook, Anthony Grafton, Bill Jordan, Arno Meyer, Ted Rabb, Jim Searing, Laurence Stone, Robert Tignor, Lucette Valensi and Avram Yudevitch. Joan Dayan and Gayle Pemberton helped me more than they realise. In neighbouring Pennsylvania, Robin Kilson, Wyatt McGaffey and Hillard Pouncey fizzed as usual. The Walter Rodney Seminar at Boston University deployed its usual skills at 'shaping up' its visitors and I owe thanks to Norman Bennet, Jane Guyer, Jean Hay, Jim McCann and Jeanne Penvenne for intellectual and more material hospitality there. More recently I must thank Paul Lovejoy, Doug Hay and Paul Craven at York University in Toronto for sharing their ideas with me at a later stage of this book's production.

In Ghana my greatest debt is to Robert Addo-Fening who has forgotten far more about Akyem Abuakwa than I shall ever know. His personal and intellectual kindness reminded me that scholarship, at its most enjoyable, is concerned with mutual enthusiasm about the past shared in the context of friendship and respect. We all wait for his book on Akyem Abuakwa keenly. It was Bob who introduced me to the Okyenhene, Osagyefo Kuntunkununku II. I am profoundly grateful to Nana Okyenhene who gracefully gave me permission to use the Akyem Abuakwa State Archives and thus gave me access to a crucial resource. That archive in Kyebi is managed by A.K. Amoako Atta whose personal kindness to me went way beyond the usual courtesies of this most courtly of towns. The State Secretary, Guggisberg Ofori Atta, was no less welcoming and always helpful; I greatly miss his, the world's most infectious laugh. In Kyebi my research was greatly assisted by the kindness of Adontenhene Osabarima Kena Ampaw, Gyasehene Osabarima Kwakye II, the Mankrado of Pano and the Mankrado of Apedwa, J. Appia Danquah and Emmanuel Awuah. A wider, less specific debt is owed to the people of Kyebi and its surrounding area who, despite finding my presence decidedly odd, made me so welcome and comfortable that it is a period of my life that I remember warmly.

In Accra I should like to thank Ako Adjei, Yeboah Akua, Alfred Ammah-Attoh, Colonel Appiah-Koreng, Professor Kwame Arhin, Mrs

M.D. Asiedu, Professor A. Adu Boahen, Kojo Botsio, Dr A. Heward Mills, Kofi Ofori-Boakye, Isaac Tufuoh, and Acquiah, Eric and Minerva Twum Barima. Two special debts are owed. Joseph Anim-Asante helped me in the National Archives of Ghana beyond the usual call of duty; his ebullient scholarly enthusiasm in difficult circumstances is inspirational. And the intellectual edge and warmth of that fine scholar and good man, Kofi Baku, confirmed my long-held conviction that research in Ghana is wonderfully exciting. All of these friends and acquaintances underline my good fortune in having been connected with Ghana and especially with Ghanaians for all these years.

Lastly my wife, Frances, had to put up with long separations and worse, having to listen to me talking about minutiae which fascinate me but must bore her, during the long and obsessive generation of this book. Her patience, support and unpaid work as critical grammar coach is gratefully acknowledged and I dedicate the book to her with love. Any strengths this book might have are due to this fine company. Its awkwardnesses and sillinesses are mine alone.

Abbreviations

AASA: The Akyem Abuakwa State Archives (Kyebi). Use of these initials in footnotes indicates that a source is located there. The numbers which follow indicate firstly the class of the document and, after the slash, the actual number of the file.

AG: Attorney General.

CO: Colonial Office.

CPP: Convention People's Party.

DC: District Commissioner.

DO: District Officer.

JPC: The Joint Provincial Council of Chiefs.

Leg. Co. Legislative Council.

NAG: The National Archives of Ghana (Accra). The letters NAG in footnote references indicates that the document used is located there. The letters which follow such as ADM, SCT or EC specify the class of the document. The numbers which then follow identify the file number.

PC: Provincial Commissioner.

PRO: The Public Record Office (at Kew near London). These initials in footnotes indicate that a source is located there. The letters which follow such as CO, LCO, CAB indicate the class of the document; the numbers which follow the class letters are those of particular files.

UGCC: United Gold Coast Convention.

CHAPTER ONE

The Land and its Peoples

This book is about the murder of a minor chief or *Odikro* of a small town in southern Ghana.[1] Initially it was a local matter, although for those involved it was a matter of life and death. In a short time it was front-page news not only in the Gold Coast but also in Britain's press. Although the Odikro disappeared in February 1944, rancorous reverberations can still be heard today. The case is of importance for an understanding of the texture of post-war politics in Ghana as well as those of a region of that country. But the book is also implicitly concerned with what written and oral records dealing with an explosive issue like this tell us about politics and emotions in a small part of Africa in the mid-twentieth century. This study is an attempt to understand what these events and their repercussions meant to those involved in and around what came to be known as the Kibi murder case.

Many of the questions raised by what was almost certainly the murder of the Odikro of Apedwa are incapable of resolution; any historian's capacity to reconstitute the past is obviously limited by the extent of the available evidence as well as by his or her ability to use that evidence sensitively. The extensive documentation thrown up by the police inquiries, court cases, appeals and petitions and political in-fighting which ensued allow us to unravel at least some of contemporary 'readings' of this confusing and untidy bundle of events.[2] As will become apparent, the exceedingly bitter struggle for the 'truth' took place between a variety of protagonists both literate and pre-literate, rich and poor, African and European.[3] The many versions of 'reality',

1 The name adopted by the country's rulers when the Gold Coast became independent of British control in March, 1957.
2 Such investigations are rich gifts for historians. This is beautifully elaborated in Carlo Ginzburg's essay 'The Inquisitor as Anthropologist', in his *Clues, Myths and the Historical Method* (Baltimore, 1989), pp. 156–65.
3 'Struggle' in the sense used by Hans Medick: 'It would be false to assume that such processes take place on a neutral field under conditions of equal abilities and opportunities. The issue is ... one of the ongoing struggle for meanings. [That] is formed in the context of social relations of individuals, groups, classes and cultures which at the same time are constituted by the struggle. Reciprocity, dependency and resistance – and their mingling – are therefore not structurally

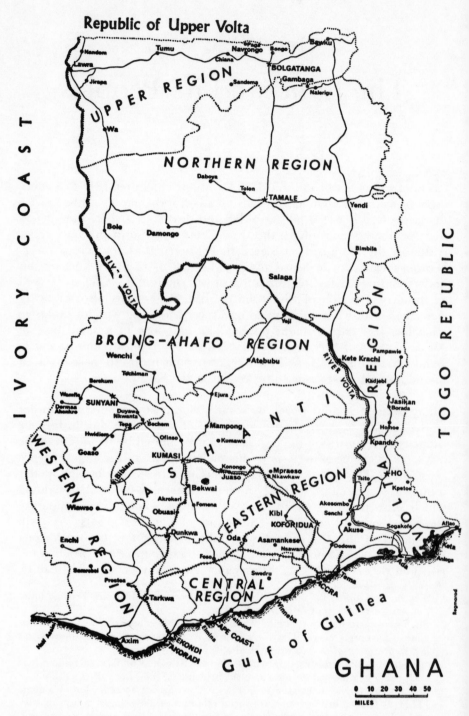

Ghana, *c.* 1960 (from Dennis Austin, *Politics in Ghana*, Oxford University Press, 1964).

of what happened and what it meant were constructed by groups and individuals in different ways and at different times, although each contending account shared many of its building blocks with other narratives. There were major disagreements not merely about motives and meanings but also about what actually *did* happen; but there was a common understanding that something important had occurred on the date of the Odikro's disappearance. The distinctions between these different readings became more vivid and deeper over time as each party, in its eagerness for its version to prevail, added more and more detail to its initial account.[4] In this exponential process of elaboration, the original narratives became increasingly irreconcilable. While some of this struggle was based on profound intellectual differences, much of it was clearly generated to support the instrumental intentions of interested parties. Each protagonist, at different times and in different ways, wanted to achieve particular goals; defeating their enemies was, however, a common ambition for all. There were many other more subtle and better-concealed agendas. A study of these fights, games and debates does not imply that the people of Akyem Abuakwa were an especially quarrelsome bunch of people in the 1940s; they were neither more nor less so than any other human community. But their vivacity highlights the intense disservice done to our understanding of the African past by essentialist generalisations about cultural or political communities.[5]

The large African kingdom in which much of the action takes place comprised a profoundly diverse society. Akyem Abuakwa had been constructed by its peoples' complex history of ancient and modern migration and conquest. The state had been physically defined by conflict, population movement and more recently by the formal carto-graphy of a colonial power, Britain. Before the British, that state had not been infinite. Boundaries and rights to regard valued resources such as watercourses or river crossings as being in its control were the stuff of constant struggle with Akyem Abuakwa's neighbours. An imaginary pre-colonial map could only have been an approximation and would

given. In reality they come into being only in the struggle for meaning.' See 'Missionaries in the Rowboat? Ethnological Ways of Knowing as a Challenge to Local History,' *Comparative Studies in Society and History*, 29 (1987), p. 98.

4 The importance of the ways in which mounting arguments gather more and more contending 'facts' over time becomes apparent. I am indebted to Peter Brown for the insight that as court cases were at the core of this dispute, the resulting arguments on both sides were to some extent 'formatted' by the style of the courtroom.

5 A point made vigorously by Paulin Hountondji in his *African Philosophy* (Bloomington, 1983). Amongst his most valued insights is the reminder of the vacuity of assuming that entire communities – collections of individuals after all – think in the same way. People in Akyem Abuakwa did not do so.

have become rapidly invalid after its drafting. Colonial maps were no less contentious; among the agendas of colonial cartography was that of fixing boundaries, a somewhat vain hope as the value of land and other resources increased throughout the twentieth century. In many cases the task of delimitation increased the number of disputes between contending states for parcels of space and people. Although its African rulers proclaimed its cultural and political homogeneity, the reality was much more exciting. The people of Akyem Abuakwa had diverse origins; by the twentieth century they were ethnically and confessionally plural, economically stratified, and both divided and united by the ties of family. But it was always a population of individuals who acted and reacted in accordance with the promptings of perceived personal or group interests and, as importantly, thoughtful reflection, and did what accorded with their personal moralities and individual instincts. These two elements of motivation were not necessarily fused.

The Odikro disappeared in the space left by the death of one of the most remarkable figures in African history. On 20 August 1943, the twenty-ninth remembered *Okyenhene*[6] or King of the state of Akyem Abuakwa,[7] *Nana* Sir Ofori Atta I,[8] died. Akyem Abuakwa then had a population of over two hundred and fifty thousand.[9] It was, and is, a rich forest state whose wealth was based upon the proceeds of cocoa cultivation but also, by the twentieth century, upon gold- and diamond-mining concession rents and royalties. Its history as a discernibly independent polity dates to the seventeenth century, although the origins of its people still excite hot debate in both Akyem and Academe.[10] It was predominantly an Akan state; most of its people

6 Recent analysis makes Ofori Atta the twenty-ninth ruler. See R. Addo-Fening, 'Akyem Abuakwa: a Study of the Impact of Missionary Activities and Colonial Rule on a Traditional State', unpublished Ph.D thesis (University of Ghana, Legon, 1980), and the regnal list on pp. 30–31 of the Odwira festival held in Kyebi, 5–13 January 1991, drafted by Addo-Fening and senior *Akyeame*. The king is also called *Omanhene* – state chief – and by the honorific *Nana*.
7 Old orthography renders this as Akim Abuakwa. Throughout I use the modern form – Kyebi rather than Kibi, for example; the 'ky' sound is 'ch' as in 'cherry'.
8 A royal name adopted on installation. He was baptised Aaron Kwadjo Dwa on 11 October 1881 and knighted in 1927.
9 And a land area of about 2,750 square miles. Census data before 1948 is patchy. Its present population is at least half a million.
10 See Addo-Fening, *op. cit.*, and K. Afrifah, 'Akyem *c*.1700–1874. A Study in Inter-state Relations in the Pre-colonial Gold Coast', unpublished Ph.D thesis (London University, 1976); also F. Ofori Atta, 'Amantoomiensa in the Political and Administrative Set-up of Akyem Abuakwa', unpublished BA history dissertation (University of Ghana, Legon, 1978); J. Simensen, 'Commoners, Chiefs and Colonial Government: British Policy and Local Politics in Akyem Abuakwa, Ghana under Colonial Rule', unpublished Ph.D thesis (University of

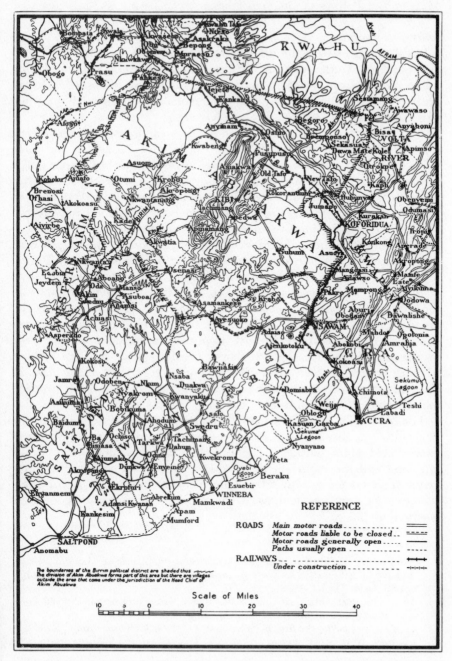

Akim Abuakwa (from J.B. Danquah, *Akim Abuakwa Handbook*, Forster Groom & Co., London, 1928).

shared a language, Twi, many cosmological ideas and social and cultural practices with the better known Asante (Ashanti) to the north and with the Fante states to its south-west; but it had enjoyed long independence from its Akan neighbours, something its local historians greatly relish; consequently Akyem Abuakwa developed its own particularities.

While he was only sixty-two when he died, the *Okyenhene* had suffered a series of mild heart-attacks before his terminal attack in the third week of August. He was rushed to Korle Bu, the Gold Coast's major hospital in the capital Accra; there he died after a week of unsuccessful treatment. So momentous was this news for Akyem Abuakwa that an exercise in 'news management' was undertaken. His death was not announced formally until three days after it had occurred.[11]

Akan funerary rites, and especially those for kings, are long-drawn-out.[12] Those for the late king drew to an end in February 1944. On the final day of his rites, 28 February, the *Odikro*[13] of one of the senior towns of the Three Counties that comprised a politically salient grouping in the state (the *Amantoo Mmiensa*), disappeared whilst he was in the kingdom's capital, Kyebi. He was one of three elders of the Amantoo Mmiensa who were charged with important procedures at this stage in the obsequies. Despite extensive enquiries and searches, Akyea Mensah was never seen again. By the end of July 1944, eight men, all descendants of previous kings of Akyem Abuakwa, had been arrested and charged with his murder.

The old king's 'going to Banso'[14] and his second funeral provided the backcloth for this tragedy. These events initiated violent conflict and exacerbated older tensions. The personality and achievements of the late king and the nature of the kingdom he dominated for over thirty years are vital for any understanding of what happened. Accordingly this account begins by looking at where, when and around whom these events took place.

Trondheim, 1975); J.B. Danquah, *Akim Abuakwa Handbook* (London, 1928); and Kumi Attobrah, *The Kings of Akyem Abuakwa and the Ninety-nine Years War against Asante* (Tema, 1976).

11 In a vivid oral culture like this it is unlikely that many people did not know that he had died within hours of his passing.

12 Held in two parts; the first is called *doteyie* – the 'rough-and-tumble funeral' – from *dote* (clay, dust) and *ayie* (funeral). The second *ayie* follows considerably later.

13 Literally head of a small town – a *krom*. His honorific was *Barima* – 'Brave'.

14 The circumlocution for saying the unsayable: 'the king is dead'. '*Nana ko Banso*' evokes the final removal of the king's remains to the royal mausoleum at Banso, north-west of Kyebi, the site of an earlier royal capital.

The Land

The main road from Accra to Kumasi takes a traveller into the kingdom of Akyem Abuakwa when it crosses the River Densu at Nsawam. By this time the visual dullness of the Accra Plains, relieved only by strange grassy outcrops, is behind you. From Nsawam onwards you are in the rainforest and, until extensive road repairs in 1992, on a much-ravaged road which degenerated into mud-slides in the rainy season and potholed dust-storms in the dry season. For centuries the forest has been cleared and re-cleared by generations of farmers so that the tree cover is largely made up of recently self-seeded softwoods and varieties of cultivated palms which yield, for example, palm-oil, palm wine, bananas and coconuts. Even more ground is given over to farmland on which cocoa, cassava, maize and, more recently, pineapples, predominate.

From a speeding lorry much of the land looks wild and overgrown, but on foot you can see that it is intensively farmed by the large population of the area.[15] Farming styles favour inter-cropping,[16] which is ecologically sound but looks casual and even untidy for eyes more used to the dull, unvarying geometric symmetry of European or North American farms.

Small towns[17] are scattered along either side of the road's length. At the roadside, women trade from small stalls; they sell a range of goods such as locally baked sweet bread, which tastes rather like brioche, cans of evaporated milk, soft drinks, pineapples and oranges to cater to the needs of the regular passenger and freight transport that trundles up and down this, probably the most frequently used interregional road in Ghana.

In daylight the towns look sparsely populated and almost abandoned. Sometimes this is because those portions of them visible from the road are only segments of much larger settlements which often extend deeply into the bush. But for much of the year most of their inhabitants are, during the twelve hours of daylight,[18] away working on their farms,

15 The 1970 census records a population of over half a million and rates over five hundred settlements as towns.
16 For example young cocoa seedlings must be shaded, and consequently new trees are inter-cropped with big-leafed crops.
17 Quite when a village becomes a town is a problem familiar to those learning Latin and worried about what a town or a small island is. People in Akyem talk of their 'villages', but these can prove to be big and more populous than that cosy word suggests.
18 Kyebi is only six degrees north; day length and the times of sunset and sunrise vary little over the course of the year.

which often lie many miles' trudge away from their homes. In the early mornings and in the mid-afternoon large numbers of children in yellow and brown uniforms are to be seen walking considerable distances to and from their local schools. As seems to be the case in all the world's rural areas, the most ancient inhabitants sit patiently absorbed watching the road traffic.

At the town of Apedwa the road divides; the right-hand branch loops off to Kukurantumi. The main Kumasi road dives sharply to the left and now begins to follow the lush valley of the River Birrim. On either side of the road, the valley's sides become steeper and steeper; while farmers have colonised the lower slopes, the heights are tree-covered and wild. Hunters[19] range these forests and offer their surplus prey – buck, squirrel and cane-cutter (a large and tasty herbivorous rat) for sale at the roadside. The road swings through the towns of Amanfrom, Petroase and Akwadum; and then the valley broadens out and the scenery becomes even more impressive as the hills to the east and west are now joined by the Nkawkaw range to the north.

The first signs that the capital of the kingdom, Kyebi, is in sight, are groves of royal palms: the towering, grey-barked, fat-bottomed but tapering palms that most accord to the popular western image of what an honest-to-God palm-tree should look like. Appropriately these trees were planted at royal insistence in the 1930s and add the grandeur intended; some of them, especially those which shade the first half-mile of the road from Kyebi northwards, have come to the end of their natural life and are now enjoyed by huge colonies of fruit bats and weaver-birds. To the right of the road, in the middle of the valley floor, is a low hill; and it is on that hill that the royal capital is sited.

Few people in transit between the great cities of Accra and Kumasi would take much notice of it. From the road, Kyebi is no more than a small, dusty lorry park and a cluster of market stalls serving travellers, surrounded by undistinguished swish houses; amongst them is the sadly decaying house of one of Akyem Abuakwa's greatest sons of modern times, Dr J.B. Danquah, the lawyer-philosopher and pioneer of nationalism. You must walk away from the road and up the hill to get into Kyebi. The undemanding climb is instantly rewarding. The views of the valley from the middle of the town are stunning. To the south, the Apedwa hills follow the bend of the Birrim. To the east and west the valley walls are the lush, shiny, deep greens of the *Douanier* Rousseau's imagined jungle. During the rainy season, the hills are shrouded in wispy low clouds that trail through the treetops like silk scarves. After the rainy season, the green is relieved by wonderfully vulgar splashes of bright yellows, reds and oranges as trees and bushes explode into

19   Usually farmers who own guns rather than men who do nothing but hunt.

flower. The valley is home to a huge variety of butterflies; and the river is host to a dazzling and varied collection of dragonflies.

Away from the dust and racket of the main road, the valley is alive with the song of a spotter's guidebook-ful of birds, from minute bee-eaters to vultures hovering expectantly on the thermals. Even further away from the road, birdsong is augmented by the harsh warning calls of spotted monkeys. Unseen more often than not are large numbers of smaller things including mambas, cobras and a variety of the nastier vipers. Against these horrors farmers now protect themselves by wearing knee-high Wellington boots, preferring the discomfort of sweaty feet to the risk of a speedy and painful death.

Kyebi, after the teeming chaos of any big modern town, is a quiet, orderly and house-proud town laid out on a grid like a tiny tropical Manhattan. To the north is that part of town still called Oburonikrom, the white man's town. In the late nineteenth century this area was developed by the Basel Presbyterian missionaries with the tolerant permission of an animist king. By choice Christians were segregated by a single narrow road from what they continued into the 1950s to call 'the town': by this they meant the pagan capital. No *Oburoni* lives in the 'white man's town' now. For generations the Presbyterian ministers and their flock, who built their rather fine houses around the church and its free-standing cluster of bells and the mission house, have been African. From the early days of their mission, Presbyterians worshipped in Twi, the Akan language,[20] and taught the young in the same language using translated prayer-books, Bibles and school-books which they generated themselves. Despite its name, Oburonikrom is a full part of Kyebi.

The church, whose tower is the highest point in the town, was built in the 1870s. Like the mission house it is unmistakably Swiss, or at least Alpine, in conception; their corrugated iron roofs were angled by an unconscious architectural imperative which worried about accretions of heavy snow rather than tropical rain. The surrounding houses' roof angles are notably flatter. In the handsome, balconied mission house, which remains the Presbyterian Church's local centre and the manse, parts of the great work of the missionary, J.G. Christaller, such as his Twi–English Dictionary and his Twi Testaments, were written. From the church northwards, the town plunges steeply down the north face of the hill from whose foot farmland extends towards the town of Pano and the present site of Akyem Abuakwa State College, the town's famous secular secondary school.

---

20 Basically the same tongue as that spoken by Asante and Fante. Akyem Twi is, however, a distinct dialect and has forms and vocabulary as well as pronunciation of its own. For some help with this variety see Florence Abena Dolphyne, *The Akan (Twi-Fante) Language; its Sound Systems and Tonal Structure* (Accra, 1988).

Walking southwards from Oburonikrom and into 'the town' you emerge into an extensive square, divided by a single east–west road. The square is neatly edged with shady trees and seats conveniently placed under them on which the town's ancients gossip and watch the world go by; it looks much more like a Provençal or South American town centre than that of a Ghanaian town; old men in berets playing *petanque* would not look out of place here. But this large open space of about three acres is where the great seasonal festivals of this Akan state are celebrated. To the south-west of this open space, an ancient tree stands, its roots surrounded by whitewashed stones. At its foot lies a large copper bowl with three great stones in it. Into this bowl the blood of sacrificed sheep is tipped on high days and holidays.

Twenty feet southwards are the imposing gates of the royal palace, the Ofori Panin Fie or Ahenfie.[21] The palace covers about five acres, surrounded by high, whitewashed walls. Although the site is ancient, many of its most eye-catching buildings date from the 1930s. Its outward simplicity belies its complex interior. The main part of the palace comprises a two-storey building which houses the two great chambers in which the State Council, the Okyeman Council and the two State Tribunals[22] are held. To the east lies firstly the administrative offices of the State and then further east still, the old harem or *Ma'am* which is no longer used. To the south of the administrative offices are the king's living quarters, the *Dabre*, and his state rooms. Beneath these are a series of small courtyards linked by covered passageways. And further to the south is a now sadly neglected but once rather grand garden, which in turn leads to an overgrown tennis-court, built in 1930.

Ofori Panin Fie is impressive and mysterious. Parts of it are closed to all but the ritually qualified few. The mausoleum and the Stool House, where the ancestral stools or thrones are stored can be visited only by those very close to the royal stool, and a large number of prohibitions prevent casual visitors, even if they are Akyemfo – Akyem Abuakwa people – from entering these sacred places.[23] The court in front of the great tribunal and council chambers houses the state drums.

Every day numbers of state officials and chiefs bustle through this courtyard on their way to consult the State Secretary or the Okyenhene.

---

21 From *Fie* meaning 'house' in Twi. Ofori Panin, the thirteenth Okyenhene, is celebrated as the architect of the modern Akyem Abuakwa state at the beginning of the eighteenth century. In his honour the royal throne or stool is called the Ofori Panin stool and the palace also bears his name.

22 That of the Okyenhene, whose jurisdiction covers the state, and that of the Abontendomhene, which is more concerned with matters in Kyebi.

23 This, very politely, ruled out the author. I rely on the testimony of others as to what these areas actually look and feel like.

Robed in handsome and often very expensive cloth, worn in the same manner as Roman senators, these dignified bureaucrats and aristocrats give the palace an air of timelessness only jolted by their digital watches and, on occasions, sunglasses. Ofori Panin Fie is unmistakably royal; and in its decorousness and quiet confidence, Kyebi is unmistakably a royal capital. Its quietness by day is explained, as is that of smaller towns, by the absence of many of its inhabitants at their farms which ring the town. But at weekends, especially when there is a local funeral, and on festival days the town fills up with the sons and daughters of Akyem Abuakwa who now live in the livelier economic centres of Accra, Kumasi, Koforidua – or Chicago and Toronto.

Many Ghanaians, while acknowledging the beauty of the Birrim valley and the quiet but warm charm of Kyebi, told me that it was too dull, and in their words 'too underdeveloped' for their tastes. Unlike many other Ghanaian urban centres it boasts no movie-house, no obvious nightspots, few bars, no modern hotels, restaurants or shops. You can walk safely in Kyebi's streets, as do its children, sheep and goats, for few cars are driven through town. Physically, despite more recent additions such as a Community Centre and the half-finished and very modernist new Presbyterian Church (all cantilevered roof and reinforced concrete), it does indeed look much as it did fifty years ago.

There are very good or, rather, very bad reasons why this is so; part of this book implicitly attempts to explain why Kyebi feels like a town that time has forgotten, for it was not always so. During a substantial part of the colonial period the state of Akyem Abuakwa and its capital were regarded by colonial authorities and other Africans as synonymous with modernisation and progress. It was an area in which model farms, early experiments in cooperative agriculture, innovative trade schools and extensive road-building were to be found. Kyebi has since been studiously ignored by a succession of governments whose intention has been to punish, by neglect, the state's royal family and, by extension, their subjects for their political positions and actions.

If governments have treated the area harshly, the Creator has smiled upon it. The entire state contains some of the best farming land in Ghana. Kyebi receives between sixty to ninety inches of rain per annum and is one of the wetter areas of Ghana; additionally the hilly nature of the region means that it is well watered by many spring-fed rivers which are carefully used by farmers for irrigation in the dry season. This mitigates the relatively low natural fertility of the lateritic soils which characterise much of the West African forest area. The temperature range is narrow, rarely exceeding the high eighties Fahrenheit and seldom falling below the low seventies, even on the coldest of wet nights. On average, more than two hundred days a year are spent in full sunlight. To the untrained urban eye, the area looks remarkably abundant; there seems to be something growing everywhere. The fact that for the last one hundred and fifty years large numbers of immigrants from other parts of Ghana and even other parts of West Africa have sought to establish farms within the kingdom suggests that the reality of the visible fertility is more substantial than a mere impression.

The area was one of the pioneer regions of cocoa cultivation in the late nineteenth century, and cocoa remains an important cash crop. Farmers also cultivate many other food and export crops such as plantain, maize, sugar cane, cassava, oil palm and bananas with considerable success. In recent years the growing of excellent pineapples, largely for export, has become more evident. The historical record suggests that even at very low points of the economic cycle such as the 1930s, Akyem Abuakwa was not afflicted by hunger.

The local staple, *fufu*, is usually made here from a mixture of plantain and cassava pounded together in a pestle and mortar. Yams are widely eaten but are imported from further north, as is rice, which is a more recent addition to the local diet. Protein sources include sheep and goats which are to be found roaming widely, not least upon the roads. Although tsetse fly infests the forest, small herds of cattle graze in the southern part of the state where the bush has been cleared. Fish are caught in the rivers as well as imported from the sea-fishing areas of the coast. Additionally many valley farmers have fish-stews, small ponds filled when rivers flood, in which river fish, mostly the tasty but formidably bony tilapia, grow sufficiently large to be regularly 'cropped'. Local diets are enriched by small game from the forest, along with giant snails and, oddly, bats, which seem to have no more meat on them than small anorexic birds. Wealthier people also augment more traditional menus by buying tinned pilchards and sardines, and now eat bread made from imported wheat flour.

Akyem Abuakwa's natural advantages do not stop above ground. The lower Birrim area is diamondiferous, and large-scale diamond mining around the Akyem towns of Akwatia, Asamankese, Topiramang and Kade dates back to the early 1920s. Gold is also found in the region. Some of this is alluvial; old people remember a time when the Birrim was less polluted than it is today and tiny specks of gold were visible, glinting and tumbling in the stream. Mothers collected these flecks and placed them on small children's heads in conformity with an old wives' tale that this would produce tall children. It is doubtful whether anyone really believed that this happened, but a child so haloed must have looked enchanting.

While most of Ghana's gold is mined north-west of a straight line drawn between Takoradi and Mpraeso, people in the Kyebi area have mined gold time out of mind. Amongst the hazards encountered when walking across farmland around Kyebi are the ancient gold-miners' pits which were never filled in after working ceased. These pre-colonial and sometimes very ancient workings are both deep and perfectly round in shape. More recently, commercial gold mining moved into the area in the twentieth century. Gold prospecting and development has recommenced in the area after a break of thirty years following the liberalisation of the Ghana's exchange control and profit repatriation regimes, and is already providing some local employment. Both diamond and gold mining have provided individuals and the Akyem Abuakwa state with a considerable income from leases and royalties.

The People

Akyem Abuakwa is a compact state. Although people express vociferous local loyalties to their villages or towns, the distances between settlements are small. By the mid-1920s most centres were linked by roads. These were for the most part built and maintained by 'the Chiefs and people in Akim Abuakwa'.[24] This road system had to cope with the growing number of motor lorries which linked areas of production with local and metropolitan markets. The records of the Presbyterian Church[25] and the Palace Archives[26] suggest a population relying increasingly on motor transport for physical mobility. In the course of the twentieth century and especially after 1918 the physical space of Akyem Abuakwa seemed to shrink as journeys, which had taken days on foot, now took hours by motor transport. The eastern marches of Akyem Abuakwa were, moreover, served by the mid-section of the Accra–Kumasi railway line after 1917. These developments helped reinforce Akyem Abuakwa's identity.

The ancestors of the dominant people of Akyem Abuakwa originally came from further north. All their traditions agree that Adanse was their original home.[27] Early in the seventeenth century internal pressures, including an increasing incidence of war provoked by the military rise of firstly Akwamu and then Asante itself, initiated a period of

24   *The Gold Coast Handbook* (London, 1924), pp. 229–30.
25   Some of which are to be found in the National Archives of Ghana, henceforward NAG, EC 1 series.
26   Henceforward AASA. They also suggest that more and more people were using the telegraph network. By the 1920s the Okyenhene used telegrams to summon meetings of the Okyeman Council or his Tribunal. In turn, wing-chiefs and sub-chiefs used the system to inform the Palace of local events.
27   Oral tradition in Adanse confirms these accounts.

migration to the south and east of their homeland.[28] The evidence suggests that a discrete, centralised Akyem Abuakwa state was in being by the middle of the seventeenth century. By the end of the third decade of the eighteenth century the state's inhabitants had gradually and for the most part peacefully settled, alongside earlier populations, into the area which is today identified as Akyem Abuakwa.[29]

It is, like the better known Asante to the north-west, an Akan state.[30] Most people in Akyem Abuakwa speak Twi, are matrilineal and have much in common with other Akan speakers. The state structure, like that of Asante, is derived from a structure of military command.[31] The Okyenhene is normatively and undisputedly paramount. Subject to him are five chiefs, *Amanhene*, who are often referred to in translation of a military idiom as 'wing-chiefs'.[32]

Technically all wing-chiefs are equal but the *Adontenhene*, the commander of the vanguard in war, is regarded as the most senior. In Akyem Abuakwa the Adontenhene's capital is at Kukurantumi. The commander of the left wing, *Benkumhene*, has his stool in Begoro. *Nifahene*, the commander of the right wing, sits in Asiakwa. The commander of the unit whose duty in wartime is to protect the sacred Ofori Panin stool,[33] the essence and symbol of Akyemness, is *Oseawuohene*, whose own town is Wankyi. Lastly *Gyaasehene*, whose divisional role

28 See R. Addo-Fening, 'The "Akim" or "Achim" in seventeenth and eighteenth Century Historical Contexts: Who Were They?', in *Research Review* (New Series), 4.2, 1988. The first capital was Banso, which remains the last resting place of royals.

29 Pre-colonial state borders are hard to define historically; they were constantly the substance of inter-state litigation. Where the legal authority of one state ended and another began was and is a matter of great concern for both royal authorities and their subjects; such litigation is not only a matter of land- or resource-grabbing but marks, rather, contestation over jurisdiction and authority.

30 There is a huge ethnographic literature on the Akan culture area. The most famous are R.S. Rattray, *Ashanti* (Oxford, 1923) and J.B. Danquah, *The Akan Doctrine of God* (London, 1944). An overview of Akan political thought and structures is to be found in Kwame Arhin, *Traditional Rule in Ghana: Past and Present* (Accra, 1985). More general but short is Dennis Warren's overview of the ethnographic literature, *The Akan of Ghana* (Accra, 1986), the edition well revised by K. Ampom-Darkwa and K.N. Bame.

31 Although in this, as in much else in the state, there are important differences between Asante and Akyem Abuakwa.

32 Together they constitute what is known as *Mpasua num*.

33 Stools are elegant, backless thrones carved in wood. Each design has a precise association with an Akan saying. Kings' and chiefs' stools symbolise the greater importance of the office than the incumbent, and mention of 'the stool' is often a reference to kingship itself; they are accordingly accorded great respect. See Peter Sarpong, *The Sacred Stools of the Akan* (Accra, 1971).

was to defend the state's hearths and homes whilst the army was away on campaign, has his stool at Kwaben. These divisions are of unequal size.[34]

Akyem Abuakwa's origins are as a clan state; that is to say that the leaders of the migrants, and those who came to dominate it once the politics of migration developed into those of a settled state, were, with one exception,[35] drawn from the Asona clan or *abusua*. As the Akan kinship system is sternly exogamic, this meant that whilst the dominant clan was Asona, the migrants and, later, the state's citizens were necessarily drawn from all the Akan clans. A person's clan is determined by his or her mother's clan. From one's father's side one inherits *ntoro*, which in some senses is synonymous with 'character', though these attributes do not necessarily outlive their 'owners'.[36] But it is from the matriclan and hence through one's mother that heritable blood relationships extend, and these have real, immutable permanence.[37]

For a stranger to such a social structure it is constantly confusing that, irrespective of where a person lives, his or her 'home' is always identified as that of the mother. Thus when Akyemfo talk of 'my village' or 'my town' they usually mean the original town or village of their mothers. Naturally some people also live in their mother's village. Many marriages are made locally and thus the usual tradition of virilocality does not necessarily separate a woman and hence her children from 'home'.

The Akan kinship system, an immensely complex and fascinating moral system as well as a functional solution to the universal problems of marriage and inheritance, insists that marriage, and indeed even more casual liaisons, can only lawfully be conducted exogamically. Thus virtually every village and town of Akyem Abuakwa consists of people from all eight Akan clans. Each clan has a senior male elder, *abusua panin*, who is regarded as the ultimate arbitrator of disputes within clans. In Akyem Abuakwa, such elders sit on the great Council of State, the Okyeman, alongside the wing-chiefs and the other royals.

34 In 1970 the Adonten division comprised 119 towns, Nifa 73 towns, Benkum 130 towns, Oseawuo 135 towns and Gyaase only 49 towns.
35 *Nifahene* is always a member of the Oyoko clan.
36 There is, however, an indestructible quality to *ntoro* which resurfaces when a grandson bears the qualities of his father's father. This is reified in naming practice: boys are often given the name of respected grandfathers in the expectation that this will perpetuate both the ancestor's status and personality. This is elegantly set out in Tom McCaskie's essay 'Konnurokusem: an Essay on Kinship and Family in the history of the Oyoko Koko Dynasty of Kumasi', unpublished paper given to the West African seminar at University College London, October 1991, pp. 23–5.
37 A Twi proverb insists that *abusua baako, mogya baako*, or 'one clan, one blood'.

As the Okyenhene and all but one of his wing-chiefs are themselves Asona, it follows that they can be succeeded only by their uterine brothers or by their sisters' sons.

The people of Akyem Abuakwa, Akyemfo, are accordingly laced together by an indescribably complex cat's cradle of affinity through blood, place and history. These interrelationships are constantly being deepened and extended by marriage. People today have extraordinary knowledge in depth and width about other people's genealogy and place of birth,[38] so while the state is physically extensive and populous it feels, and actually is, remarkably intimate. Intimacy does not prevent sharp rivalries and divisive competition; it can create the claustrophobic atmosphere of everyone knowing everyone else's business. But it is an important dimension of what constitutes Akyem-ness.

That integrity is, however, something of a myth. The relative homogeneity of the Akyemfo was achieved by the integration, over time, of other populations. At the beginning of the modern state, the migrants 'overlaid' local populations.[39] As a successful military state, its army leaders frequently brought in large numbers of slaves from outside whose descendants have, to a large extent, been incorporated.[40] But much more significantly Akyem Abuakwa has become, especially since the nineteenth century, a magnet for in-migration by non-Akyem and even non-Akan peoples. The 1948 Gold Coast census, the first which can be relied upon, suggests that by this time Akyemfo were a minority population in their own state. No fewer than sixty percent of the population were defined as non-Akyem 'strangers'.

The explanations of this are numerous. Akyem Abuakwa had initially welcomed an influx of refugees from the Asante state of Juaben

38   Invaluable to me because Akans do not bear patronyms. The only obviously determined part of their names are day-names. The rest are given names; in later life these can change to commemorate an ancestor or loved relative. Without specific knowledge it is usually impossible to divine an individual's parentage on the basis of names alone. While genealogy can be fictionalised because of the promptings of politics or economic expectations, it is difficult to do so without an undercurrent of knowing rumour – which itself can, of course, be based upon creativity rather than fact.

39   Like that of Pano, $\frac{1}{2}$ mile north of Kyebi on the main road. Their traditions speak of scouts of the main body of the Akyem migrants asking for advice about where to settle and being advised by Pano's rulers to move into uncleared land a little further south in the Birrim valley where Kyebi now lies. This is related with pride in Pano. Pano enjoys a position of some power in the Akyem Abuakwa state as one of the Amantoo Mmiensa villages.

40   I was surprised by the awareness people had of the slave antecedents of others. This stigma can be formally obliterated by those with power and wealth, just as it can be created for those without access to power and wealth. In this sense all such genealogy is socially constructed rather than being a factual account of past affinity.

(Dwaben) when that state was defeated in the course of civil war in Asante. In time this large influx of Dwaben refugees created tensions; by the twentieth century both the Dwabenhene and the Okyenhene were claiming that these people were their subjects; each claimed jurisdiction over them and sought to extract taxation from them. Less dramatically, some of the southlands of the Akyem Abuakwa state had been gradually settled by Ga and even Ewe-speakers, and by immigrants from Akuapem, who were amongst the pioneer cocoa farmers celebrated in Polly Hill's remarkable work.[41] Although their contribution to the wealth of Akyem Abuakwa is undoubted, they too posed problems of divided loyalties.[42] And as wealth was created throughout the late nineteenth and twentieth centuries, Akyem Abuakwa attracted new trading communities to its towns. Traders from as near as Kwahu and from as far as Lagos began to form significant communities within the state, as did Muslims from further north of the region who were attracted to Akyem by the developing trading and wage-labour opportunities.

Thus despite the constantly invoked homogeneity of the state, a traveller will often be told that this or that settlement is a Dwaben town, an Akwapim village or that this or that block of land is farmed by Krobos or Kwahus. Akyem Abuakwa comforts itself with a frequently proclaimed ideological package wrapped up in a variety of often-stated positions which insist upon cultural, political and historical homogeneity.[43] The reality is, however, that for well over a century it has been an increasingly plural society.

The fault-lines of that plurality are not only the obvious ones of ethnicity. Local rivalries over the siting of markets, the provision of pipe-borne water, the routes of new roads abound as they do in all rural areas. Perceptions of unfair favour and its logical corollary, relative deprivation, inform inter-regional and local rivalries. But the modern population is also divided confessionally. In the sphere of traditional religion, the local shrines vie with one another in rather the same way as European pilgrimage sites competed for the sacred and commercial

---

41 *Migrant Cocoa-Farmers of Southern Ghana* (Cambridge, 1963).
42 They moved in because of the willingness of many Akyem sub-chiefs and even wing-chiefs to sell land to them, although the meaning of 'sale' was often contested – did it involve freehold or only usufruct for example? These communities created tensions not merely by their presence but also because Akyem Abuakwa's kings bridled at the unregulated sale of 'Akyem' lands by citizens of Akyem Abuakwa.
43 See e.g. *Ofori ko Banso*, the commemorative programme for the funeral of Nana Ofori Atta II (r.1943–73) by Kwame Kesse-Adu and Fraser Ofori Atta, Accra, 1973 and the sumptuous programme for the Odwira festival held at Kyebi, 5–13 January 1991.

attention of prospective pilgrims. The coming of Christianity[44] to the area added confessional competition to older divisions. Akyem Abuakwa's earliest experience of Christianity was dominated by the Swiss Basel mission's Presbyterianism.[45] By the 1920s Methodist, American Methodist Episcopal Zion and Roman Catholic missions had also arrived in the area, opening not only churches but also schools.

In more recent times a large number of Pentecostal, Evangelical and 'born-again' churches have opened in the region, all competing energetically for the hearts, minds – and financial contributions – of the population. Anyone walking around any Akyem Abuakwa town on a Sunday moves from place to place accompanied by the often extra-ordinarily good hymn and psalm-singing of numerous religious communities.[46] Moreover the Moslem populations in many of Akyem Abuakwa's larger towns support local mosques and Qu'ranic schools.

Other divisions within wider Akyem Abuakwa are more difficult to label. There are wide and visible discrepancies in wealth. While some writers on the Akan have insisted on using the language of class, it is hard to recognise the distinct cleavages and self-awareness that are implicit in that discourse in Akyem Abuakwa past and present. People have numerous confusing identities which intersect and divide in different circumstances. One of the most observable cleavages, that between royals and traditional office holders, is not necessarily based upon wealth. Many senior chiefs and even royals are significantly poorer than some of their subject commoners. Similarly activists in *asafo* companies, the organisations of commoners to be found in most Akyem Abuakwa towns, are sometimes notably well-heeled rather than being the wretched of the earth.

While it is dangerous to generalise, it does seem that the corporate natures of family, lineage or village tend to have the dual effect of protecting the most vulnerable from indigency and of forcing the affluent to share some of their wealth to that end. Very poor people have usually become vulnerably disaffiliated for some reason such as

44   Which arrived in the 1830s but took root in the 1860s.
45   Their work was taken over during World War I by the United Free Kirk of Scotland. In 1926 they adopted the name of 'The Presbyterian Church of the Gold Coast.' From the beginning, Presbyterian insistence on the use of Twi in worship and tuition has itself contributed to the making of Akyem Abuakwa's Akan identity.
46   Evidence of religious revival is widespread in modern Ghana and is not unique to Akyem. The PNDC government was suspicious of these developments and new churches required government approval before being granted church status. Government fears rested on two concerns: approved churches enjoy tax concessions and some have been 'fronts' for more obviously profane activities. Secondly the diffusion of American-style video evangelism has created unease which, in the light of the Swaggart and Bakker crusades, seems justified.

rancorous divorce, bitter family dispute, mental sickness or even barreness where women are concerned. But this complex of rights, obligations and expectations neither works inevitably nor is it necessarily as benign as it might appear. It creates a sometimes demeaning dependence for the recipients of crumbs from rich men's tables. The well-off are often 'served' by entourages of poorer relatives or townsmen and women whose lives as drivers, house servants and 'gophers' frequently seem abject and anachronistic to the point of servility. But expectations can, in turn, impose such onerous pressures upon the successful that they will redefine, unilaterally, what is meant by 'family'; or they will remove themselves from everyday obligation by absenting themselves in towns like Accra or Kumasi.

The experiences of poverty or of wealth were enormously important determinants of behaviour in Akyem Abuakwa as elsewhere. But other considerations were and are no less important. Akyemfo have a strong sense of acceptable and unacceptable behaviour. While a successful man or woman might be envied, he or she will not be admired if relative affluence is not moderated by humanising behaviour such as personal generosity, respect for age and appropriate personal humility. One of the most revealing sources we have for the sensitivities of the Akyemfo for the period this book is concerned with are the records of the two Tribunals conducted in the palace in Kyebi.[47] A substantial amount of the criminal jurisdiction was devoted to hearing and deliberating on cases in which private citizens summonsed one another for using 'slanderous and insulting words' or 'slanderous and defamatory words' against them. These insults are many and various; some read as essentially trivial: '. . . have you once built a house?',[48] 'you are a fool . . .'.[49] But the overall impression is one of a society with a profound sense of propriety and impropriety, in which due respect was demanded and disrespect punished.[50]

Honour is important to Akyemfo and its defence can be bitter and sometimes violent. Many non-Akyem Akans said that they regard Akyemfo as violent people with long memories. While thinking about what this reputation meant to people in Akyem Abuakwa I was helped by V.S. Naipaul:

---

47 A partial run of these records is in NAG ADM 32/1. The full manuscript record is held in AASA.

48 NAG ADM 32/1/16. Kwabena Young v. Kwame Kagya, 10 June 1939.

49 NAG ADM 32/1/16. Native Authority Police v. Kwaku Amoako, 13 January 1938.

50 In the first of these cases the defendant was fined £3.18s; in the second he was fined £30 or six months' imprisonment with hard labour. £30 in the 1930s was a large sum. A blacksmith earned about 3 shillings, a day-labourer about one shilling and sixpence per day at this time.

... in the Indian countryside of my childhood in Trinidad there were many murders and acts of violence and these acts of violence gave the Trinidadian Indians ... a fearful reputation. But to us to whom the stories of murders and feuds were closer, other things were at stake. The family feuds ... often had to do with the idea of honour. Perhaps it was a peasant idea; ....[51]

It is this strongly ingrained ethic which in part explains a further division which is of considerable importance as context for the events with which this book is concerned. Many Akyemfo resent Kyebi and its people; that is to say, many non-Kyebi people feel that the capital is a privileged town that has conspired at granting itself that privilege at the cost of other parts of the state. The allegation in the inter-war years, as now, is that Kyebi as the seat of the king, the site of the major traditional organs of state government, waxed fat from its position of prominence whilst being resistant to the ethic of limited redistribution. In particular it was felt that the royal family, which played a significant role in the state's institutions, had acquired by taxation, tribunal fines, shares of land rents, concessions and even by 'cheating', more than its 'fair share' of available funds in the wider state. In this it failed to deploy the appropriate respect to the less fortunate, was proud and overbearing. Perhaps such suspicions inhere in all monarchical systems. But there is abundant evidence over the past eighty years that both the Okyenhene and the royal family have attracted both the respect and disdain of their subjects, and have often done so in equal measure at one and the same time.

We are then dealing with a rich state; but we are also concerned with a human population who were divided and united by a large number of objective and subjective circumstances, some of which were ancient, some of which were more recent. In the first half of the twentieth century, a great sovereign lay at the heart of all that vibrancy. And it is to that man that we now turn.

51   *A Turn in the South* (London, 1989), pp. 161–2.

CHAPTER TWO

The King

We are concerned with the impact of a great king's death. He was Okyenhene Nana Sir Ofori Atta I. The basic political history of his long reign has been chronicled.[1] The intention of this chapter is, therefore, more thematic; my focus is upon the king, his personality and the construction of his state and family. This more intimate history helps explain why Ofori Atta's death was such a profound loss for Akyem Abuakwa; that matters because the tragedy began in that intensely personal space.

Ofori Atta's Immediate Predecessors

Ofori Atta's three predecessors were confusingly all called Amoako-Atta. The first with this stool-name ruled from 1866 to 1887. Amoako-Atta I bore the brunt of the bewildering changes which beset Akyem Abuakwa. To begin with, the Presbyterian mission finally established itself in Kyebi under the controversial and abrasive leadership of the Reverend David Asante.[2] Asante's Christianity was uncompromising and out of sympathy with what he deemed to be the pagan customs of the Akyem Abuakwa state. By 1868 Church and palace were at daggers drawn. Amoako Atta I's toleration of the mission did not extend to the increasing and occasionally successful attempts to convert palace

1 See especially J. Simensen, 'Commoners, Chiefs and Colonial Government. British Policy and Local Politics in Akim Abuakwa, Ghana', unpublished Ph.D thesis (University of Trondheim, 1975) and Robert Addo-Fening, 'Akyem Abuakwa c.1874–1943: a Study of the Impact of Missionary Activities and Colonial Rule on a Traditional State', unpublished Ph.D thesis (University of Ghana, 1980).
2 Son of Akuapemhene Owusu Akyem, the king of Akuapem, first cousin to Okyenhene Amoako Atta I. Ordained after study in Scotland (begun in 1857), he returned as minister of the mission in Kyebi. What follows is distilled from the informative account in Robert Addo-Fening's thesis, *op. cit.*, pp. 106–12. See also E. Reynold's 'The Basel Mission and the Akuapem State', unpublished paper given to a conference on Christian missions and the state in the Third World (Roskilde, Denmark, May 1992).

officials and royals. Although Amoako Atta I was portrayed by the mission as an unalloyed heathen, his vision was more complex than this allows for. Akan kingship was bound up with much that was sacred in traditional religion but which was now denounced as the devil's work. The king provided a link with the royal ancestors who had ruled the Akyemfo time out of mind. He performed vital, regular rituals of renewal, invoked the wisdom and sought the benedictions of the ancestors through propitiation.[3]

Any Okyenhene would have found it difficult to combine kingship with scrupulous nineteenth-century Christianity; to espouse the new faith was to discard much of the essence of Akan kingship. This was no less true of the many officials of the Ahenfie. Confronted with obdurate Christian attitudes towards many traditional practices, Amoako Atta I was left with little choice; he openly supported a traditionalist, anti-Christian movement in Akyem Abuakwa.

This conflict would ordinarily have worked out in favour of the Okyenhene. But the timing was, from Amoako Atta's point of view, disastrous. Akyem Abuakwa had not been part of the British sphere of influence which spread from the coast in the wake of the Bond of 1844.[4] Akyem Abuakwa was a pragmatic ally of Britain because of their mutual hostility to Asante. But by its own reckoning Akyem Abuakwa remained unequivocally sovereign: while the British regarded the Okyenhene as a 'protected chief', this did not permit the British to encroach upon his jurisdiction. This was all to change in the wake of the Anglo-Asante war of 1874 in which Akyem Abuakwa had proved a valued military partner of the British in the anti-Asante alliance. No less importantly, Akyemfo saw the British as valued partners in *their* campaign against Asante.

Despite the proclamation of a colony in 1874, within whose boundaries it lost its formal independence, the impact upon Akyem Abuakwa was initially slight. This frustrated the Reverend David Asante. He sought to reduce the Okyenhene's power by invoking one of the earliest laws of the colony, the Emancipation Ordinance of December, 1874. Akyem Abuakwa was a slave-holding state and amongst the state's slave-holders was the Okyenhene. David Asante's problem was that despite the liberal pretensions of that legislation, it was an ordinance more often ignored than acted upon. Without the revenue or manpower

---

3   Despite early Christian views, there was no question of ancestor 'worship' in Akyem Abuakwa. See J.B. Danquah, *Ancestors, Heroes and Gods* (Kibi, 1938).

4   The first of a succession of treaties in which signatory African rulers acknowledged the power and in some cases the jurisdiction of the British, though not as subjects but as allies. Akyem Abuakwa was not a signatory.

1 Nana Sir Ofori Atta, Okyenhene of Akyem Abuakwa in 1927.

to extend colonial rule, the British depended upon friendly local rulers even if they were slave-owners; slavery, deodorised by the circumlocution of 'domestic slavery', had to be tolerated if alliances were to survive.

David Asante felt free to harass the Okyenhene and the Palace in the absolute conviction that his prejudices were divinely inspired and that, more mundanely, British rule would confirm his monopoly of the moral high ground. In an important court case in 1877, David Asante prevailed upon the colonial law officers to deal with the assault on the wife of a local deacon by the Okyenhene. As Addo-Fening points out, both David Asante and the Okyenhene lost out in this process. By this time the Governor had had enough of Asante's tactless provocations which threatened disturbances in the new colony, and used the case to force him to leave Akyem Abuakwa. But at the same time the Okyenhene had allowed the first cat's paw of British jurisdiction to intervene in his own bailiwick by permitting himself to be tried under its rules.[5]

Amoako Atta I believed that the Governor's action had confirmed his own authority and exonerated his harassment of the growing body of Akyem Abuakwa Christians. By May 1880, the continual complaints of the Basel missionaries to the British about the king's persecution bore fruit. The Okyenhene was accused of involvement in a ritual murder carried out during the funeral customs of Nifahene Duodo in 1874. The all-African, and all-Christian, jury exonerated him on that charge; but he was found guilty of 'malicious arson', a charge relating to the destruction of church property, and was sentenced to five years' penal servitude. He was exiled in Lagos from 14 May 1880.

His exile ushered in a dreadful period for the Akyem Abuakwa stool. During this time two senior chiefs, Adontenhene and Gyaasehene, died, as did the Queen Mother, the *Ohemaa*. Tradition also suggests that, horror of horrors, several members of the royal family converted to Christianity.[6] The Christian community, especially in Kyebi, had become powerful. Addo-Fening argues that these early adherents were not only the familiar figures of many accounts of African conversion – ex-slaves, ex-pawns, the indigent and women – but were also those with a history of antipathy towards the stool or the stool family.[7] In 1883 for example they were successfully to champion the candidacy of a Christian, Joseph Bosompen, for one of Kyebi's most senior local stools.[8] Further erosion of royal authority emerged from the colonial power's virtual guarantee of protection to Christians. Colonial government pressured local rulers such as the Adikrofo of Apapam and Apedwa to sell land to the Basel missionaries on which they were to build mission stations and schools.

Amoako Atta's exile ended in December 1884. During his absence royal authority decayed. Symbolising that, several of his wives had run away with members of the Christian community. This was the ultimate in indignity. Seduction of a royal wife was a capital crime; the traditional death penalty in these circumstances was exemplary, horrific and long-drawn-out. Amoako Atta I returned to Kyebi determined to reassert his authority and that of the Ofori Panin stool. He recommenced his persecution of the Christian community. Despite the patient attempts at reconciliation in 1886 by the tactful new minister, Esau Ofori, the tension between the mission and the stool was renewed. The

---

5   Addo-Fening, *op. cit.*, p. 117.
6   Addo-Fening, *op. cit.*, pp. 135–6.
7   *Op. cit.*, p. 144.
8   That of the Kyebi, as opposed to the Akyem Abuakwa, Gyaasehene. Bosompen, who came from Apedwa, had converted in 1876.

colonial government, arguing that they were merely honouring their promise of protection to the Christians, intervened again and again in the affairs of Akyem Abuakwa, finally sending in an armed detachment to 'keep the peace'. On 8 January 1887, the humiliated Okyenhene left Akyem Abuakwa for Aburi and died of pneumonia the following month.

Amoako Atta I was succeeded by his younger brother Kwesi Kuma, who adopted the stool name of Amoako Atta II. The early months of his reign were no more peaceful than the last months of his brother's. Amoako Atta I's funeral was the occasion for anarchy, which suggested that Kyebi at least was in the grip of something close to a civil war. Akan funerals are always short periods in which chaos is sanctioned.[9] In this case, vindictive acts by Christians against traditionalists and vice versa were rife. Crops and buildings were burnt, livestock shot. By the end of October 1887, Akyem Abuakwa had been allotted its first District Commissioner, Captain H.B. Lethbridge.[10] He toured the district to make it known 'throughout Eastern Akim that the DC's Court is now open for the hearing of all cases'.[11] This overtly challenged Amoako Atta II's jurisdiction over Christians, and to underline this Lethbridge was accompanied by a significant show of strength.[12]

Amoako Atta II's prestige was inevitably reduced by this colonial intervention, even if it was not yet a permanent presence. The Christian community could now defy his authority[13] by threatening to summon that of the colonial government. But Amoako Atta II was also defied by traditionalists. The rulers of the towns who traditionally were charged with defending the routes into Kyebi against invaders and

9 A king's death ushers in a period of chaos. This is beautifully caught in one of the funeral dirges for a dead Asantehene: '*Nana atu kineye, awia ne ebekuyen. . . .*', 'The king has removed his umbrella/We shall be scorched to death by the sun.' (from the text and translation by the late A.A.Y. Kyerematen, *Kingship and Ceremony in Ashanti* (Kumasi, no date but 1965)). The significance of trees and shade in Akan allegory is raised in R.S. Rattray's *Religion and Art in Ashanti* (London, 1927). Asante describe the death of a king by saying *dupon kesee atutu'*, which evokes the uprooting of a huge *gyadua* tree. The inherent chaos can be extremely violent. For an especially harrowing example, see T. McCaskie, 'Death and the Asantehene: a Historical Meditation', in *Journal of African History*, 30, 3, 1989.

10 No DC was permanently stationed in Kyebi in what became known as Birrim District until 1908. Before then the DC was essentially a peripatetic figure of colonial authority.

11 NAG ADM 11/1/1094, 11 October 1887.

12 '1 sergeant, 2 corporals, 3 lance-corporals, 1 bugler, 20 privates, a colonial surgeon and a magistrate R.B. Acquay', *ibid.* Acquay was an African.

13 The extent of that remained unresolved until as late as June 1899; only then was the Native Jurisdiction Ordinance, which spelled out the matters that could be heard by the 'Native Tribunal' or by the colonial courts, extended to Akyem Abuakwa. The ordinance had been promulgated in 1883.

with defending the king's person, the Amantoo Mmiensa (the Three Counties), deplored the manner in which Amoako Atta I had been pressured by the colonial state. They condemned what they saw as Amoako Atta II's impotence in the face of colonial incursions. In August 1894 the Odikro of Apedwa 'publicly abused and insulted the king' at the royal tribunal and later expelled royal messengers from Apedwa.[14]

In 1900, following what many Akyemfo felt to be a weak reaction during the military campaign in Asante of that year, the Amantoo Mmiensa were again prominent in an attempt to turn Amoako Atta II out of office.[15] Perversely it was the colonial government which saved the Okyenhene's bacon. They invoked a section of the Native Jurisdiction Ordinance to defy the wishes of many of the state's sub-chiefs to have him removed.[16] That Amoako Atta II survived in office until his death in February 1911 owed much to the diplomacy and bureaucratic skills being deployed in the palace by the man who was to become Ofori Atta I.

He and his older brother had taken over the secretariat in Ofori Panin Fie in August 1903. He was only twenty-two years old. Between 1903 and his accession in 1912, he was to steer the state and traditional office in that state through the shoals of transition. As his half-brother J.B. Danquah later expressed it, the state was 'emerging from the old order of affairs into a new era in which the principal care of the men at the head of affairs was so to blend the new with the old as to effect and adjust a desirable equilibrium in the peaceful government of the country'.[17]

That is very precisely the point. Towards the end of Amoako Atta I's reign, the 'old order', exemplified in the office of Okyenhene and the power of the palace, showed every sign of impending collapse. In the early 1900s it was partly shored up by a colonial government which sought increasingly to maintain what they regarded as law and order and a decent trading climate by using 'natural rulers' as auxiliaries. Ofori Atta's genius, a word used advisedly, was the recognition that kingship could be modernised and made more powerful than it had ever been during the pre-colonial period.

He had only a short time to wait before being able to exercise direct power rather than simply advising the Akyem Abuakwa monarch.

---

14 NAG ADM 11/1/1095, Amoako Atta II to the Colonial Secretary, 3 August 1894.
15 Such attempts are usually known by the ungraceful expression 'destoolments'.
16 Addo-Fening argues that this owed less to affection for Amoako Atta II than to apprehension that he would be succeeded by Ofori Atta's elder brother, Alex Eugene Danquah, of whom they thought very little. *Op. cit.*, p. 394.
17 *Akim Abuakwa Handbook*, p. 111.

Amoako Atta's successor, Amoako Atta III, who was known as Kwaku Sreko before his enstoolment, was a disaster. As J.B. Danquah tactfully put it, 'he had allowed his exuberant generosity to over-run the limits of a sober-minded person';[18] in other words, he spent state money and was a drunkard. He was destooled on 26 November 1912. Four days later A.E.B. Danquah was enstooled as Okyenhene Ofori Atta I, Akyem Abuakwa's first literate monarch and its greatest since Ofori Panin, the founder of the modern state.

Biography of a Prince

Ofori Atta's enthusiasm for the written word allows us to get a picture of the kind of man he was.[19] The future Nana Ofori Atta was born on 11 October 1881. His father, Yaw Boakye, was a senior official at the palace in Kyebi, one of the *Atumpakafo* – state drummers – to Amoako Atta I. This office implied much more than musicianship: drummers are heirs and repositories of a significant genre of Akyem Abuakwa's traditions; they were hence experts in protocol and precedent.[20] He was impeccably well connected, being the nephew of Omanhene Asafo Agyei of Dwaben.[21] Before Amoako Atta I's accession as Okyenhene of

18 *Op. cit.*, p. 115.
19 The records in the Ofori Panin Fie, the minutes of the State Council and his Tribunal, the minutes of both the Legislative Council and the Executive Council and the numerous writings of J.B. Danquah about his half-brother afford us a remarkable picture of this man. While he was unusual in being a literate ruler in this early period, he was not the only person to be so. A survey in 1913 in the southern third of the Gold Coast suggests that over a third of Eastern Province 'chiefs' were literate (12 out of 33) as opposed to 4 out of 25 in Central Province and 0 out of 43 in Western Province: NAG ADM 11/1/498. These figures cannot be entirely accurate, but they do show that Akyem Abuakwa, Akuapem, Krobo and Kwahu were well served by literate leaders.
20 Something they share with the Amomafo, the court's minstrel poets, the blowers of the state horns such as the Asesebeng as well as the Akyeame, or linguists. Akyem Abuakwa's 'traditions', assemblages of accounts of and reasons for the past and the present, come in multiple voices, each of which emphasises different aspects. Informants said that Yaw Boakye combined his formal role with being the keeper of the Okyenhene's privy purse.
21 Dwaben in Asante (also spelt Juaben). Yaw Boakye's uncle led the Dwabens during the Asante invasion (October 1875). The defeated Dwabens retreated into Akyem Abuakwa, with whose ruler they had a military alliance. Asafo Agyei's attempts to regain his state from Asante were seen as disruptive by the British; he was deported in 1877 (to Elmina). He returned in 1879 to what was now called New Dwaben, a town and region carved out of Akyem Abuakwa territory. He plotted against Asante and was deported in 1881 to Lagos where he died in 1886. See R. Addo-Fening, 'The Background to the Deportation of

Akyem Abuakwa, Yaw Boakye had reputedly been the future king's best friend.[22]

What was even more important in this matrilineal society was that Ofori Atta's mother was Akosua Buor Gyankromah. Her blood-line could not have been more distinguished. She was a direct descendant of the great Ofori Panin, the thirteenth Okyenhene, who died in 1727, the founder of modern Akyem Abuakwa. She was moreover the grand-daughter of Nana Dokua who, unusually for a woman, had been Akyem Abuakwa's twenty-third recorded ruler,[23] and an exceptional one at that. Akosua Buor Gyankromah was accordingly first cousin to Amoako Atta I. While Amoako Atta I had a great many cousins, she was particularly close to the Okyenhene. He is remembered as having called her 'Yeyere' or 'darling wife' in public, an affectionate name obviously usually reserved for a wife. Both were members of the Asona clan and thus there was no question of marriage between them; nor is there anything which suggests any sort of affair. Such a liaison would have been dangerous; if discovered it would have been a prima facie case for Amoako Atta's being thrown out of office. It would also have led to serious punishment, for endogamy was regarded with absolute abhorrence by Akans. All that we can conclude is that she was unusually close to her kinsman. It is believed today that it was as a token of the affection between Yaw Boakye and Amoako Atta that the latter, in effect, 'gave' his obviously adored first cousin in marriage to his much admired friend.

Ofori Atta, or more properly Kwadwo Dua as he was known as a child, had parents who were thus both highly respected and well-placed in Akyem Abuakwa. In normal circumstances he, and his brothers and sisters, would have looked forward to the privileged upbringing of princes and princesses of Akyem Abuakwa. Through their mother they were members of the Asona clan and the royal house; the boys were potential heirs to the stool and the girls potential mothers of kings. But their father, who was already middle-aged, decided to convert to Christianity in 1876.

By any judgement this was an extraordinary decision. He was at the peak of a career that owed much to the reputation he enjoyed in the eyes of his monarch. But his king was already involved in a sometimes violent campaign to reduce the growing influence of the Presbyterians in

King Asafo Agyei and the Foundation of New Dwaben', in *Transactions of the Historical Society of Ghana*, vol. XIV, no. 2, December 1973.

22 NAG SCT 2/4/12, *Civil Record Book*, vol. 4B, p. 580.
23 From 1817–35, when she abdicated to be succeeded by Atta Panin. The Akyem royal family has been, since the early nineteenth century, a 'house' within the Asona clan, who are descended from Nana Dokua through the female line.

Akyem Abuakwa. By his apostasy, Yaw Boakye had unequivocally placed himself in the camp of the king's, his friend's, enemies. It was a recipe for a family disaster.

In tune with the prevailing Presbyterian ethos in the Gold Coast, Yaw Boakye, or Emmanuel Boakye Danquah as he now preferred to be called, denounced the 'heathen' practices of the court. He piously refused to drum on Sundays or on 'pagan' festivals such as Addae.[24] In what must have been a terrifying test of conflicting loyalties, Akosua Buor Gyankromah, who since her conversion in 1877 was known as Susanna, stood by her husband as royal anger turned from shock and affront into active persecution of these royal apostates.

This was not the result of the blind fury of a simple bigot. It was as much the result of Yaw Boakye's provocations.[25] Yaw Boakye had acted as one of David Asante's key witnesses in his first court case against the Okyenhene. This led to an uncompromising vendetta between the two men in which both seem to have forgotten their earlier mutual affection. Shortly after his return from exile, Amoako Atta saw Yaw Boakye at the State Council. Tradition says that Amoako Atta rose from the stool and, defying protocol by not speaking through his Okyeame or linguist, shouted at his *quondam* drummer: 'That is Boakye. That is Boakye. That is Boakye' whilst pointing his right forefinger at him. So threatening was this that it is said that Yaw Boakye fainted and had to be carried out of the palace unconscious.

Ofori Atta's parents moved to the Oburonikrom and built a large house, Yiadom Hall, to the west of the church. It still stands today, a magnificent courtyard house only slightly smaller than the capacious mission house itself. Its front door lies fifty yards from the doors of the church and close to the free-standing carillon of church bells. By moving from 'the town' to Oburonikrom the family had symbolically as well as spiritually sided with the Church against the king and the court in Ofori Panin Fie.

The Presbyterian establishment thought well of Emmanuel Boakye Danquah; he had not only learnt to read and write but was by the middle 1880s felt to be the ideal, committed 'native' evangelist. Their eventual use of him and his little family was, however, to prove dangerous. Given the pressure the family were under in Kyebi, the mission's decision to send them to evangelise at Asuom in October 1886 was foolhardy. The mission clearly hoped that an evangelist with such an enviable genealogy would succeed where others of more humble origins might not. While Asuom is some thirty-five miles distant to the

---

24 He told the king that he 'could not join in anything done in honour of the fetish'. NAG SCT 2/4/12, *Civil Record Book*, vol. 4B, pp. 513–14.

25 For an analysis of Amoako Atta's actions see Addo-Fening's thesis, *op. cit.*

west of Kyebi as the crow flies,[26] the story of Yaw Boakye's conversion was widespread in Akyem Abuakwa and was, to traditionalists, a notorious matter.[27] Asuom was, moreover, the site of one of the Akyem Abuakwa's greatest shrines, that of Apenin.

On his arrival, the new evangelist promptly and properly presented himself to the local ruler, who was accompanied by his chief priest, Okomfo Anene. At a formal meeting, the kind of courtly environment in which he had spent so much of his career, Yaw Boakye earnestly announced the Good News and warned of the implications of ignoring his message. It was a grim meeting of opposed and unbending convictions. The court at Asuom was unimpressed and angered; the Omanhene ordered the townspeople not to sell food to the family and thus, in effect, put them under siege in his town. In the meantime the local priests at the shrine consulted the *Obosom*,[28] which ruled that if the evangelist and his entourage were not immediately driven from Asuom the results for the town would be dire.

Two days later Yaw Boakye and his young family were first roughly manhandled and then literally thrown out of town by night; their property was destroyed. These dreadful events were sufficiently traumatic, the family insists to this day, to cost the life of Ofori Atta's recently born younger brother, Kwaku Dua, who died shortly afterwards.

The family arrived back at Kyebi, visibly shaken by recent events, on 2 November. Kwadwo Dua was just five years old at this time; he was certainly old enough to share his parents' fear and young enough for this to have been a dreadful memory to take into adult life. But it was a very confusing set of messages. On the one hand he knew that he was a young aristocrat, not least because of the ways people addressed him. Despite the Presbyterian Church's feud with the Palace, much of that church's practice was unusually supportive of what they regarded as the more benign sides of Akan culture. And despite their appalling proximate experiences, both his father and mother are known to have shared some of their great pride in the past with their children. Ofori Atta was certainly not brought up to view his own history in a negative light.[29] But he had also witnessed, and felt at first hand, the power and

26 Significant hill-climbing was involved before the era of road-building.
27 There was moreover a family link with Asuom. Yaw Boakye's uncle, Asafo Agyei, had set up headquarters there in 1875 while re-grouping his Dwaben force against Kumasi. The colonial authorities however insisted that his forces move from there by the end of that year. NAG ADM 1/7/10, Moloney to Hay, 3 December 1875.
28 The usual translation of this term is 'fetish', which, thanks to wilful Christian – and Moslem – misunderstanding and later appropriation by Freudians, has become a pejorative term. The *Obosom* at Asuom is amongst the most powerful of the *Abosom*.
29 He was very proud off it. As king he wrote to Akyem's chiefs: '... it is highly necessary that such history should be preserved ... any Stool or family without

fury of what Danquah called 'the old order'. One did not have to be very old and experienced to see the essential conundrum. Ofori Atta was to do more than see this problem: he was to live it.

Akyem Abuakwa's very integrity and distinctiveness were threatened by the incursions of both Christianity and colonialism. His immediate family was Christian and had suffered greatly for that. Ultimately, colonial rule and its predilection for its own version of law and order had protected his family, and others like them, from what in pre-colonial days would have been condign, and hence capital punishment for what was unequivocally treasonable behaviour. For the rest of his life he was to seek an accommodation between these contradictory forces; and it was to be more than an accommodation but rather an attempt at synergy whereby both Akyem Abuakwa and its kingship could be reinforced and reconstructed by using some of the properties of the two forces which were undermining the state at the end of the nineteenth century.

It is hard to believe that Ofori Atta's childhood was happy. First he and his family had to endure further exile when Yaw Boakye was sent to establish a new mission station about ten miles north of Anum which now lies on the eastern shore of the southern end of Lake Volta. The children he played with were more likely to have spoken Ewe than Twi, and perhaps the need for a playtime *lingua franca* contributed to what became a very fine grasp of formal and colloquial English. When it was time for him to go to school, he had to do so at the Basel mission school at Anum, for his father's mission station was still without a school. In a period before the advent of the motor-lorry he had, during the week, to board with the schoolteacher, for it was too far for a small boy to walk there and back each day.

But very much more tragically, his mother died when he was only eight years of age. Premature loss of a mother is tragic in any culture. It is devastating for an Akan. For Kwadwo Dua, his father's stern monogamy meant that there was no stepmother to cuddle him at this terrible time. He was to live with his maternal grandmother during his secondary education in Kyebi; this was an important relationship, for her death on the eve of his assuming the kingship hurt him greatly.[30] Yaw Boakye and his little family are remembered as a close and affectionate family; apart from considerations of natural love and affection,

tradition loses its intrinsic value . . . it is . . . essential that Akyem Abuakwa shall have its history retained . . .'. Okyenhene to all Akyem chiefs, 19 December 1925, AASA 3/266.

30 In March 1890. While the relationship between a young boy and his grandmother is obvious enough, the importance of grandmothers in the childhood of young Akans has scarcely been touched by scholars, although it is much spoken of in the vernacular.

their harsh experiences can only have reinforced family bonds. Only four days after his mother's death, this already grieving family learnt that Emmanuel Yaw Agyei, one of Ofori Atta's older brothers, had died at the Presbyterian theological seminary at Akropong. The family were clearly shattered by this double loss. Yaw Boakye's life seemed almost Job-like, and the mission gave him some months' compassionate leave, which he took in Kyebi.

This involved yet another move for the eight-year-old boy. And these disruptions were added to when, at the end of 1890, his father was appointed to the mission station at Bepong in Kwahu. Ofori Atta was now registered at the Presbyterian school in Kyebi, and thus able to spend only school holidays with his father at Bepong. After a year at the Kyebi school, where he successfully completed his Standard I examinations, he spent two years, again in a Presbyterian school but this time at Abetifi, closer to his adored father's mission station than Kyebi. He completed the three years that took him to Standard VII at the middle (grammar) school at Begoro in Akyem Abuakwa. His reports and his reputation indicate that he was a clever and likeable little boy. At his father's insistence, the next step was to be the cloth, and he was duly enrolled in the theological seminary at Akropong.

It did not take long to realise that he lacked a vocation. After less than a year he returned to his disappointed father[31] with his decision to leave the seminary. Given the great sophistication that characterises his career, his fluency in both Twi and English, the wit and style of his writing, it is a shock to realise that his considerably disjointed formal education ended when he was only eighteen years of age.

Quite why his career now took him to Accra is unclear. We know that a family friend, J. Wilson Buobai, who was later to become ruler of Apinaman in Akyem Abuakwa,[32] had given him a letter of introduction to the formidable Accra lawyer Thomas Hutton-Mills.[33] The young man was to be employed as a solicitor's clerk. At this stage of his life, oral evidence suggests that he wanted to become a lawyer; this is an impression supported by the fact that Ofori Atta actually lived with the

31 Disappointed as his oldest son had died eight months short of ordination. Another son, Alex A.E. Danquah, had also withdrawn from the seminary and was now a Police Superintendent at Prampram on the coast. Any hopes that Yaw Boakye had of passing on the torch were accordingly dashed.
32 With the stool name of Barima Kofi Boaten.
33 The scion of a distinguished complex of Accra families, he was educated in Freetown. He began his career as a clerk in the office of the Queen's Advocate but was dismissed, on silly grounds, for alleged involvement in a riot in Accra in 1886. As a result he went to England to read for the Bar and was called in 1894. Thereafter he practised in Accra. He was to be President of the National Congress of British West Africa.

Hutton-Mills family in their grand Accra mansion for some of this time, a privilege which would hardly have been extended to someone destined to remain simply a clerk.[34]

As with the theological seminary, Ofori Atta stuck with this attachment for no more than a year. There is no evidence which explains why he did not proceed with his legal training. There is no question of a rift with Thomas Hutton-Mills; they were to remain on friendly terms until the 1930s and Hutton-Mills was to be retained by Ofori Atta, after his accession, as legal adviser to the Akyem Abuakwa stool.[35] It cannot be explained by boredom either. Ofori Atta remained fascinated by law throughout his life. As Chairman of the Native Tribunal in Akyem Abuakwa he was to spend a very large proportion of his reign dealing with legal niceties – and nastinesses – and he loved it. The records of these hearings show how much he relished the cut and thrust of the adversarial process, enjoyed exploring versions of the 'truth' and delighted in revelation.[36] He was to develop into one of the colonial government's most respected sources on 'customary law', a role in which he both interpreted 'custom' and also 'invented' tradition and codified it for a grateful colonial government.[37]

The *guondam* solicitor's clerk was to become a colonial Solomon by the late 1920s.[38] His enthusiasm for law owed much to his perception of its importance as a weapon of defence and offence.[39] That is visible in the

34   At this stage few people would have singled the youngster out as the successor, to the stool. There were other eligible men including the Okyenhene's brothers. Hutton-Mills did not, I believe, accommodate him because he was royalty; many Africans were. Nor did he do so because the family were rich; at this stage it is clear that the young man lived entirely off his small salary.

35   They were however to be antagonists over the attempted secession of Asamankese and Akwatia, who were legally represented by Hutton-Mills, from Akyem Abuakwa in the 1930s.

36   Many of his judgements are recorded in J.B. Danquah's *Cases in Akan Law Delivered by the Hon. Nana Sir Ofori Atta* (London, 1928).

37   He was to slip into this role early in his career. He was consulted, as the most authoritative expert, on the 'rules' of destoolment amongst the Akan in 1918, only six years after his accession. See Ofori Atta to Colonial Secretary, 13 August 1918, NAG ADM 11/1/720. The language of this letter, which was drafted by the Okyenhene, immediately reveals its author as someone who relished the ornate quality of legal English.

38   He was by then defining what 'customary' law actually was for the colonial government. See *Minute* Sequence 23–25 April 1929, NAG ADM 1/11/1016. The Native Administration Ordinance of 1927, which David Kimble sees as giving 'a firmer foundation to the power of the Chiefs and to some respects to extend it, notably in judicial matters ...' (*A Political History of Ghana*, Oxford, 1963, p. 493), was largely drafted by Ofori Atta.

39   'We can use colonial laws to defeat our enemies and to prevent ourselves from being defeated by them. Only those who understand the laws and see how than

strong support afforded to his half-brother, Joseph Boakye Danquah, during the latter's legal studies in London and the appointment, in 1928, of J.B. Danquah as solicitor to the State Council.

But if boredom does explain his abandonment of Hutton-Mills' chambers, then his next port of call was a jump from the frying-pan into the fire. He joined the correspondence branch of the colonial Customs Department in Accra as a clerk. He now sent and received letters which were rarely if ever other than sleep-inducing. His half-brother later suggested that tedium pushed A.E.B. Danquah, as the young man was now called, into joining the Gold Coast Volunteer Corps in 1900. He was a good soldier and within the year was made up to Sergeant. He served with distinction with the Akyem Abuakwa levy in the Asante campaign of 1900, although from the point of view of this detachment, the campaign was a disaster.[40] For a few months after this challenging and life-threatening interruption in the tedium of his life, Ofori Atta returned to the Customs Department.

This employment was not destined to last long. His unusual written fluency in both English[41] and Twi was wasted in the Customs Department. By the end of 1900 he had been transferred to the Governor's Office as a correspondence clerk. His language skills and his easy, open manner were quickly noticed and despite his age, he was to serve as the Governor's[42] interpreter on several occasions. In 1902 he resigned from government service. At a greater salary than he enjoyed as a civil servant he became a senior clerk with the mining company, Goldfields of Eastern Akim (Akim Abuakwa) Ltd. This appointment owed everything to the Okyenhene's[43] influence. The company had opened a mining base and office in Kyebi in late 1901.[44] They were actively prospecting in the Birim valley in the first decade of the twentieth

they can be related to native [sic] law will prevail.' Ofori Atta to J.B. Danquah, 26 November 1928, AASA PF/7.

40 Nana Amoako Atta II's 'unsteadiness' at Fwereso, which along with some rash tactics by the two young European officers contributed to a rout of this force, prompted some of his subjects to try to destool him. Ofori Atta comes well out of this. He had 'a good war' and won the Ashanti Medal; this was useful to his career as the electors to the stool continued to see military courage as a strong qualification, amongst others, for a future Okyenhene.

41 Better than many of the ex-patriate, native speakers of English with whom he corresponded at this time, whose grammar and style could be wretched.

42 Sir Matthew Nathan, KCMG, Governor 1900–4.

43 By employing the young royal the company not only obliged the Okyenhene but got their hands on a fluent, bilingual employee.

44 With headquarters in London. It had a variety of addresses until its liquidation in 1928 after which it was reconstituted as Akim (1928) Ltd. The firm's addresses included 56 Cannon St and Finsbury Pavement House, both of which were in the City of London.

century and were dependent upon the Okyenhene for the grant of concessions to prospect. This was not to be the last mining or trading enterprise which sought to influence the Okyenhene by acceding to requests for appointments for young royals.

While J.B. Danquah suggests a degree of intention behind this sequence of employment, a step-by-step apprenticeship in the new governmental and economic order,[45] there is no documentary evidence which supports that. But by 1902, when he left government service, there can be little doubt that he was now being placed as an important client of the stool. At the suggestion of the directors of the gold mining company, and following an introduction by them, he spent nine months working in the larger gold-mining operations at Obuasi before returning finally to Kyebi in August 1903.[46] A month later, he and his elder brother A.E.A. Danquah, to whom he was close, were appointed to take over the secretariat in the Ofori Panin Fie.

This was a taxing job. The bureaucratic demands on the Akyem Abuakwa state were increasingly onerous. Government directives and requests for information became more frequent as colonial rule established itself.[47] The negotiation of agreements with mining and trading companies became a frequent function of the Okyenhene and his court. But the king and his councillors were illiterate; they were dependent upon a handful of young clerks whose education had taken them no further than basic literacy and numeracy.[48] None of them knew much of the world outside Kyebi; none of them before the arrival of the two Danquah brothers was royal, and hence they were not intimate with the court they served. As blood relatives of the Okyenhene, the brothers could be trusted in a way that other civil servants could not be.

While the family tradition insists that A.E.A. Danquah was highly

---

45 *Akim Abuakwa Handbook*, p. 111. Danquah's account, written during his half-brother's lifetime, was partly dictated by the Okyenhene. There is an element of rationalising the random after the event in the way the sequence is put together.

46 His interest, in both senses of the word, in the gold industry during his reign was stimulated by these experiences. John Saxton, the British mining engineer who was to be Ofori Atta's business partner and agent in Britain until his death in the late 1920s, got to know the future king during this period.

47 The demands were even more taxing given that before 1908 Akyem Abuakwa had no resident District Commissioner and hence no locally based bureaucracy to whom they could turn for advice.

48 They were however part of a growing cohort of western educated southern Ghanaians. André Gide, meeting an agent of the Forèstiére company in what is now Gabon, found out that he had worked in the Gold Coast and asked if he preferred working there. '"Don't!" cried he, "There's nothing whatever to be done over there. Just think! Nearly all the Negroes know how to read and write. . . ."' *Travels in the Congo* (Penguin edition, 1986), p. 70.

intelligent and as skilled as his younger brother, all agree that he lacked application. Unlike him, Ofori Atta was a glutton for hard work throughout his life. As king, his daily schedule recalls the devotion to detail and personal involvement with all the affairs of state of a Philip II or a Louis XIV. Of course he relaxed but never before he had completed his daily tasks. As Tribunal Chairman he resisted adjournments, never hurried the proceedings and was always insistent on seeing that all stages of a process were properly gone into. Tribunal sittings were long and there was none of 'wretches hang that jurymen may dine' about his court. Even the minor administrative work in the Ahenfie was never totally devolved and he went through his staff's drafts before fair copies were made. He was never satisfied with his bureaucracy.[49]

The palace archives speak volumes about this revolution in the king's bureaucracy. There is no doubt that the creation of an extensive palace bureaucracy was an innovation. The Danquah brothers instituted a proper filing system, recorded Tribunal and Council meetings in impeccable minutes, had a letterhead printed and generally transformed the state's administration. One of the mysteries of that revolution was the decision to use English in a high proportion of its business. While it made sense to use English in exchanges with colonial authorities and the firms, its use in Tribunal and Council minutes is harder to understand. Because of Presbyterian education, all of the palace bureaucrats were literate in Twi and meetings were conducted in Twi, yet the minutes are usually in English. Record-keeping was thus a draining task of simultaneous translation; the sometimes exhausted handwriting show that these are simultaneous records.[50]

Amoako Atta and his councillors were clearly well-pleased with these developments. That confidence is visible in the increasing frequency with which the king and the Okyeman Council turned to this very young man for advice.[51] With greater frequency the king's and the state's interests were publicly represented by Ofori Atta.[52] He was now

---

49   'In dealing with letters received I still have my memory to thank . . . and I still have to deal with almost everyone myself,' he snarled at the State Secretary in 1935. Okyenhene to K.T.A. Danquah, 20 April 1935, AASA PF/7.

50   Tribunal registrars and clerks to the councils became fine record-keepers. About twenty-five percent of the State Archive is in Twi, for the most part occasioned by an incoming letter in Twi which attracted a reply in the same language. I believe that Ofori Atta felt that English was somehow a 'natural' language of a modern bureaucracy. The Presbyterians had, however, no trouble with being thoroughly and often tediously bureaucratic in Twi!

51   This is a culture which reveres the wisdom that age confers. Calling someone a 'small boy' is a conventional suggestion that his opinion is not worth entertaining.

52   This was against custom. The king enjoyed the services of about fifteen Akyeame, linguists, who traditionally both advised him and acted as his

acting as the Okyenhene's confidential secretary. The king's favour[53] was clear to all members of the court and to the colonial regime. Travelling Commissioner J. Philips noted: '. . . the Omanhene . . . is either utterly helpless in the hands of his elders and councillors or extremely clever. . . . I am inclined to think he is the latter. He is ably assisted by his clerk Mr A.B. Danquah . . . who is now in my opinion the brain power behind the Omanhene's throne. . . .'[54] All this suggests that he was becoming a very powerful young man.

Amoako Atta II died in February 1911, sincerely mourned by Ofori Atta who had become very fond of his master. His successor's[55] unhappy reign lasted no more than twenty months.[56] He was destooled in November 1912. In the period leading up to the announcement of the nomination of new Okyenhene there is no record of serious discussion of any candidate other than the young A.E.B. Danquah. And so it was that on 30 November 1912 he was duly enstooled as Ofori Atta I at the age of thirty-one.[57] Thus began his reign of thirty-one years.

Dynasty

Ofori Atta was not just an impressively bright and administratively able prince who became a king; he was also an ambitious man with firm ideas about re-forging his ancient kingdom. Those plans included the deployment of his immediate family as the instruments of positive change. His concepts were not essentially democratic although he genuinely sought to better the lives of his subjects. He believed in aristocracy as strongly as he believed in the benefits of technology. His ideas combined elitism and modernisation. While there is no immediate evidence of his having read the works of the nineteenth-century pioneer African nationalist Edward Blyden, much of the thrust is identical. Africa's dependent and dominated status could only be overcome by the

spokesmen. Although Ofori Atta was always accompanied by an Okyeame in colonial courts, or at meetings with colonial officials, he acted on his own.

53   He spent more time in the presence of the Okyenhene out of office hours in the Dabre. Despite having no traditional office at this point, he was more intimate with the king than the most senior of the wing-chiefs.

54   In a letter to the Colonial Secretary, 25 July 1909, NAG ADM 11/1/136.

55   Amoako Atta III was a younger brother of the old king.

56   Kwaku Sreko, who took the stool name of Amoako Atta III, died in 1918.

57   An installation not formally recognised by the colonial government, as required under the Native Jurisdiction Ordinance, until February 1913. There was nothing sinister about this. Colonial bureaucracy was habitually slow. Ofori Atta was highly thought of and the succession of a literate, able man to an important stool was welcome in Accra.

development of sturdy self-sufficiency. Above all, Africans would have to emulate the technical and institutional merits of the West if they were to hold their own in the modern world. And once they could hold their own, they could successfully defend those aspects of traditional life which were estimable. That kind of progress, a favourite word of Ofori Atta's, rested on the rapid acquisition of western education.

If the state was to survive, its rulers must be guaranteed in office by being themselves educated and being served by educated people. Its rulers and their families must also succeed in the creation of wealth which was also, he believed, a logical result of the acquisition of education. The Kyebi royal family must provide an example to the wider population. But because of their achievements, they would be able to retain control without serious challenge from below.

These ideas were not particularly traditional. His enthusiasm for 'progress' was a deeply felt reaction to the weakening of a once mighty state sandwiched between the upper and nether millstones of colonialism and Christianity. The Akyem Abuakwa state, which had been badly shaken in the lifetime of his father and himself, could only be resurrected by adapting to the new demands. And his proximate experiences had convinced him that the management techniques he had learnt about in Accra were the way forward.

That much is easy and implicit in the very course of his career. But the perception of the centrality of his family to this change owes more to his apprehensions about the tenacity of the 'old order' and to even more visceral feelings. While it is possibly psychologistic to do so, it is important to remember how surrounded by death in the family he was. He was concerned not merely with commoner usurpation of royal authority: he was also worried about the gradual extinction of the royal house. He had, after all, lost in childhood his mother, a younger and an older brother. In 1903 his uterine sister Elizabeth Otiwa died. And in 1912 both his maternal grandmother, with whom he had stayed whilst at school in Kyebi, and another uterine sister, Ama Kyerewa, also died. In 1915, a niece, Ama Kyerewa's only daughter, also died.

This was a threatened family tree. His mother's early death had denied this house of the Asona clan large numbers of children; and the death of his brothers and sisters meant that the succession was unusually restricted. His affection for his own children owed something to the brutal fact that he had very few nephews upon whom to lavish affection or favour.[58] Given the ways in which he wrote and spoke about his

---

58 Had he wanted to. Relationships between nephews and uncles can be unbearably tense. The Twi adage *'wofase ye dom'* roughly means that a nephew/heir is hostile to his uncle. This is examined in the context of nineteenth-century Asante by T. McCaskie in 'Konnurokusem: an Essay on Kinship and

immediate family[59] it seems that family tragedy had left its harsh mark on him. It drew him close to his immediate kin. He certainly talked to and of his sons and daughters in an unusually intimate fashion for an Akan dynast; his was a close family despite his public position. His control over his immediate kin allowed him to mould their upbringing, and this was most easily done with his children. It seems likely then that pragmatic concerns and his own more personal experience directed him to choose to staff his modern kingdom largely with his own children and close relations.

But he also promoted his children and the children of previous kings within the more obviously traditional structure. This too was innovative. Before Ofori Atta's reign only the post of Gyaasahene, of all the palace posts, had been traditionally offered to a king's son. The institution of state Danquah called the Executive Council, more correctly known as *Ankobea, Apesemaka ne Kyidom*, became more important in his lifetime. It was a council largely composed of the Kyebi traditional elite resident in the royal capital.[60] By 1919 Ofori Atta had created a new stool for the post of *Abontendomhene*, who was to become the first Councillor of State. It is true that in 1858 the Okyenhene had pre-figured this by creating the post of *Apesemaakahene*, with the role of controlling the passionate rivalries between heirs and their lineages. That post was filled by a man Danquah described as 'the best son of the king'.[61] But the new post had real administrative clout. Local legal matters were heard before the Abontendomhene's Tribunal; the Abontendomhene chaired the Executive Committee in the absence of the Okyenhene. While the traditional, matrilineal hierarchy of wing-chiefs retained power in the State Council, the day-to-day running of the state undoubtedly fell more and more into the hands of the king's close family in the course of his reign. This did not occur without resentment. The sons who were placed in the growing palace bureaucracy were almost always educated, and educated at the state's

Family in the History of the Oyoko Koko Dynasty of Kumase', unpublished paper delivered to the West African seminar, University College, London, October 1991.

59   In many family letters the frequency with which he used terms of affection, unlike the formulaic addresses of kingship, is striking. He used 'beloved', 'devoted' and, when loss occurred, 'tragic' and 'sadness' very often. Psychologism is perhaps a vice but there is enough evidence to suggest that his emotions were as frequently engaged as his brains.

60   Danquah, *Akim Abuakwa Handbook*, p. 66.

61   *Ibid*, p. 67. Danquah suggests that this patrilineal office conferred neutrality, as such a man 'has no interests to represent, other than those of the State' – a neat bit of family special pleading. Of course Abontendomhene had other interests and especially those of the king's immediate kin, and that was one of the reasons why this office was created.

expense. Their nobility entitled them to that state support and then, in turn, that education equipped them for office.

Reconstructing the family details is difficult. There are two sets of written sources which augment the oral material. The palace archives contain partial lists of his children in the 1930s.[62] The Presbyterian Church also listed some of his wives and children in 1933.[63] Both listings are, if the oral material is reliable, incomplete. By the mid-1930s, the palace sources credit him with fifty-one children. The Presbyterian records for roughly the same period allow for only forty-four children. Informed Akyemfo suggest that either number should be at least trebled by the time of his death. So far as wives are concerned, the palace archives record forty-four by the mid-1930s. The Presbyterian record allows for only eleven. But it seems that he had over fifty, as well as numerous, less formally acknowledged, liaisons. We have registered births, and hence accurate birth dates, for only twenty-seven of his children.

His first marriage was to a Kyebi woman called Ellen Kwakoa in 1903, and this marriage was solemnised in church as well as celebrated traditionally. He was a reasonably regular communicant of the Presbyterian Church until his accession and thus was almost certainly at this stage a monogamist.[64] After his coming to the stool, none of the subsequent marriages were solemnised in church.[65] He is remembered as a man who liked women very much and not only as sexual objects. He played a large part in extending western-style education to girls; many young women, both his daughters and other girls in Kyebi, benefited from his unusually enlightened educational sponsorship and encouragement, although this was sometimes at variance with the distinctly non-feminist feelings of his elders. There was, for example, criticism in Okyeman Council when he insisted that his daughter Susan should go to Britain for medical training in the late 1930s. This antipathy was certainly influenced by her gender.[66] While he married many

---

62   AASA 3 series.
63   NAG EC 1/54.
64   Presbyterian records suggest that it was hard to conceal sexual adventurism from members of the congregation. Flirtations and betrayals were obvious in this face-to-face society and privacy was impossible. 'Backsliders', as such miscreants were called, had to account for themselves before the Presbyters and were often excluded from communion (Lord's Supper).
65   The Church continued to list a proportion of his immediate family because a substantial number of children were church attenders and communicants as well as pupils of the schools run by the Presbyterians.
66   Her training was a success and Dr Susan de Graft Johnson, as she became, had a distinguished medical career in Ghana until her death in 1985.

women, he had liaisons with even more. He is remembered as discrete and dignified in such matters, a courtly seducer rather than a ravisher emboldened by a sense of *droit de seigneur*.[67] While many of these liaisons were occasioned by straightforward sexual attraction,[68] he was also consciously building a very particular kind of dynasty.

Those of his wives we know about were in part chosen because they bound the Kyebi stool even more closely to other centres in the kingdom. While some wives came from Kyebi, even more came from each of the major towns of the state; and almost without exception every one of them was a royal in her own right. The intended upshot of that was that by his death a full twenty to twenty-five percent of the chiefs and officials sitting on his State Council or on his Tribunal were his biological sons, who derived their authority to represent towns and villages from their mothers' clan blood-lines.[69] And because he promoted western education, especially amongst his own children, few of whom were illiterate, Akyem Abuakwa's institutions were accordingly 'modernised' in the way Ofori Atta intended. Thus two agendas, one firmly rooted in a concern for binding the state by the traditionally sanctioned method of multiple marriage and the other rooted in his strong sense of 'modernisation' and 'progress', were brought together in the persons of his children and especially his sons.

The atmosphere in the palace must necessarily have been bewildering, hovering as it did between Ofori Atta's enthusiasm for what he regarded as 'progressive' and his insistence on respect for custom. For example his relationship with the church was ambiguous.[70] The parish record books and diaries show that the Presbyterian ministers were frequent visitors at the Ofori Panin Fie. While many of these visits were clearly courtesy calls, numerous such entries record that prayers were said for the Okyenhene in the palace. Ofori Atta did not attend

---

67 Lack of virility and fertility are regarded as profound tragedies for a man. A childless man is called *Okrawa* from the humiliating jibe '*Kote krawa*', or 'wax penis'. As this is rooted in a terror of the extinction of a family line, fecundity and sexual activity of the most important member of the royal family are viewed positively.

68 There is evidence of an affair during his visit to London in 1934 as a member of the joint Aborigines' Rights Protection Society and Joint Provincial Council delegation. A charming intimate letter dated 27 July 1934, sent from Camberwell in south London from someone with an indecipherable signature and prefaced by the valedictory 'Your loyal little friend', suggests that Ofori Atta enjoyed some relaxation whilst in London. This was the only love letter I encountered in the palace.

69 An average of the estimates of a number of informants who were well-placed to make such calculations.

70 An ambiguity brought out admirably in his *Memorandum to the Presbyterian Church of the Gold Coast by the State Council of Akim Abuakwa* (Accra, 1941).

church as a communicant after his succession. But the saying of
Christian prayers in the palace was a commonplace event. These
prayers were usually said in the Dabre, the king's personal quarters.
And the Dabre is no more than seventy-five yards away from the Stool
House where the blackened stools of Akyem Abuakwa's most distinguished past rulers are enshrined. The stools are the repository of
ancestral spirit, wisdom and life, and the rites which surround them
were anathema to the Christians. These abrupt and apparently incon-
gruous juxtapositions typify Ofori Atta's Akyem Abuakwa.

The Presbyterians correctly regarded him as being closer to them
than to other Christian confessions. While he and some of his family
were enumerated in Presbyterian parish censuses, it is notable that
neither he nor his wives or children are credited with paying the
Presbyterian Church's quarterly contributions or the payments that are
listed as 'Lord's Supper dues'. But he and, after his death, his family
were to use Presbyterian ministers as arbiters and peacemakers, and
this as much as anything demonstrates the intimacy of the court with
the Presbytery.

Ofori Atta's attitudes towards religion were complex and enlightened
if pragmatic. As Okyenhene he had, necessarily, to avoid alienating any
of his subjects. Privately he expressed a commendable liberalism. One
of his daughters contemplated conversion to Roman Catholicism in
1942; her priest wrote to her father to canvass his attitude towards this
prospect.[71] Ofori Atta replied: 'Every son or daughter of mine who has
reached puberty has the fullest freedom in regard to choice of whatever
religion he or she desires to embrace....'[72] She was to become a
Roman Catholic. His attitudes towards traditional religion were, despite
his searing childhood experience, no less tolerant. The veneration of
ancestors, the acknowledging of the force of some 'fetishes' and the role
of their *Akomfo* or priests was inescapably part of kingship in Akyem
Abuakwa. Traditional religion lay at the heart of those great reaffirma-
tions of the kingdom and its kingship, the cyclical celebrations of the
Odwira, Addae and Akwasidae festivals. Towards the end of his life he
spoke of these as 'assemblies where the people of Akim renew their
attachment to the soil and love of country and also loyalty and devotion
to the holder of the revered office of the ruler of the *oman*'.[73] Rather
remarkably for someone of his parentage and his era, he appears to
have felt it utterly unnecessary to rationalise or apologise for this central
fact of his office.

Ofori Atta fought successfully for the due recognition of what he

71   Emily Dokua.
72   Ofori Atta to Rev. Father H. Rigney, 4 September 1942, AASA 11/59.
73   Ofori Atta, *Memorandum, op. cit.*

called 'fetishes' and for colonial government to hold its hand[74] when
dealing with the complaints which often arose around practices at
shrines and groves.[75] Believers, he argued, should not be 'left without
any substantial object of faith and worship so vitally essential for the
sustenance of a good civic life'.[76] In this correspondence and in others,
he usually referred to 'cult' members in the third person plural, inten-
tionally conveying the sense that while he did not necessarily himself
believe, others did and their feelings should be respected.[77]

While Ofori Atta and the Okyeman Council recognised, and to some
extent protected, existing shrines in the state, they did so by the issuing
of official licences; and this yielded revenue to the state, for these
licences, like all licences issued by Okyeman, had to be paid for.
Anyone importing a new 'fetish' into Akyem Abuakwa had to appeal to
the State Council for recognition. The Council could and sometimes did
resist new cults. When the Odikro of Suhum announced the arrival of
a new fetish, Tongo, from Upper Volta,[78] Okyeman doubted that
the people of Suhum 'really need these foreign impositions', not least
because of Tongo's possession of witch-finding properties, which 'are
nearly always undesirable'.[79]

Palace life was accordingly a mosaic of ancient and modern. When in
Kyebi, many royal wives lived in the *ma'am* or harem and the palace

74 He encountered little resistance. It was policy to recognise shrines, priests and
    cults when these did not threaten public order. Government dropped heavily
    on Christian missionaries who attacked fetishes. In a minute (9 May 1933), the
    Secretary for Native Affairs recalled an abrasive conversation with a literally
    iconoclastic Catholic missionary: 'Father McCoy . . . gave me an assurance that
    he would support government policy. . . I added that any person who created
    civil disturbances through the destruction of fetishes would be removed from
    the area. . . .' NAG ADM 11/1/824. Government's, like Ofori Atta's, concern
    was that shrine priests should not overcharge devotees, make outrageous claims
    for their powers or get involved in witch-finding campaigns.
75 Like that at Osino when a shrine directed that a woman undergo trial by
    ordeal. The tragic upshot was that the woman never regained her sanity and
    was committed to the asylum in Accra in 1926. AASA 3/272.
76 Ofori Atta to the Governor, 14 March 1928, AASA 3/272.
77 Informants differed over Ofori Atta's 'real' feelings. His writings and
    judgements on matters spiritual is that of an agnostic with a respect for the
    spirituality of others who enjoyed rituals for their inherent theatricality.
    Nothing suggests that he was apprehensive about death or that he believed in
    divine retribution for himself or others. While traditional priests were part of
    the court he seems to have been utterly uninterested in the advantages or
    disadvantages he might enjoy or endure through attempted manipulations of
    the supernatural. If he felt these things, he was careful not to record them or to
    be recorded as saying them.
78 As Burkina Faso was then known.
79 Ofori Atta's report of Okyeman decision to DC Birrim District, 11 May 1928,
    AASA 3/272.

was an extensive, and by all accounts often rather noisy, family home as well as an administrative centre. The younger children, when not in school, played in the palace's main north courtyard and in the Ahenfie's extensive and then beautifully planted gardens.

But homework and games of football were only part of their childhoods. At home their lives were also governed by the routines of the palace. Although there was much about this routine that we should characterise as 'modern' government – the drafting of letters, the filing of correspondence, the sending of telegrams – there was also much that was traditional. The king's apartments, the Dabre, were penetrated by few outside his immediate family. Here he would eat and be bathed, clothed and adorned in seclusion in much the same way as his ancestors had been. Traditionally he could neither be addressed by, nor reply directly to, anyone; his Akyeame, his linguists, acted as his mouthpiece. This owed little to any perception of his divinity, for Akan kings are not so perceived. It was, rather, a function of the fact that the Okyenhene's utterances were definitionally *ex cathedra*. When he spoke, he spoke for the whole state or *oman*. Technically his statements enjoyed the sanction of the Okyeman Council. The Okyenhene was a respected, but not worshipped, institution as well as being a man; his children's experience of his fatherhood was understandably complex.

His surviving children remember, and the documentary record shows, that there were occasions on which he cast off the somewhat grave protocol of the palace. Although he seems to have been deeply embroiled in administration, he spared time for his immediate family. He shared his love of Akyem Abuakwa's history and his ambitions for the state and for the Gold Coast with his children. He discussed, sometimes with rancour, their school reports, their demands for more pocket money and what they should do with their futures. He was a demanding father[80] who had high and sometimes excessive expectations for his children. He was intolerant of failure but enthusiastic about success. He was stubborn and forceful but capable of great warmth.

Such an extensive family suggests that not all the wives and children could enjoy his personal attention. He assuredly had favourites and it remains a mystery why some were favoured and others were not. This was expressed by a close British friend of his, Walter Austin, who acted as his business partner in many ventures. 'Now please tell me why it is that among all your children you have favoured William. . . .[81] At one

---

80 By the post-Spock generation's standards he was undoubtedly an overly demanding father.

81 William Ofori Atta, or Paa Willie as he was widely known in Ghana before his death. He was Ofori Atta's fifth child and the fourth-oldest son. He was later to act as Treasurer of the Akyem Abuakwa Treasury and headmaster of the

time I thought it may be due to this young man showing more promise than any of the others and yet I doubt this. Then again it might be due to a greater affection for William than the others. But I must be wrong on this as you have already indicated your affection for A.E.B.D.[82] Another suggestion is that this boy's mother[83] might in some ways have closer affection for you than others and so you have shown your appreciation by giving William this great opportunity. . . . I am baffled . . . . Maybe you select one boy and girl[84] of your children with some special object in view. . . .'[85]

Sadly there is no record of an answer to these perceptive questions. But there is little doubt that an honest reply would have emphasised that he did indeed 'have some special object in view'. Ofori Atta's options at the beginning of his reign were limited by a variety of factors. While he enjoyed great initial popularity in the state, he enjoyed no more room to manoeuvre than any of his predecessors. Akyem Abuakwa's kingship, which some of his family have sought to portray as living democracy, was no such thing. It was, rather, a fragile autocracy in which kings were ringed by 'overmyghty subjects' whilst having no clear personal monopoly of coercion with which to overcome them.[86]

Kings-to-be in Akyem Abuakwa emerge through an intense political process, the most important aspects of which take place in private in the Akan equivalent of 'smoke-filled rooms'. While some institutions and offices[87] have the official function of 'announcing' the nomination, they are not the sole king-makers. Nominations, which were invariably recorded as being 'unopposed', were the end of a process of metaphorical arm-wrestling in which some factions had prevailed and others lost. All Akan rulers necessarily have a number of potential heirs; both their brothers and their nephews are eligible. While the selection process ideally emphasises the potential of the candidates,[88] it was and is a

Akyem Abuakwa State College before moving into a long and distinguished political career, including unsuccessful candidacy in Ghana's 1979 presidential election.

82   A.E. Boakye Danquah, his oldest surviving child. He was one of the eight accused of the murder in 1944 and was manager of Dua and Company, a trading concern set up by the Okyenhene and Walter Austin which was created for Ofori Atta's sons.

83   A royal from Pramkesse.

84   A reference to Susan Ofori Atta, then studying medicine in Britain.

85   W. Austin to Ofori Atta, 12 April 1939, AASA 9/64.

86   Colonial rule limited the king's judicial powers severely. His Tribunal was unable to hear cases of great gravity, and its sentencing powers were restricted.

87   Such as the Amantoo Mmiensa and the Queen Mother/Ohemaa.

88   The Queen Mother is supposed to be capable of a good assessment of character as ideally she has seen the candidates develop from childhood. Not all Queen

political process in which segments of the lineage vie for power.[89]
Accordingly all kings take office with debts to their supporters and
strained relations with their opponents, for they all know who were for
and who against them.

Thus Ofori Atta assumed the stool with a stack of obligations to those
wing-chiefs, lineage elders and palace officials who had supported his
nomination formally and informally. In this respect he differed little
from his predecessors. But his vision was of a different kind of state, a
modern kingdom. Colonial rule had ended the old military rationale of
the state forever; Akyem Abuakwa would never again take up arms.
Successful rulers and wing-chiefs had now to be more than good
tacticians and brave warriors. The new state would have to take the
colonial presence seriously. The state's and hence the king's room for
manoeuvre was now circumscribed by colonial ordinance. If colonial
incursions into the powers of the king and his court were to be held off,
the new state must perforce use a new armoury which would comprise
bureaucratic competence and colonial legal expertise.

By the early twentieth century Akyem Abuakwa's aristocracy and
court were almost universally illiterate and hence, in Ofori Atta I's
opinion, ill-equipped for these new demands. One of the explanations of
Ofori Atta's unusual power as an Akan ruler was his domination as
the most experienced and literate member of the Okyeman Council.
Secondly, Akyem Abuakwa was embarking on a totally new economic
era. By 1913 the Gold Coast had become the largest cocoa-growing area
in the world and Akyem Abuakwa was one of the major centres of
production. The Akyem Abuakwa state had consequently become
extensively monetised. Local exchange as well as revenue was increasingly in currency and not in kind. Accordingly, if the king was to
command this burgeoning economy, he would need to be served by
numerate as well as literate aides. Lastly the great boom in mineral
exploitation had brought with it numbers of smooth-talking mining
executives who sought to strike hard bargains over concessions, rents
and leases. The king needed courtiers with business acumen.

Mothers had been in office and hence placed for such acute observation for
long.

89   Much information about these processes is found in the questionnaires filled in
by each stool on the election and installation of new rulers. SNA Form no. 6
was distributed to paramounts in the inter-war years by the Secretary for
Native Affairs and thence distributed to sub-chiefdoms. There were forty-one
questions, prepared in the light of prevailing ethnographic wisdom and
bureaucratic need. Sadly the form which should have covered the election and
installation of the new Okyenhene in 1943 was taken from the palace archives
by the CPP government in the course of its struggle with the Paramountcy.
There is no record in the National Archives of these data, nor is there any
account of why and how these forms were devised in the first place.

The need for a revolution in style posed immediate problems. While both Ofori Atta and his brother had been brought into the palace to take on these new and daunting tasks, the rate of change was rapid. The evidence suggests that the literate population of Akyem Abuakwa was at the time of his accession almost entirely commoner. The few literate Christian royals – the two attributes of Christianity and literacy were often conditional upon one another – had endured proximate experiences of a stool which was hostile to their confession at the end of the nineteenth century and could not necessarily be looked upon as loyal supporters of the king.

Accordingly his tactics, throughout his long reign, were to create the core of a modern state by deploying close kin in these roles. Central to this ambition was his insistence that his children should attend school. Virtually all of his children appear on the roll of Kyebi's Presbyterian primary school throughout Ofori Atta's reign. He read and filed their school reports, upbraided the lazy and praised achievement. Those with palpable talent were singled out and sent on to secondary schools in the Gold Coast and in exceptional circumstances for further training overseas. There simply were so many children that accounting for each and every one proved to be very difficult. The records certainly suggest that Ofori Atta found the task difficult. He was, for example, an extremely slow payer of school bills; the files are full of letters from aggrieved school bursars asking for payment.[90]

The scatter of placements suggests careful thought about which child was best suited to which school. This personal selection gradually extended to a growing number of children from Kyebi and ultimately from Akyem Abuakwa at large who were awarded scholarships by the Okyeman Council for study.[91] The most detailed evidence is for the early 1930s. In those years there were children, both royal and commoner, paid for by the Akyem Abuakwa state, attending the technical school in Accra,[92] Achimota, Accra Academy,[93] St Mary's

90   His record with Achimota, the great secondary school in Accra established in 1928, was especially bad. In 1934 the Bursar had to ask the lawyer Henley Coussey (who had children at the school and was one of the stool's legal advisers until appointed to the Bench in 1944) to help get school fees from the Okyenhene: AASA 11/43. Plaintive letters from the children suggest that he also forgot to give them pocket money. These princes and princesses seldom had the price of a bottle of lemonade or a bag of sweets. If it were not for the abundant evidence of his being generous it might seem that he was mean. It seems, rather, that he always left bill-paying to the last moment in an arrogant if regal fashion.
91   Scholarships were mostly in the form of loans to children outside the royal family. These were to be repaid over a period of years following the child's graduation. AASA 11/31 and 11/42.
92   Ransford K. Birikoreng.
93   L.E. Koroduah.

Convent Cape Coast, Krobo Girl's School in Odumase, St Monica's,[94] Mampong, Adisadel, the Methodist girls' school, the Methodist senior school[95] and the Womens' Training Institute, both at Nsawam.[96]

The expense of all this was considerable. In 1931 he had seven children on the Achimota roll.[97] The school bills for that year and for that school alone show that tuition alone amounted to £280 per year. Both the Presbyterian and government schools in Kyebi also charged fees, although these were much lower than those of the prestigious secondary schools such as Achimota. All the same, Ofori Atta had no less than twenty-eight of his children on the local school's role in 1934. The high cost might explain his readiness to pull under-achievers out of school. In January 1933, following poor reports on them from Achimota at Christmas, he simply removed three of his children.[98]

He was no less assiduous in attempting to get his children, and those bright local children he favoured, into training posts and apprentice-ships both in the private and government sectors. He persistently cor-responded with the Public Works Department, the Sanitary and Prisons Department in Accra as well as a scatter of trading and mining companies in the Gold Coast with whom he had some kind of relation-ship; and he was frequently successful in 'placing' young people in this fashion. While he and the Palace bureaucracy were sensibly careful not to promise them jobs after they completed their training, the majority of them were to join the various branches of the native authority in due time.

Sponsorship and encouragement went very much further with the especially favoured. By the early 1920s the first two young men from Akyem Abuakwa were sent to the United Kingdom for training.[99] In 1921 Ofori Atta's younger half-brother J.B. Danquah,[100] and his son

94   Maria Ofori Atta.
95   Rosina Ofori Atta.
96   AASA 11/52.
97   W.E.A, A.E.A, Kofi, Clifford, Susanna and Akyeampong Ofori Atta and Ama Gyankromah.
98   Kofi Asante, Kwaku Atta and Akyeampong Ofori Atta were simply removed at the end of the Christmas term of that year.
99   They are the first two listed in the records. The lateness of this initiative is explained by the Great War. There were sons and nephews who were sent to Freetown, Sierra Leone earlier than this. Daniel Opoku, Ofori Atta's successor, for example, was sent with an elder cousin to the Albert Academy in Freetown in 1915 where they stayed as guardians of Dr Easmon. Daniel Opoku was later found employment, through Ofori Atta's influence, first with Akim Ltd, the mining company, on whose board Ofori Atta sat (with John Saxton), and later with the government's Public Works Department.
100   Son of Yaw Boakye's second marriage contracted after the death of Susanna, Ofori Atta's mother.

George Twum Ampofo, were sent to Britain. Danquah successfully studied law and returned in September 1927, armed not only with a law qualification but also with a University of London Doctorate in Philosophy. George Twum Ampofo's stay in Britain was designed to train him in commerce. This experience proved far less successful than Danquah's. He drifted from job to job despite the help given him by John Saxton, a business partner of Ofori Atta who lived in Britain. He married an English woman in Sheffield and they had a child. Ampofo was successfully prosecuted for indecent assault on a hotel chambermaid in 1926. In disgrace, he had his legal fees and fine paid by his father but his allowance, more than £100 per annum, was withheld and he was forced back to Akyem Abuakwa by Ofori Atta in late 1927, leaving his wife and child in England.[101]

Sending relatives abroad was expensive. The best evidence we have of how this worked in the cases of J.B. Danquah and George Twum Ampofo emerges from some of the detail in the balance sheets which were sent to Nana Sir Ofori Atta after John Saxton's death. These show that between the 3 December 1921 and 7 September 1927 Danquah received, through Saxton's hands, a grand total of £3,460. This money was found in two ways, so far as one can see. First, and without the apparent knowledge of the Okyeman Council, Ofori Atta kept sums of money raised by director's fees and dividends which were managed by firstly John Saxton and thereafter by another business partner based in Britain, Walter Austin. Walter Austin explained his role after Ofori Atta's death:

> ... I used to pay all the University fees of William Ofori Atta and from time to time the late Omanhene would instruct CayCo (London) Ltd [a mining consortium with mines in Akyem Abuakwa] to pay me such part of his share of the profits which would discharge the obligation. ... When Susan Ofori Atta came over to this country I used to pay her fees and advance money for her maintenance, then later I would be refunded by your Uncle's instructing CayCo ... to pay me.[102]

It is clear that Austin realised that such money belonged by right to the stool rather than to the Okyenhene personally, for his letter mentions

---

101 The deserted wife's lawyers badgered Saxton for maintenance. Ofori Atta I harshly rejected any responsibility for his daughter-in-law and grandson. 'With regard to Mrs Ampofo, I ... trust that the Solicitors will look no more to us as people responsible for her maintenance. ...': Ofori Atta to John Saxton's executors, 14 January 1928, AASA 11/30. Twum Ampofo returned to a kind of gentle oblivion. He is remembered for doing little other than fishing with rod and line in the River Birim for the rest of his days in Kyebi.

102 Walter Austin to Ofori Atta II, 29 December 1943, AASA 3/14.

that Ofori Atta I's successor's share of CayCo's profits was seven and a half percent and '... I should imagine that your share of the profits should be paid over to the Stool Treasury'.

The record of these sums is far from complete. But we know that by the early 1920s he was receiving £100 per annum as director's fees from Selection Trust, another mining company active in Akyem Abuakwa. It also seems clear that he either bought, or more likely was given as an inducement, shares in the same diamond-mining concern. He sold £4,000-worth of these in the six years between 1921 and 1927. In 1934 he transferred, by sale, his shareholding of five hundred £1 shares in Akim Ltd, of which he was also a director, to a Mr S.A. Bentsil of Cape Coast.[103] In addition there are sundry sterling cheques made out in Ofori Atta's favour which were then banked in his UK accounts.[104]

Secondly it is also clear that concession rents were, in some cases, retained and used, again without the obvious knowledge of the Okyeman Council, as personal finance. The most obvious example of this occurred when Danquah was brought before the Council for insulting Ofori Atta, a dispute which is expanded upon below.[105] At this inquisition on 23 October 1936, Danquah let slip that he received £150 per annum from the Adadientem concession. Okyeman minutes show that the Council were extremely interested to hear of this and Adontenhene tartly asked for more information. Sadly there is no record of that information being supplied to him or the Council in open session. Danquah's mother came from Adadientem and as a royal of that stool, the family suggest today, she and her heirs were entitled to that revenue. This is not an opinion that is widely shared in Akyem Abuakwa. In this case there seems little doubt that the entire sum was retained and used by Ofori Atta himself.

The whole question of these funds is a grey area. By custom, created and then enshrined in Okyeman Council bye-laws, such rents and royalties should have been split three ways. The Okyenhene was himself the legal recipient of one third of such money, the Stool Treasury a further third and the stool in the locality in which the concession was sited, the final third. While a close examination of the Stool Treasury's accounting shows that it did indeed receive some concession shares,

103   AASA 9/39.
104   Two cheques amounting to £687 were paid to Ofori Atta by John Walsh Ltd between November 1923 and September 1924. I have been unable to find out anything about this company. A further cheque for £1,000 was sent to him by John Saxton in February 1923, which possibly represents fees and dividends from Akim Ltd. None of these payments seem to have reached, in part or in full, the State Treasury, as custom and bye-laws required. These were very large sums by 1920s standards.
105   See Chpt 8.

there are cases, such as this one, where no such payments are recorded.

Stool Treasuries were neither officially nor thoroughly audited until the Second World War. In the event it is extremely difficult to be certain of how complete earlier accounts are.[106] Neither Ofori Atta nor his civil servants kept a set of accounts which clearly distinguished Ofori Atta's personal affairs from those of the state. A certain amount of what accountants call virement, both accidental and intentional, characterised this rickety system of accounting.[107] This all led to wild surmise and hence suspicion within Akyem Abuakwa about Ofori Atta's use of state funds.

A deal of this, as we shall see below,[108] was unfair speculation. But some of it was clearly reasonable suspicion. What is abundantly clear is that Ofori Atta's income as Omanhene,[109] which never technically exceeded £3,000 per annum, could not cover his outgoings.[110] These, to be fair, included a remarkable number of charitable payments to the host of people who wrote begging letters to him, and the fairly frequent payment of debts run up by the more prodigal members of his family. He also spent a great deal of his 'own' money on the state. The planning and eventual building of the Akyem Abuakwa State College in the 1930s was very largely bank-rolled by the Okyenhene personally, for example.

106   Impressive as the State Archives in Akyem Abuakwa are, some of the archive is still retained in the Dabre and is not open for consultation. It is possible that some of the answers to such questions will be found there.
107   Correspondence in 1921 mentions the Akim Abuakwa National Fund or Abuakwaman Fund, for the general betterment of the state, which was raised in 1921 by setting aside five percent of state land sales proceeds. On 7 December 1921, the Bank of British West Africa sent £150 by cable to John Saxton in England, for unknown purposes, and debited the Abuakwaman Fund's account for this purpose. The 1920s accounts suggest that the most frequent drawer on the Abuakwaman account was named Danquah; given the frequent use of this surname amongst the royal family, it is hard to know who this was. It is even more difficult to account for the ways the fund was used in this period: AASA 5/30.
108   See Chpt 8.
109   This sum, agreed by the colonial government, came out of native authority funds, which also paid salaries to chiefs, native authority personnel and palace staff. Most of this was raised by local taxation, fines and fees.
110   He was for example a lavish host. Guests at the palace frequently drank champagne, claret and port in the evenings. Much personal expenditure was the dull round of the maintenance of a large house with leaky roofs and a household with a propensity to buy things on credit, but the flashes of extravagance are delicious. He had a taste for Foyer Burlington cigarettes (Virginia and Turkish), whose boxes were embossed with his name. He liked large American cars and was driven in a Studebaker and a Chrysler in the inter-war period; the last such car boasted whitewall tyres.

As well as his chiefly income, he claimed one third of the value of all land sales in the kingdom, although it is abundantly clear that many such sales were concealed from him and the Okyeman Council precisely to avoid these imposts. Indeed it was this taxation which provoked the two chiefdoms of Asamankese and Akwatia to attempt secession from the Akyem Abuakwa Paramountcy in the 1920s.[111] He was, moreover, the recipient of one third of all taxes, fines and licence fees imposed or levied by the State Tribunals and the State Council.

But what entered the books misrepresented the situation. Part-confirmation of this suspicion emerges from the extraordinary change which took place in 1940. In March of that year, under government pressure, the State Council appointed a Finance Board which acted with the advice of the District Commissioner. In the financial year preceding this, state revenue was stated to be £6,043 and expenditure £5,973. A year later, and in the midst of a war which had, initially at least, depressed trade and producer prices, revenue had jumped to £18,275 and expenditure to £17,276.[112] Accordingly the official numbers must be treated with considerable suspicion, and the rather anecdotal and episodic evidence accorded rather more respect than it would usually enjoy.

While we shall never be able to reconstruct this important element of Akyem Abuakwa's economic history, it is clear that Ofori Atta I's casual accountancy at best or chicanery at worst were rooted in his relentless efforts to 'privilege' his close kin and especially his children. While by the standards of Akyem Abuakwa his personal lifestyle was opulent, such was expected of a king by most of his subjects, not least because he was a generous donor to those in real need.[113]

But if there is a discernible organising principle to Ofori Atta's financial activities, it seems, like so much in his life, to have been based upon his perception of the necessity to promote his state by promoting

---

111 A stand-off only finally resolved in 1939. This extremely important and divisive case is dealt with fully and admirably in Simensen, *op. cit.*

112 NAG ADM 32/1/131, *Annual Report* (Birim District, 1940).

113 The records show him to have been a soft target for a begging letter. Many such letters were ignored, but he found it hard to say no. There was a technique to writing a letter which appealed to him. He was vulnerable to anyone with a project which would establish assertive African independence in business or intellection; an example of this was his sponsorship of the Society of African Herbalists in Sekondi. 'I am glad', he wrote, 'to observe that something is being done to promote knowledge and interest in regard to African herbs. I have for a long time advocated some system whereby the application of African herbs be placed on good and scientific basis so that the Africans may continue to enjoy the benefits of the efforts made by our forebears. . . .': AASA 3/280, letter dated 19 March 1932. Sadly little came of this initiative.

his immediate family. In this project he created an extensive network of clientage and dependence. The important elements of state and palace activity were dominated either by kin or by those whose careers he had sponsored. At the heart of that network lay Ofori Atta's remarkable gifts, and its smooth operation rested upon his mastery of its complexity.[114]

His death, accordingly, was more than a sad event. It was, rather, the creation of devastating uncertainty. Things threatened, quite literally, to fall apart. At the centre of that threatened chaos lay his immediate family who by 1943 were a fundamental element in the system Ofori Atta had created. They were accordingly plunged into a confusing void in which some, quite literally, did not know where their next meal would come from.[115] Unsurprisingly the very depth of that void prompted some of them to attempt to re-establish order by an act which would pacify the elements, and to signal their great grief by an appropriately great sacrifice. Eight close kinsmen were to be found guilty of taking the life of Akyea Mensah, the Odikro of Apedwa.

114   Thinking about how this worked I was drawn to a simile of Lewis Mumford's. Writing about Dante and echoing Henry Adams' metaphor of the Gothic cathedral in temporary harmony between conflicting forces, he said that medieval society was 'a great French cathedral . . . load, thrust, tension, counter-thrust, living, pushing, acting forces, all pitted against each other so as to produce a stable fabric. Such equilibrium as the society had was a dynamic one; it implied constant effort.' *Findings and Keepings: Analects for an Autobiography* (London, 1976), p. 176. Akyem Abuakwa's tragedy was that Ofori Atta's 'constant effort' did not outlast him.
115   This was not a baseless fear. By 1946 the Okyeman Council's Select Committee on the Estimates was deploring the 'perpetual idleness of those of the [royal family] receiving allowances . . . [they] should seek employment . . .'. At their next meeting they withdrew the annual allowance paid to royals who did not serve on the State Council *Minutes*, February 1946, AASA 8/37.

CHAPTER THREE

Transforming the Inherited State

Ofori Atta I's rich agenda was ambitious. What obstacles stood in his way? Unusually in colonial Africa, his most persistent opponents were not the agencies of colonial rule but, rather, African institutions and individuals. The Okyenhene ruled Akyem Abuakwa for much of his reign in a situation of remarkably indirect Indirect Rule. This policy became the watchword of good 'Native Administration' in the inter-war years, although it had been practised pragmatically before it acquired its capital letters. In brief it was a policy which recreated and, in some cases, created pre-colonial polities within colonial territories. It then devolved powers to the traditional rulers of these reconstituted states as recognised local governments or Native Authorities. These included limited and localised legislative, judicial and policing powers and rights of local taxation and expenditure through 'Native Treasuries'. Until the mid-1940s, the policy allowed colonial administrations to remain remarkably small and hence cheap in British West Africa. From both the administration's and Nana Sir Ofori Atta's point of view, it worked well in Akyem Abuakwa.[1] Accordingly many of the most significant changes which took place in Akyem's Abuakwa's daily life were ordered by the Okyenhene and his court.[2]

Unusually the District Commissioner who was 'responsible' for the kingdom for the early part of the inter-war years,[3] W.J.A. (later Sir Andrew) Jones, spoke Twi, and became so identified with Akyem Abuakwa that he was known in the local press as 'Kibi' Jones;[4]

---

1 After 1945 indirect rule was gradually liquidated as it was recognised that the new goal of 'development' was impeded by this conservative policy.
2 Which is to say the State Council or *Okyeman Nhyiam* which, in this period, had statutory recognition as the local legislative body.
3 DC from 1916–24.
4 Later Secretary of Native Affairs, Gold Coast, then Chief Commissioner, Northern Territories. It was a close relationship. Jones' diaries (NAG ADM 12/5/13) show respect and affection. On 6 May 1928 he notes 'arguments with Ofori Atta invariably stimulate one's reasoning facilities'. There is more in the same vein. The admiration was mutual: Ofori Atta named one of his sons Jones

2   Nana Sir Ofori Atta and his retinue after being dubbed a Knight of the Order of the British Empire at Buckingham Palace, 1927.

throughout the longest period of his kingship, Ofori Atta I was usually supported by sympathetic colonial officers and by the power of the colonial state when he needed it. Much of that was not to be found in actual positive interventions, although such did occur most dramatically in 1918 and 1932, but, rather, in giving Ofori Atta a relatively loose rein. Nana worked hard to achieve room to manoeuvre; it was not a free gift from a genial colonial regime.

Any impression of a 'hand in glove' relationship would be false. British sources suggest discomfort with dependence on Ofori Atta I. Akyem sources suggest unease with doing business with the colonial state. Both sides were wary of one another and had no illusions about its being other than a working relationship. The colonial state was to frustrate some of his policies and he was no less frequently to challenge the government.[5]

Ofori Atta I's state building was a centralising project. In working

Ofori Atta. By the mid-1930s Jones came to doubt the probity and political viability of Ofori Atta's policies and became an open advocate of measures of democratisation for native authorities.

5   Most notably in his support for the retention of the cocoa crop in an attempt to raise producer prices in the famous 'cocoa hold-up' of 1937.

towards this he alienated sections of his population from the highest to the lowest. His reign undoubtedly gave more power to the palace and his family; in the process, the relative autonomy of wing-chiefs was eroded. But his policies were also highly directive. He sought to create a command economy in which the centre would control not only taxation but also resource allocation. He tried to control land sales and entrepreneurial activity. In this too he made enemies; and because of this the potential support of the colonial state was an important element in his arsenal.

Control of land was a vital part of all this. In Akyem Abuakwa popular ideology and varied recensions of 'custom' endorsed the idea of communal land tenure. Akyem was no different from many others parts of Africa where the ideological construct of 'communal tenure' has been assumed by some to record reality. In practice, long-term usufruct can and did become tantamount to freehold, and in many parts of the Akan-speaking world such rights have been and are sold. At the same time outright alienation of land was also practised.[6] Technically all land belonged to the local stool and hence to all those who owed allegiance to that stool. Had this actually reflected reality, usufruct would have been the closest anyone could get to outright land ownership. But it is clear that land sales and freeholding go back at least to the 1870s; as cocoa growing, copal-gum and rubber extraction, and gold and diamond prospecting (and hence concession-hunting) expanded, so did the cash value of land in a rapidly monetising economy. Akyem Abuakwa, like neighbouring Akuapem, was the location of much of the dramatic expansion of capitalist cocoa farming.

Ofori Atta's overt policy after 1912 was to prevent the alienation of land by sub-chiefs to immigrants. In this there was more than a whiff of chauvinism, which Ofori Atta would have called patriotism. This was set out in his public pronouncements, which frequently stressed the abomination of losing Akyem lands to 'strangers' even if some of those strangers spoke Twi, owed allegiance to the local and national stools and in some cases had lived locally for generations. This is nicely caught in his letter to Tafohene on 7 April 1917:

'If in ancient times the responsibility of defending the territory against foreign invaders devolved upon the shoulders of my great ancestors, it becomes an obvious corresponding duty of mine as their humble successor in this time of peace to protect the rights of the Stools of Akim Abuakwa against foreign visitors, who employ modern weapons of civilisation to dispossess the stools of their inherent rights

6 This has not been accompanied by the growth of either extensive landlordage or proletarianisation in Ghana. Part of the explanation of this was, until relatively recently, the relatively large pool of uncleared land.

and aim at the confiscation and despoilment of the riches and rights which these Stools should otherwise enjoy for years to come.'[7]

Behind that rhetoric, the evidence suggests however that he was not entirely averse to countenancing alienation to strangers so long as he and his Council were rewarded for granting leave, especially to sub-chiefs, to sell land to strangers.

But the prohibition on land alienation to 'foreigners' was widely flouted during the inter-war years. On the face of it there was ample substance in Ofori Atta's justification for increasing central control of land and land sales on the grounds that Akyem sub-chiefs had failed to safeguard Akyem resources from immigrant farmers and African and European concessionaires.

Accordingly by the 1920s he and the Okyeman Council had come to command the probably entirely untraditional central control of all Akyem land. It was untraditional because tradition suggested that the Paramountcy, through conquest, originally 'owned' all land in the kingdom and this land was vested in the stool. But it went on to insist that the Okyenhene had given that land to various chiefs in the remote past. The idea of ostensibly collective but, in reality, central control over the destiny of land was new.

He and his State Council also tried to impose a differential taxation regime on 'immigrants'. In 1918 a stiff tax of £1 was imposed on each 'produce-raising farm', which essentially meant cocoa farms; additionally the Okyeman Council sought to levy 10/- on each 'foodstuff farm'. Both taxes were to be imposed upon 'non-natives of Akim',[8] a category defined by the State Council. Such definition was frequently arbitrary. It was primarily aimed at the immigrant population who farmed around the area of New Juaben. Many here protested against this levy and were arrested and tried by the Native Tribunal in Kyebi.

This was an onerous tax. The right to tribute from outsiders farming on a chief's land was old but had been paid in kind at the annual Odwira festival;[9] it became monetised towards the end of the nineteenth century. In Asante, by contrast, as late as the 1930s, the Asanteman Council levied no tribute on stangers' food farms. Moreover that Council charged cocoa tribute at the rate of one penny per eight bearing

---

7   See NAG ADM 11/136.
8   I am grateful to Adu Boahen for sharing his New Juaben family's memories of this period. These struggles were part of older wrangles with neighbouring rulers about who was or was not the suzerain, not of territory but of populations. This was not merely a matter of jurisdiction but also concerned who payed taxation to whom.
9   For an account of this festival see Nana Ofori Atta II's published lecture, *The Odwira Festival in Akim Abuakwa* (Accra, n.d.).

trees until the 1950–1 season when cocoa prices were many times higher than those of 1918. Had Akyem Abuakwa's State Council proposed to tax on the Asante criteria, a cocoa farmer would have had to have been cultivating nearly two thousand bearing trees before he attracted the flat fee of £1. Most cocoa farms had large numbers of young, non-bearing trees, as trees take six to seven years to come to maturity; Akyem's rates took no account of that. Using the Asante criteria, Akyem's annual cocoa tribute assumed a considerable acreage, as optimal tree density is reckoned at no more than four hundred trees per acre on good land. Moreover new plantings have to be intercropped with leafy crops to afford the saplings shade from the sun. Although the cocoa price was to double its 1918 value by 1920, it thereafter oscillated at considerably lower levels until the late 1940s. In 1938 it was estimated that the income of a cocoa farmer was about £12 per season. Accordingly many stranger farmers were being very heavily taxed in Akyem.[10]

By the end of the 1920s, one penny per cocoa tree was being levied.[11] While the colonial government formally disallowed this impost,[12] they did not prevent the exaction of money in the guise of rents from strangers paid by 'consent'. There are court cases which suggest that strong-arm methods were sometimes used to obtain consent from such farmers whose security was often fragile; very few of them had written title to their farms.[13]

Ofori Atta I also used his State Council's legislative powers, essentially those of enacting local bye-laws, to attempt to ensure that the stool acquired one third of all land rents and royalties from leased land in the kingdom. This was upheld when an arbitrator, Mr Justice Roger Evans Hall, ruled that the Akyem paramount stool was entitled by

10   See Asanteman Council *Minutes* for 1937, 1940, 1946 and 1948. On cocoa tribute see the revised edition of *Warrington's Notes on Ashanti Custom Prepared for the Use of District Commissioners* by J.N. Matson (Cape Coast, n.d. but late 1949), p. 72. This was prepared with the participation and approval of the Asanteman Council.

11   £1 per 240 trees or just under £2 per acre of cocoa farm.

12   The Attorney General held that it was *ultra vires*. Simensen suggests that the voluntary nature of the 'tax' was concealed from the populace and that both the Okyenhene and the DC presented it as compulsory. See Simensen, Ph.D thesis, *op. cit.*, p. 106.

13   Simensen notes the harassment of Kwahu traders who enjoyed much of the cocoa-carrying trade to the coast. After a inter-state demarcation dispute had been resolved in Kwahu's favour in 1923, Okyeman demanded that all Kwahus without title to their farms should be evicted from Akyem. The colonial authorities forced the Okyenhene to back down, arguing that such powers inhere only in sovereign nations rather than in parts of larger states. By the time Okyenhene agreed to comply, many Kwahus had been evicted from their stores in favour of Akyem Abuakwa 'nationals'. See Simensen Ph.D thesis, *op. cit.*, p. 108.

'native custom to one equal third part share of all rents and profits of lands alienated . . .'.[14] There was in fact little that was 'customary' about it, if that meant hallowed by time and practice. In 1902 Amoako Atta II had secured Okyeman Council's agreement to his right to exact one quarter of land purchase prices in the kingdom, but the evidence suggests that this was more honoured in the breach than in the observance. The nearest analogy in 'custom' in commentary by Akan legal authorities was the traditional right of chiefs to gold nuggets found on the land and to parts of hunted game beasts.[15]

The major reason for this concentration on taxation rather than outright sale was that the stool and hence the royal family had scarcely any land in Akyem Abuakwa which came directly under its control and was therefore unable to act as a direct vendor. The Okyenhene could only achieve a share in the profits of land commoditisation and commercialisation[16] by rent taxation and by in effect taxing the land sales of others.[17]

Ofori Atta's recognition of the importance of law in the colonial situation lay at the heart of such policies. His status and that of other traditional rulers in Akyem Abuakwa ensured that local legislation and the legal processes which remained under the control of recognised Native Tribunals would be favourable to his interests. When it came to the courts run by the colonial state and concerned with colonial law, success in them demanded access to the small but powerful group of African lawyers who practised in them. Their services were expensive and there is little doubt that in the early years of the twentieth century triumph in these courts had much to do with the wealth of the litigant. The Akyem Abuakwa stool kept some of the Gold Coast's best lawyers on retainer throughout Ofori Atta's reign.[18]

Legal processes do not for long empower only one set of actors if they are genuine legal processes. Law can be used by those seeking redress or protection. By the 1920s, some of Akyem Abuakwa's sub-chiefs had learnt about the force of colonial law and began to use it to resist the stool's controls and exactions. They were increasingly able to do this because, quite simply, the entire area had been creating wealth since the end of the nineteenth century. Many more people and many more

14 See *Gold Coast Law Reports 1926–9*, p. 302.
15 See A.A.Y. Kyerematen, *Inter-state Boundary Litigation in Ashanti*, African Social Research Documents, vol. 4 (Afrika Studiecentrum, Leiden, n.d.), pp. 116–17.
16 Land values were soaring throughout most of the inter-war period. Migrants seeking to open up new cocoa farms were not the only element in this. There was a growing scramble for land around areas where either gold or diamonds had been discovered.
17 This is essentially Simensen's conclusion in his Ph.D thesis, *op. cit.*
18 Such as T. Hutton-Mills and Henley Coussey.

stools could afford to go to law by the 1920s. The Gold Coast by this
time had, in effect, a binary justice system. The state recognised two
sets of courts. On the one hand there were courts established *de novo* by
colonial rule. This system began with the lower, magistrates' courts and
extended upward through a series of courts presided over by judges
appointed by the British authorities, up to the West African Court of
Appeal. At the same time the laws of the colonial state also recognised
those courts called Native Authority Tribunals which were hybrids of
the traditional courts of the past and the introduced, colonial system.
At different times in the colonial period the jurisdiction of these two
systems changed. Whilst the colonial courts retained jurisdiction in
serious criminal matters and heard complex civil matters, 'traditional'
courts, recognised by ordinance, came to enjoy an extended jurisdiction.

The relationship between the two systems was volatile. In terms of
colonial policy this reflected several imperatives. Certainly devolution of
legal powers was inherent in the ideology of Indirect Rule as it was
elaborated in the inter-war years. But it was also the case that political
imperatives dictated that 'native rulers' must be seen to be more than
figure-heads. Kings and their councillors could and did exercise just
such powers through their State Councils and through their Native
Tribunals. There was a clear growth in the strength of Native Tribunals
following the amendment of the Native Jurisdiction Ordinance in 1910
whereby Native Tribunals became compulsory courts of first instance in
matters not falling clearly under British law. Ofori Atta recognised this
when he said that chiefs owed 'an incalculable debt of gratitude [to the
amended law of 1910] which restored the basic principles of Native
Administration, the foundations of which had for many years been
gradually weakened by the loss one after another of its inherent functions and duties until the whole structure was . . . rapidly tottering to its
fall'.[19]

At the same time the British wished to control the Native Tribunals.
This desire was informed not only by the wish to maintain authority but
also by the abundant, uncomfortable evidence that such courts could be
arbitrary and corrupt. Indirect Rule in the Gold Coast posed a constant
problem to the British. For the system to work, chiefs and kings had
both to wield and be seen to wield devolved powers. At the same time,
constant popular complaint about 'irregularities' from the subjects of
native authorities could not be ignored. A balance between autonomy
and intervention was never satisfactorily struck. So far as the Native
Tribunals were concerned it is clear that amendments in 1910, such as
the requirement that Tribunals keep detailed records, were an attempt

19   Quoted in Simensen Ph.D thesis, *op. cit.*, p. 91.

to iron out some of the wrinkles in the system. It was, however, a manifest failure.

The crucial aspect of this binary legal system was that individuals getting access to colonial courts could evade the necessity to pursue justice in the Native Tribunal.[20] The most important tribunal in Akyem was composed of the Okyenhene and his senior chiefs;[21] but they were to some extent authors of a proportion of the distress being complained about. For example in two chiefdoms in Akyem Abuakwa, Akwatia and Asamankese, diamonds had been discovered shortly after the end of the Great War. Both chiefdoms used the colonial courts to attempt virtual secession from the control of the Akyem stool, hoping thus to avoid paying heavy taxes[22] on the royalties from concessions they had sold to mining companies.

That dispute was finally settled in 1939.[23] In the course of the case the Akyem Abuakwa stool had paid out at least £100,000 and Asamankese £80,000 in lawyer's fees. The high costs of legal actions undertaken by stools constantly concerned the colonial administration. The figures quoted are based on a report commissioned by the colonial government in 1945 undertaken by C.R. Havers, KC. He described this case as 'protracted and ruinous litigation'. He noted, *inter alia*, that

> some States are able to borrow money from rich Elders or friends.
> Others who are less fortunate are compelled to resort to money-

20 Under the 1910 amendments, tribunals enjoyed a monopoly of hearing cases of petty crime, civil cases involving values up to £25, property succession cases involving values up to £50 and all land cases not involving formal, written documentation. In such matters the District Commissioner had no right of intervention.

21 Danquah lists its members in 1928 as the Okyenhene as court president and the 'Omanhene's Stool Elders who reside with him at the capital'. *Akim Abuakwa Handbook*, p. 11. The tribunal had no set membership and was composed of a variety of notables on any one hearing day.

22 Okyeman Council's decision to increase the stool's share of concession rents from one quarter to one third in 1920 was intimately related to the discovery of diamonds in 1919.

23 The main adversary fuelling this dispute was his late mentor and *quondam* legal advisor to the stool, Thomas Hutton-Mills, who had acquired large land holdings in 'prime sites'; he was happy to represent Akwatia and Asamankese in this attempt to resist royal encroachment into their freehold rights. The other major lawyer in the case was Kobina Sekyi, who had negotiated a ten percent annual share of all mining royalties in Asamankese instead of a fee. Additionally Sekyi was to present a bill for over £3,000 to Asamankese in 1940 for professional services in 1932–7. In one bill for what was a long series of hearings, Sekyi was paid £1,180 in 1932. Both men cleverly used their connections with coastal politicians to portray Ofori Atta as an uncompromising feudalist but clearly had more than just radical politics on their minds. It was accordingly a bitter battle.

lenders who have seldom lent money at a rate of interest lower than
50 per cent and sometimes at the rate of 100 per cent. Usually they
are compelled to mortgage part of the Stool lands as security for
the loan.... Not infrequently, States... raise a levy upon their
subjects.... Similar disputes have given rise to widespread indebted-
ness of Divisional Chiefs, Chiefs, villages, communities, families and
individuals.[24]

Considering the contemporary value of such sums it is clear that this
was indeed a wealthy region. Because of that it was also an area in
which struggles over control of wealth-producing resources could be
very bitter.

Ofori Atta used the law skilfully within the Indirect Rule structure,
and not only in matters which were obviously economic. Throughout
the inter-war period his State Council awarded itself increasing formal
and informal power over the election and destoolment of minor and
increasingly dependent chiefs in the Akyem Abuakwa state.[25] The
growing capacity of the Okyeman Council to ordain what was and what
was not 'customary' law was enhanced in 1927.

Ofori Atta's power within the Akyem state and his growing ability to
influence policy within the colony transformed his local initiatives into a
colony-wide enactment, the Native Administration Ordinance of 1927;
he played a major role in the drafting of this bill and it was, until
the local government reforms of 1951, to give considerable and unprecedented power to paramount chiefs.[26] Ofori Atta was favoured by
the colonial administration. Akyem was, according to Governor Hugh
Clifford,[27] the 'most progressive and leading of all our native states in
the Gold Coast'. Government was, he said, 'prepared to support Akim
Abuakwa in every possible way'.[28] In 1923 Clifford's successor, Sir
Gordon Guggisberg,[29] admitted to the Secretary of State for the Colonies

24 PRO CO 96/780/3. This thrust is supported by Mrs J.M. Matson's *Report on
    land Disputes in the Adansi Division, Obuasi District, Ashanti* (1947). In this she, *inter
    alia*, costed a long land case and concluded that it '...illustrates...not only
    the expense of litigation but... that this high cost was, to a very great extent,
    caused by the exploitation of an illiterate people by lawyers': pp. 33–4.
25 The Okyeman Council actually initiated destoolment proceedings against 'sub-
    chiefs' who broke ranks. The most famous cases are those of the chieftaincies of
    Abomosu and Apinamang.
26 According to Danquah, writing a year after the ordinance became law, a
    'renewed accession of strength came to the law-making and law-enforcing
    powers of the State Council...'. *Akim Abuakwa Handbook*, p. 10.
27 Governor from 1912–19.
28 A speech in Kyebi on 11 August 1920, quoted in *Gold Coast Leader*, 14 August
    1920.
29 Governor from 1919–27.

that while Ofori Atta was certainly exceeding both his customary and colonial rights, the Okyenhene's general policies should be supported as they 'were in accordance with the general tenets of British policy in native affairs'.[30] He was favoured because he was extremely able and because of his enthusiasm for the development of chiefly rule. This accorded with the logic of Indirect Rule policy, as opposed to the demands of many, largely coastal, intellectuals for more local democratisation; Ofori Atta was extremely skilful in parleying that favour into local power.[31]

In these processes he not unnaturally alienated some of his subjects. Divisional chiefs who sat on the State Council were mostly content to accede to his policy of centralisation. They were content because the system of taxation of rents and licensing led to the division of such income within the State Council; for example the imposts on 'strangers' came firstly to them as local suzerains, and they were statutorily required only to pass on a third of the take to their paramount. Members of the 'Native Tribunal', themselves chiefs of divisions of the kingdom or members of the state's growing bureaucracy, divided fines levied in the tribunals as well as the hefty fee (*apasobodee*) required to secure a hearing and the *aseda*, literally 'thank you money', if the tribunal found in your favour. The Akyem native authority, like other native authorities in the Gold Coast, vastly expanded its powers to license, for a fee, a large range of social and economic activities.[32] As Native Treasuries were unaudited before 1939, such income was in effect personal and tax-free income.[33]

But the commoners and their ancient associations, the *Asafo* companies, shared in little of this largesse, or at least perceived that they did not.[34] Asafo companies, in common with much of the state

30 Guggisberg to Secretary of State, 31 March 1923, PRO CO 96/638.
31 Simensen suggests on a number of occasions that the dubious legitimacy of some Okyeman Council bye-laws was fudged by the willingness, especially of 'Kibi' Jones, to act in favour of the stool. An example of Jones' role as 'enforcer' was his heavy-handed intervention in the row over land sales between the Tafohene and the Okyeman Council in 1915–18. Jones was opposed to outright illegality but at the same time was an enthusiast of strong chiefly government in his district, even if it involved bending rather than breaking the rules.
32 Such as the licensing of letter-writers and the vendors of 'native medicine'.
33 Income tax was not levied until 1943, not least because of a protracted struggle against its imposition. The amazingly low volume of the tax 'take' after 1943 seems to suggest that assessment and enforcement were ineffective and could penalise only the salariat.
34 The '*Asafo* movement' and its struggle with the Okyenhene is admirably dealt with by Simensen in his Ph.D thesis, *op. cit.*, although I dissent from his overall suggestion that Asafo resistance was, in effect, class-based.

structure of Akyem Abuakwa, had their origins in military formations. The 'companies' are composed of commoners, 'youngmen' or *nkwankwaa* or *mmerenta*. At the head of each company is an *Asafoakye* or Captain, and his *sirpis* or lieutentants. In 1917–18 major unrest broke out in Akyem Abuakwa, occasioned in part by a serious bottleneck in the cocoa industry, caused by official policies on the allocation of limited shipping space.[35] This hit hardest at the least well capitalised and, I suspect, at the most indebted farmers.[36] Part of Ofori Atta's response was an attempt to create a cocoa sales organisation and to rent a merchant ship; he began this project by raising a large loan from the Colonial Bank. His local enemies accused him of literally mortgaging the stool. In reality he had pledged Akyem state revenue against the loan. Unrest grew and he eventually called in the colonial state's forces. The Gold Coast police were summoned by Ofori Atta using the telephone recently installed in the Ahenfie. This was to prove an affront to his enemies: a king, they argued, could only speak directly to others through his linguists. The telephone enabled him to avoid the Okyeman councillors' knowing what he was up to. The unrest in the area was ultimately smashed by a very heavy-handed police intervention.[37]

Amongst the most active in this agitation were the 'Three Counties' comprising the towns[38] of the Amantoo Mmiensa. This group of towns girdled the capital and protected it by their control of the approaches to it. Apart from monitoring access to Kyebi, they constituted the Okyenhene's bodyguard. They call themselves 'Ofori's warriors', invoking the state's founder's (and his stool's) name. This prominence, and more importantly the pursuit of aggressive politics when the state was at its weakest, allowed them to drift into the state's administrative structure over time. To demand what this role precisely was is unreasonable, as this was disputed from the last quarter of the nineteenth century. They had an advisory role, the privilege of calling upon the Okyenhene in his capital without summons and of laying proposals before the State Council. The Amantoo Mmiensa also accrued a kind of legislative monitoring role, as tribunes of the plebs perhaps, and it was this which encountered strong resistance from the Okyenhene and the

---

35   This is analysed in Jarle Simensen's Ph.D thesis, *op. cit.*, pp. 141–60.
36   There is no sustained study of credit and debt amongst Ghanaian cocoa farmers although it is important. Some of this is brought out in Gareth Austin's 'Indigenous credit in West Africa, 1750–1960' in Austin and Sugihara (eds.), *Local Suppliers of Credit in the Third World; 1750–1960* (London, 1993).
37   Petition from the Odikro and elders of Akwatia, 23 April 1943, NAG ADM 32/1/29.
38   The major towns of the Three Counties are: 1. Apapam, Afiesa, Afwenease, 2. Apedwa and 3. Tetteh, Pano and Wirekyiren.

State Council. Because of the latter's pressure, the Amantoo Mmiensa received no statutory recognition under the general ordinances of the Colony. Danquah described them as one of the 'national constituent bodies in the State'[39] but it is clear that he meant that they only enjoyed advisory powers. At the same time they retained status as the *Werempifo*, the 'tough guards', the group who conducted the *Wirempe* ceremonies at the death of kings and as such enjoyed a voice in the nomination of a new Okyenhene.[40]

Amongst the dissidents' stated ambitions in 1918 was the destoolment of Ofori Atta.[41] They failed. But it was not the first time they had tried. They had been inserting themselves into the state structure, by confrontation, in the half-century before colonial rule finally overlaid Akyem Abuakwa. Throughout the 1860s and 1870s, this group had attempted to secure a more powerful legislative position in the evolving constitution of the state; in some of these struggles they had gained new prerogatives and privileges, in others they had lost. The tensions between them and the paramount bubbled up in a serious clash with the paramount and his State Council in 1894 when, fearing an unfavourable judgement from the State Tribunal in a land case, people from Apedwa broke up the tribunal, drove messengers from Kyebi out of Apedwa. Insulting the king and his emissaries was perceived as treason by the paramount and his advisers. Events in 1918 were in part elements in this sequence. Unsurprisingly in the 1927 Ordinance, in whose drafting Nana Sir Ofori Atta played such a huge part, the Amantoo Mmiensa found themselves excluded from any statutorily defined political role in the governance of the state.

Two divisions in the state as well as the Asafo companies rose in near-revolt over local taxation in 1932 but this was again ultimately contained by the Gold Coast police. Some sources insist that the Amantoo Mmiensa were complicit in this insurrection. The Amantoo Mmiensa however claimed that they supported the Okyenhene throughout these ugly incidents.[42] Whatever the truth of this they were undoubtedly

39 *Akim Abuakwa Handbook*, p. 68.
40 By far the best account is that by Fraser Ofori Atta, 'The Amantoo Mmiensa in the Political and Administrative Set-up of Akyem Abuakwa, unpublished BA dissertation (University of Ghana, October 1978).
41 This was not a wild ambition: there were thirty-five destoolments of divisional (senior) chiefs in Akyem Abuakwa between 1904 and 1944. See NAG ADM/11/2/14 and Gold Coast *Gazette* for this period.
42 But they used the unrest to complain about judicial centralisation, as Amantoo chiefs had lost their local jurisdiction in the 1927 Ordinance. They were less strident than they might have been; they were under surveillance by the local police and remembered what had happened in 1918 when thirty-nine Amantoo Mmiensa townsmen had gone to prison.

aggrieved at their exclusion and, as it appeared to them, relegation under the Native Authority Ordinance.[43]

That resentment re-surfaced in the negotiations about who was to succeed Nana Sir Ofori Atta. While the formal election is held in public, the horse-trading is done beforehand and *in camera*; there are no records of those discussions. Many participants insist that the Amantoo Mmiensa representatives opposed the nomination of Daniel Augustus Opoku Akyeampong, who eventually was enstooled with the royal name of Nana Ofori Atta II in September 1943. They, it is alleged, supported another nephew called Kwame Manu.[44] This is another allegation the Amantoo Mmiensa were later to deny.[45] In some ways the Amantoo Mmiensa's opposition to the ruling house was thus a combination of perceptions of political as well as economic exclusion from the rich man's table.[46] Those close to the Palace regarded them as trouble-makers whether or not they made trouble. They were, in the words of the London solicitor A.L. Bryden who was to act for the Kyebi royal family in the 1940s, 'a political group which had been hostile to Sir Ofori Atta and were historically opponents of the Paramount Chief and his Court'.[47]

These examples suggest that Nana Sir Ofori Atta's policies attracted considerable opposition both within Akyem Abuakwa and outside it. The wider project of making Akyem Abuakwa great once again begs questions. The most important of these revolves around what he meant by Akyem Abuakwa. Manifestly many inhabitants of the Akyem state felt that they were the victims rather than the beneficiaries of his state-building. In political and economic terms the gains appeared to amass

43   See the long minute by Ofori Atta I in the troubles of 1932 (AASA 4/69) and Okyeman Council *Minutes* of 14 May 1937 (AASA 8/14), which suggest that relations between the Amantoo Mmiensa and the Okyenhene were strained.

44   A story strengthened in a contemporary (unpublished) letter Danquah sent to the London *Times* on 29 June 1947. It was not published because it is over sixty pages in length! The letter is entitled 'Stalins in a colony'.

45   In the 'Humble Petition of the Amantoommiensa Council of Akim Abuakwa' to George VI, transmitted 6th September 1946.

46   Amantoo Mmiensa towns are far from poor, containing as they do prime cocoa land and some of the most diamondiferous areas in the state. They had participated in hectic land sales and were amongst the most affluent of the Akyem areas, but they were certainly driven away from political control over the pork barrel in 1927.

47   In the memorandum 'A Gold Coast Mystery' circulated to UK MPs (June 1946), PRO CO 96/783/5, p. 2 and repeated on p. 3 of a letter (4 July 1946) from J.B. Danquah to the Speaker of the House of Commons. Here he described them as 'enemies' of the Akyem Abuakwa state and as a 'political faction': PRO CO 96/783/5 – a far cry from his earlier description of them as being one of 'the constituent bodies in the State'. *Akim Abuakwa Handbook*, 1928, p. 68.

at the centre, in Kyebi and amongst the ruling elite. As the DC commented in his annual report for 1938: 'Native affairs are gradually passing out of the hands of local democracies into the hands of Okyeman. . . .'[48] The tensions unleashed by the murder had a deeper provenance than the events themselves. In particular, the friction between the royal family and the Amantoo Mmiensa, which was to reach frightening proportions in the 1940s, had a long history.

48   *Annual Report* (Birim district, 1938), NAG ADM 32/1/32.

CHAPTER FOUR

The Murder

As the preceding chapters have tried to demonstrate, Ofori Atta's reign was as complex as it was long; as it drew to an end he was the Gold Coast's most influential 'natural ruler'. His ideas about the 'fit' between the colonial state and African kingship had almost always prevailed. From as early as 1918 he had been looked upon by both African and colonial rulers as a leader. At his bidding senior kings and chiefs in the south of the Gold Coast began to meet regularly, a practice gradually acknowledged by the colonial state which led to the recognition of a system of Provincial Councils of Chiefs in 1924. By 1925 these councils were the electors of six of the fourteen African members of the new Legislative Council, the country's Parliament. These achievements were symbolically recognised by Britain in the knighthood he received in person at Buckingham Palace in 1927. Nana Ofori Atta sat in the Legislative Council without interruption from 1916 until his death. He also served on the Legislative Council's Select Committee on Estimates and its Standing Finance Committee.[1] In 1942 he was one of the first two Africans appointed to the Gold Coast's Executive Council.[2] He was a formidable man.

His exercise of power in the colonial state echoed his career in Akyem Abuakwa. As we have seen, his success attracted local opposition. His role in increasing chiefly power in the Gold Coast also frustrated the politicians of the coastal towns, whose more obviously democratic agenda was sidelined by the colonial government's preference for working with 'natural rulers' rather than themselves. That frustration was given vent in a deal of personally unfavourable comment about Ofori Atta in the local press which was largely controlled by his enemies. He was painted as a tool of the colonial state, a collaborator and an exploiter of his own people.[3] The eventual triumph of the more radical

1 His role on these bodies is discussed by Margaret Priestly, 'Nana Ofori Atta I and Public Financial Affairs in Ghana, 1916–43', in *Legon Journal of the Humanities*, vol. II, n.d., pp. 1–14.
2 In September 1942. The other member was Arku Korsah, later to be Ghana's Chief Justice.
3 This is most apparent in the campaign mounted by the leader of the Aborigines' Rights Protection Society in the pages of the *Gold Coast Leader*.

brand of Ghanaian nationalism after the Second World War contributed to the continuation of that view of Ofori Atta as dupe and collaborator, even in some of the scholarly literature. As we have seen, he was much more interesting than such a caricature suggests.

The extraordinary busy-ness of Ofori Atta took its toll on his health. By the end of 1942, in his early sixties, he had already suffered a series of what we now call 'coronary events'. His archive shows how busy those six decades had been. A final massive heart attack preceded his death in Accra on 21 August 1943. Immediately after his death a group of his children and wives rushed to Accra. The latter bathed his body according to custom and eventually the body was taken back reverentially to Kyebi for the first funeral, *doteyie*.

Ofori Atta's first funeral was not a peaceful affair. His successor Ofori Atta II commented: 'Whole-sale destruction of farm products at the preliminary funeral caused great havoc ... unless this practice is stopped during the final custom there is every fear that the State might be plunged into general famine'.[4] But such chaos had been traditionally sanctioned and was expected. In quieter circumstances the dead king's body was lowered into a deep pit in the royal mausoleum attached to the palace. His widows threw broken crockery into the pit. Around their waists they wore cloths which were held by kinsfolk behind them to prevent them being 'drawn' into the pit. All the while dirges were sung. The population was dressed in the sombre brown mourning cloth. The mortal remains of the king were left to the forces of nature to reduce them to bones.[5] Eight days after these rites, the immediate family performed further, less public rites and fixed the day for the final funeral. Only after that could Ofori Atta's remains be taken to Banso where they would be finally buried.

Throughout these initial ceremonies, the political process of electing the next Okyenhene was in train. On 6 September 1943 Nana Opoku Acheampong was elected. Between 25 and 27 September he was formally sworn in and enstooled; he took the stool name of Ofori Atta II.[6] Although oral evidence suggests that the leaders of the Amantoo Mmiensa had supported another candidate they were amongst those who swore their fealty to Ofori Atta II:

The council [of the Amantoo Mmiensa] has never deserted Ofori's Stools – we will never desert them. When the blade of a cutlass

4 Ofori Atta II to all chiefs, 28 January 1944, AASA 10/242.
5 Akan tradition demands that the second funeral should be held no earlier than forty days after death. Ofori Atta's *ayie* was held about six months after his death.
6 A fine account of these ceremonies written by Kwame Frimpong, described as 'Twi announcer, Department of Information', is in AASA 3/12.

breaks we make another to replace it. Today you are our sovereign lord. We have put you in the place of your great uncle. If you do not take me and my subjects as children, if you do not regard us as slave's children, we will fight to save you always. As from today if you ever call us in darkness, in fires, in the blazing sun or in rain (periods of illness excepted) and if I and my subjects turn our backs to you, I violate Okyeman's three great oaths.

What we know of the events in Ofori Panin Fie on 28 February 1944, the last day of the final funeral rites of Sir Ofori Atta, was to be paraded *in extenso* in the following year. The allegations were to be heard firstly at the Coroner's Inquest on Akyea Mensah in Koforidua in September;[7] and they were to be heard in much the same form and order at the subsequent murder trial in November. These accounts are dealt with in more detail below. Other than those who were to appear in court, there were no independent witnesses to what happened in the Ahenfie that day.

Government police were notably absent by agreement. The DC wrote to Ofori Atta II on 9 February 1944 to assure him that 'No Government Police are to be allowed inside the walls of the Ahenfie compound . . . all necessary Police duties within the Ahenfie compound to be performed by N.A. Police. . . .' There is no evidence which suggests that he had some presentiment of what was to happen but seventeen days later he qualified this in another letter to the Okyenhene: '. . . it must . . . be understood that the prohibition on Government Police entering the Ahenfie during the custom does not include entry to deal with any *serious* crime which they may see being committed or attempted. . . . This does not indicate any change in the present attitude of the Police.'[8]

What was to be alleged was that during the long funeral ceremonies the chief or Odikro of the Amantoo Mmiensa town of Apedwa had been killed in the palace. It was also to be alleged that his murderers were eight close kin of the late king, including some of his sons.[9] The Odikro,

---

7   The Coroner's Inquest, before the Ghanaian magistrate Charles Hayfron-Benjamin (who died in 1970), was held to investigate how Akyea Mensah had died. In the particular circumstances of the Gold Coast legal code and this particular case it also served as a committal procedure for those subsequently accused of his murder.

8   DC Walker to Okyenhene, 26 February 1944; both letters in AASA 10/42. The Government police complement in Kyebi consisted of about nine men at this time.

9   The precise relationships are as follows: Asare Apietu, the Abontendomhene, was a son of Okyenhene Amoako Atta I; Kwame Kagya, a grandson of Amoako Atta I; Kwaku Amoako Atta, a son of Amoako Atta II; Kwadjo Amoako and Kwasi Pipim, grandsons of Amoako Atta II; Opoku Afwenee, A.E.B. Danquah and Owusu Akyem Tenteng all sons of Ofori Atta I.

3 The only known photograph of Akyea Mensah.

4 The skull alleged to be that of Akyea Mensah. To confirm the identification, the photograph of the skull was superimposed over the image of the head – a forensic technique used with some accuracy in a number of famous British murder trials.

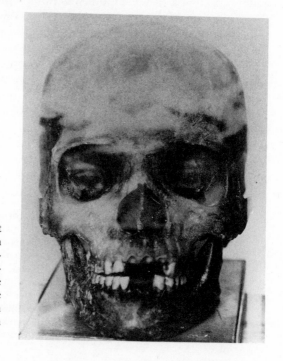

it was said, had been lured into one of the palace courtyards, had been cudgelled and then had had his cheeks and tongue pierced by the traditional executioner's knife or *sepow*.[10] Some of his blood was then collected and smeared on Ofori Atta I's stool as part of the process of blackening or consecrating the stool.[11] While this was supposed to be in progress, a memorial service was being held a few hundred yards away in the Presbyterian church, unwittingly but neatly capturing the bewildering ambiguities of Kyebi. What then was supposed to have happened to the body is more conjectural. The scatter of evidence suggests that it may have been dismembered, temporarily buried behind the royal mausoleum in Kyebi and then interred on the bank of a small stream north of Kyebi.

The Odikro of Apedwa, Akyea Mensah, was in Kyebi at this time as one of the three *Adikrofo*, or headmen, of the three towns that made up the core of the Amantoo Mmiensa.[12] On the final day of the funeral the Amantoo Mmiensa constituted the group and the rite of Wirempe. The ceremony they were charged with ends the funeral rites. They take a blackened stool into the bush outside Kyebi and stay with it overnight, during which time the stool is reinvigorated by ancestral spirits. The following day they return with both the stool and the new Okyenhene in triumph to the Ofori Panin Fie.[13]

By mid-afternoon the fact that Akyea Mensah was missing was being widely discussed in Kyebi and was made official by the sullen refusal of the Amantoo Mmiensa to perform the Wirempe ceremonies without him. A hue and cry was mounted by the customary beating of '*gong gong*' and the calling out of the young men to form search parties. There was nothing novel about this; people, especially children, often went missing in the forest, and local organisation was well geared for systematic search. The hunt was first mounted by those Amantoo Mmiensa members who were in Kyebi for the funeral and then by the wider Kyebi community under the command of the Adontenhene.

Rumours began to fly around Kyebi and then more widely. Within a very short time these had reached Accra, and thinly veiled comment about the Odikro's disappearance began to emerge in the press. The

10   *Sepow*'s purpose is to silence a victim to prevent him from uttering the Great Oath, one of whose functions is to freeze the action.

11   Washing or blackening a stool – *epun* – is traditionally done with a mixture of eggs, soot and the blood of sheep. Many accounts agree that this symbolically charged mixture once included human blood.

12   Apapam, Tetteh and Akyea Mensah's town of Apedwa.

13   This rite is carried out in most Akan states by the Gyaasehene and his men. Addo-Fening suggests that the Amantoo Mmiensa took over this role in Akyem Abuakwa in 1881 when the Gyaasehene refused to carry out Wirempe as he was a Christian convert: personal communication.

burden of this assumed that the Odikro's disappearance was sinister and that the most likely explanation of it was that he had been killed as part of the final funeral rites of Nana Sir Ofori Atta.[14]

The Amantoo Mmiensa leaders put pressure on the Okyenhene and his State Council to do something; Okyeman Council responded on 1 March by offering a reward of £8 to 'any person who would give information that will lead to the tracing of the Odikro . . .'.[15] The Amantoo Mmiensa also leant on the District Commissioner and the local detachment of the Government Police arguing that they, as well as the Okyeman Council, were being dilatory. If they were being dilatory it would have been understandable; the last thing that they or the wider colonial administration could have wanted was a major scandal involving the most dependable traditional state in the Gold Coast. But on 8 March the DC, now worried by the allegation, wrote to the Okyenhene: '. . . in order to clear up any misapprehension I should be glad if you will inform the State Council and people generally that Government is equally concerned with the Odikro's disappearance and that the Government Police are taking all normal steps in the matter.'[16]

The hue and cry and the police investigations were getting nowhere. The Odikro formally remained nothing more worrying than a 'missing person'. Adults may absent themselves without warning or explanation in free societies; accordingly the police felt that it was premature to become overly concerned. The *Police Gazette* of 20 March 1944 registered this when the following entry appeared: 'PERSON MISSING. Akyea Mensah, alias Emmanuel R. Mensah Ohemeng, age abt. 48, 5ft. 6 ins., c.lt.bk., e. big., ears small., build slender and strong, dressed in velvet cover cloth and white knickers, o. Chief of Apedwa, formerly Court Registrar of the late Omanhene of Akim Abuakwa, walks slowly and gently, last seen Kibi 27/2/44.' On first reading these brief details I was greatly, probably irrationally, moved by this oddly tender description of the one person who it is all too easy to forget in the surrounding circumstances. The suggestion of quiet gentleness was strongly reinforced by his family's and other peoples' memories of him.

But the Amantoo Mmiensa and parts of the Gold Coast press were insinuating murder. Relations between the Okyeman Council and the Amantoo Mmiensa leadership were worsening. The State Council

---

14 Gossip outside Akyem Abuakwa today continues to make that assumption, and insists that Akyemfo are the most conservative of Akans when it comes to life-taking at funerals. The events described here play their part in constructing this unenviable and probably undeserved reputation. But the speed with which the Odikro's disappearance was to be construed as a sinister mystery at the time suggests that this was an older stereotype.

15 Okyenhene to DC (Walker), 9 March 1944, AASA 3/297.

16 Walker to Okyenhene, 8 March 1944, AASA 3/297.

sought to repair the damage and summoned the aggrieved to meet them on 14 March. The Amantoo Mmiensa refused the invitation and instead gathered sullenly in the courtyard below the council chamber, insisting that every house in Kyebi, including the Ahenfie, should be searched for the remains of Akyea Mensah.[17] The Okyenhene was eager to make peace and, unusually, suggested that Okyeman join the Amantoo Mmiensa in the courtyard. Here the Okyenhene suggested that a house-to-house search was a waste of time. 'It is not probable that the missing Odikro should be still in Kyebi for if he is dead at all nobody can keep his corpse and breath it.'[18]

At this stage the Amantoo Mmiensa were also overtly conciliatory despite their terrible suspicions. Their spokesman, the Odikro of Tetteh, said somewhat sarcastically: 'Yesterday we broached the question that the Ahenfie must be searched. However if you point your gun, you stain your shoulders. We do not propose to search the Ahenfie. After all we are the slaves to be sold in the interest of the Paramount Stool. . . .' The Odikro of Apapam agreed that '. . . it will serve no useful purpose . . . and we don't want to be misunderstood'. One of the senior linguists, Okyeame Abroso, advised them 'to be calm and collected and to stop abuses and insinuation'. On behalf of the Amantoo Mmiensa the Odikro of Apapam agreed that they had 'no wish to cross words with Nana Okyenhene . . . the Amantoo Mmiensa [are] now reduced to Amantoomienu[19] . . . they will never come to Kyebi as a body and only . . . come to Kyebi whenever any of them is so invited by the Okyenhene or their wing chief . . .'.[20] Two weeks after the disappearance of the Odikro an uneasy, formal truce was being observed. But outside the staid confines of Ofori Panin Fie, the Amantoo Mmiensa were unconsoled and continued to make allegations and threats.

They were not the only people to be concerned. In the late afternoon, following the Okyeman meeting, the DC visited the palace and met the Okyenhene and his close advisers. The Akyem Abuakwa State Secretary, K.T.A. Danquah, a nephew of Nana Sir Ofori Atta, kept a record of that exchange and parts of it bear repeating in full. The DC, Walker, initiated the discussion by saying: 'Yesterday I was in Accra. . . . The Governor . . . was very sorry about the mystery and that it tends to give a very bad impression . . . to the State . . . when one reads the press. . . . The Governor remarked that this mystery is actually a stain on the good name of Akyem Abuakwa.' The Okyenhene replied:

17 There were, as we shall see in Chpt 8, some specific reasons why the Amantoo
    Mmiensa believed that Akyea Mensah had been killed.
18 *Minutes* of Okyeman Council Meeting, 14 March 1944, AASA 3/297.
19 An ironic pun; it means the council of two towns.
20 Okyeman Council *Minutes*, 14 March 1944, AASA 3/297.

'The people of Akyem Abuakwa are really law-abiding people . . . Every endeavour has been made for his discovery. . . . We have our suspicious beliefs and so men had been sent to consult many fetishes . . . £100 has been voted for the expenses that will be made in connection with the search. . . .' Walker affected naivety with his next question, the answer to which he knew only too well: 'Why is it that Amantoommiensa is more concerned in the matter?' The Okyenhene replied: '. . . they are likely to be affected if a chief . . . got missing'. Walker pressed on with his mock naivety: 'So can I take it that the attitude of Amantoommiensa in this matter is normal?' The Okyenhene countered: 'We are equally concerned in the matter and so it will be out of place if they show an abnormal attitude because Okyeman is doing its best in the matter.' Walker eventually ended his contribution to the debate by saying: '. . . something has to be done to clear out all the unkind stories going on in other States'.[21]

The widespread allegations about the Odikro's disappearance gathered and threatened. Additional police under a Superintendent[22] were drafted into Kyebi and a number of people, including four of the eight who were finally arrested, were detained and questioned,[23] but all were subsequently released without charge. The additional police detachment left Kyebi on 18 March. This did not stop the *Daily Echo* maintaining pressure on the Okyeman Council. On 15 April 1944, a leader commented: 'If an incident has occurred which has in it an element of suspicion which recalls customs of bygone days it is surely the duty of the Akim Abuakwa state to leave no stone unturned to see that the missing man is restored. . . . We trust that the Government has not let the matter drop. . . .' The State Council drafted a long statement because of the circulation of 'conflicting and libellous statements in the Press' which was published in *The Gold Coast Observer* on 21 April 1944.[24]

---

21 Okyenhene's record of a meeting with District Commissioner Walker on 14 March 1944, AASA 3/297.
22 S.C. Sinclair, the Superintendent in charge of Eastern Province police.
23 Some interviews were conducted by R. Tottenham, Superintendent of the Criminal Investigation Department (CID), and some by the Commissioner of Police (R.W.H. Ballantine). This unusual procedure is evidence of the serious view the police took of the allegations. Conversely it meshed neatly with J.B. Danquah's allegations that the colonial authorities were 'out to get' the Kyebi royal family.
24 To present '. . . the facts of the matter as far as Okyeman are concerned and it is intended to counteract the misguided statements in the press and sinister rumours associated with the affair'. K.T.A. Danquah to J.B. Danquah, 1 April 1944, AASA 3/297. The rather circuitous wording, '. . . as far as Okyeman are concerned . . .', is perhaps suggestive, but only perhaps.

Over the coming months rumours continued to fly; no material evidence of the missing Odikro, dead or alive, emerged. On 4 May the Commissioner of Police received an anonymous letter dated 26 April sent from Kyebi which claimed that a 'fetish priest', Osei Tawiah, had heard a confession to the murder from Kwesi Pipim. It is clear that the police were now convinced that a crime had been committed and they took the anonymous letter seriously.[25] Police Corporal Nuamah was sent to Kyebi and discovered, on interviewing him, that Tawiah was the letter's author. On 14 May Nuamah went to Apedwa and interviewed two witnesses who separately outlined their recollections; these were to be key pieces of evidence at both the inquest and the trial.[26] On 16 May, Tawiah took Nuamah, now joined by another African officer, Sub-Inspector Danso of the CID, to a spot close to the royal mausoleum in Kyebi where he he had been told the remains were buried. This was done at night. This was a *grand guignol* scene as men lit only by a kerosene lamp sank their spades in earth they expected was covering a corpse. Sinclair, Tottenham, District Commissioner Walker and the ADC, Levack, accompanied by the government's senior forensic officer, Dr Reid of the Medical Research Institute in Accra, had come to Kyebi in the clear hope of exhuming a body. But if anything had been there, then it had been removed before their arrival; the digging revealed nothing.

Despite this reverse the police dossier was building, as was the police presence in Kyebi; a large plainclothes squad from CID arrived at the end of May. On 21 June, the Commissioner and Sinclair again travelled to Kyebi now armed with search warrants and warrants for the arrest of the eight who were subsequently charged. Before these warrants were executed a further series of interviews took place. At one of these the Okyenhene, while denying all knowledge, eventually agreed to both a search of the Ahenfie and of the Nkonnuafieso, the Stool House.[27] At 10.30 pm on the same day, Kwasi Pipim and Kwame Kagya were

25 Berkley-Barton's memoir of the events stressed that 'experience has shown that many anonymous letters are valueless'. See 'The Case and Attendant Circumstances Relating to the Trial Rex vs. Abontendomhene Asare Apietu and 7 Others', typescript, n.d., Mss Africa S.579, Rhodes House Library, Oxford. The police were frequently sent anonymous letters but as in any country the bulk of these reflected inter-personal quarrels between, for example, neighbours.

26 Dates of these events are recorded differently by Burns (in his letter to the Secretary of State, 28 December 1944, PRO CO 96/783/1) and by Berkley-Barton in his account, *op. cit.* Berkley-Barton clearly wrote his account with the police files to hand, for his dates conform with those in the files CSO 15/3.0170.SF.73 (listed as 'Apedwa Murder Case' in the National Archives of Ghana). These match those in the Akyem Abuakwa State Archives' record (AASA 3/297); it seems that Burns' letter was hurriedly drafted.

27 The agreement of the Okyenhene and Okyeman to the search is substantiated in AASA 3/129.

interviewed throughout the night by the Commissioner, the head of CID and Berkley-Barton. By the latter's own account, 'Nothing emerged that was useful.'[28]

On 23 June, Sub-Inspector Danso went to Apedwa and interviewed 'the Elders'. Danso reported that he had been told that the remains had been removed from behind the mausoleum immediately after Nuamah had first visited the spot in May. This was, at best, hearsay evidence and Berkley-Barton recorded the following apparently contradictory comments: '. . . it will be readily appreciated how difficult investigations become when a series of conflicting stories has to be sifted and separately examined in detail. . . . This meeting at Apedwa was of much value to the Police . . . but when sifted and checked a large proportion of the information was found valueless. . . .'[29] This interview did, however, provide the police with the information that Kwame Kagya, one of those under suspicion, had visited the Kankama shrine in Ashanti whose assistant priest was later to make a statement about Kagya's confessional misery of being troubled by Akyea Mensah's ghost.

The police interviews continued with the stool carriers, two of whom, Gyekye and Mireku, were to be important Crown witnesses to the murder.[30] On 6 July, Danso and Nuamah were told where the remains were. A short period of excavation on that afternoon on the banks of the tiny River Krensen revealed a skull, a lower jaw bone, seven limb bones and a tooth. That evening eight men were arrested and were charged with murder on 10 July.

The thoughts and feelings of the royal family at this stage are imaginable but unrecorded. Eight members of the royal family, men frequently in the Ahenfie, companions as well as kinsmen, were now in custody and charged with a horrible capital crime. Akyem Abuakwa and its royal family were now being subjected not merely to a whispering campaign in the Gold Coast but the full force of the colonial state's law and order agencies. Ofori Panin Fie, until recently the splendid palace of the Gold Coast's most splendid monarch, was now alleged to have been the site of a foul murder. A once glittering state, a byword for 'progress' and its no less glittering royal family, stood uncomfortably in the searchlight of infamy.

The Okyenhene hastily summoned an emergency meeting of the Okyeman Council on 10 July. The District Commissioner was invited to attend an anodyne session at which Okyeman pledged to support the

---

28 Berkley-Barton, *op. cit.*
29 Berkley-Barton, *op. cit.*
30 Berkley-Barton admitted that: 'The taking of a statement from this type of witness is no easy matter as they are, naturally, frightened as to what will be done to them by those against whom they testify, thus they are inclined to hold back essentials and be inaccurate'; *op. cit.*

police in every way they could.[31] The police were now in a dilemma about whether to execute their search warrants in the Ahenfie. They had been told that the blackened stool they wished to examine had been removed. On 12 July they were informed that it had been returned to Stool House, and at 10.35 am the police went to the palace to make their search.[32]

This was an extraordinarily tense occasion. Senior Assistant Superintendent of Police Berkley-Barton recorded that the Okyenhene 'was in a highly nervous state and he harangued the meeting denying Akyea Mensah's death'.[33] Despite this, he was collected enough to point out the ritual exclusions which would prevent some of the police party from entering the Stool House. No Asante, no circumcised man and no one in shoes could enter and the search party was then re-selected to conform with these ritual objections. On entry they discovered seven stools and not the eight they had been expecting. The Odikro of Tetteh, one of the party, and as an Amantoo Mmiensa elder, by now an adversary of the royal family, asked where the eighth stool was. He was told that it was on Nana Sir Ofori Atta's temporary grave in the mausoleum. The party then made for the mausoleum. Libation was poured and a sheep slaughtered. In the mausoleum or *Bamu* the party found a white stool resting on a mat on the grave-mound. This, they were told, over the mutterings of the Odikro of Tetteh about this all being quite untraditional, was the stool that would be consecrated and blackened for the late Okyenhene.

Quite where this set of events left matters is unclear. If the suspected blackened stool, which, had the Amantoo Mmiensa's claims and police suspicions been correct, should have had the missing Odikro's blood upon it, been in place, then there was precious little the police could have done with it. Their forensic techniques could have detected human blood had such been on the stool, but their procedures were insufficiently sophisticated to be able to identify whose blood it was.[34] Secondly the presence of human blood would not necessarily imply murder as, for example, someone could have volunteered to be cut to provide blood for cleansing the stool. It is of course doubtful whether the Okyeman knew of these analytical weaknesses at the time.

Whatever we deduce, the number of stools in *Nkonnuafieso* (the Stool

---

31   Berkley-Barton says that this 'was a complete change of front as prior to the arrests . . . the Abuakwa State had given no assistance . . .'; *op. cit.*

32   A full account of this search is in both the police files in NAG and in Okyeman Council *Minutes* of 14 July, 1944, AASA 8.2/42.

33   Berkley-Barton, *op. cit.* See also Ofori Atta's account of this in the Okyeman Council *Minutes* for 14 July, 1944, AASA 8.2/42.

34   They had, after all, no specimen of Akyea Mensah's blood nor any record of his blood group.

House) raises real doubts about the Okyenhene's insistence that all the blackened stools were in the Stool House when this search took place. Several well-informed sources insist that today there are twelve blackened stools in that holy of holies. Akyem Abuakwa's traditions make a very good historical case for there having been thirty-three rulers of Akyem Abuakwa including the present incumbent Kuntunkununku II (Kwadwo Fredua). Ofori Atta I was the twenty-ninth ruler of the state and at least the twenty-first king for whom we have rock-solid historical evidence. However many blackened stools are actually in the Stool House, it is clear that Akyem Abuakwa honours only a select few of its rulers by the highest accolade of blackening a stool in their honour. This is the clear message of oral tradition as well as the only conclusion we can make on the basis of the limited number of blackened stools in the Stool House. But even if we accept that the white, un-blackened stool resting on Ofori Atta I's grave in 1944 was going to be consecrated and was thus the eighth stool as the defence were to claim during the trial, then were are left with a real problem. Supposing all of his successors had stools consecrated in their honour, and this is extremely improbable,[35] then the maximum number of stools in Nkonnuafieso today would be eleven. There is no doubt that the search party were not shown all the stools which normally rested in the Stool House: one or more had been removed prior to the search. When it comes to evaluating some of the trial evidence, these doubts become significant.

There is evidence of panic on Ofori Panin Fie at this stage. In a long, confused letter to the Governor, the Okyenhene made a heartfelt series of complaints.[36] Okyenhene agreed that the search was made after 'the police had asked and obtained most willing permission from me and the State Council . . . certain taboos of a sacrilegious nature were allowed to be violated . . . [but] . . . the search revealed not the slightest indication that those sacred places had anything to do with the unfortunate disappearance of Bafuor Akyea Mensah . . .'. The letter goes on to plead the inherent decency of all those arrested and charged[37] and deplores '. . . the distress and disgrace that my State, Chiefs and people

---

35   Informants were unanimous about this; the thirty-first Okyenhene, Amoako Atta IV, was a political appointment whose reign (1958–66) interrupted that of Ofori Atta II who was deposed by the Convention Peoples' Party government and was only restored after the coup that swept Dr Nkrumah's government from power in 1966. It is unlikely that this man would have been so honoured. Whether Ofori Atta I's other two successors were both so honoured is far from agreed.

36   Sent on 18 July 1944, AASA 3/297.

37   The letter first says that six were arrested and then goes on to itemise the eight accused. This I read as evidence of the pressures under which this letter was drafted.

suffer.... I ... feel it my duty to express ... our deep sense of the infamy that the course taken by the Police brings to the reputation of the State....' While the suggestion is in part manipulative – that the colonial authority was dragging down its own favoured principles of Native Administration by pursuing this matter in so open a manner – it is also clear that Okyenhene was writing about his personal pain and a gathering storm which he knew would engulf him, his family and the state of Akyem Abuakwa.

The Governor's reply, routed through the District Commissioner in Kyebi, was stern and unbending:

> ... the maintenance of law and order must take precedence over all other matters ... no personal feelings or other considerations can be allowed to hamper or interfere with their investigations. While it is appreciated that, as a result of certain measures, the good name and dignity of the Ofori Stool may inevitably have suffered indignities, the real responsibility rests, not with the authorities, but with those whose criminal activities made it necessary for such steps to be taken.... [38]

As Akyem Abuakwa's lawyer as well as a senior royal, J.B. Danquah was shown the letter soon after it was received in the palace. In his brief reply he tried to console the Okyenhene but did so without making promises that there was any immediate chance of checking this terrible reverse: '... there is no need to worry – at present ...'. [39]

But there was little other than his uncle's words to console him. On 17 July the eight accused men appeared before the magistrate's court and began a series of weekly remands in custody [40] which were to last until 12 September when the matter came before the Coroner's Court at Koforidua, a hearing which lasted until 23 September. That inquest heard virtually all the evidence which was to deployed at the eventual trial, and this satisfied Mr Hayfron-Benjamin sitting as Coroner that Akyea Mensah had been murdered. But under Gold Coast law Hayfron-Benjamin was also sitting as the stipendiary magistrate. Following his determination of the cause of death he committed all eight men for trial at the October Assizes in Accra on evidence which J.B. Danquah, who was monitoring the inquest for the Okyenhene, unhappily admitted was 'very strong.' [41]

38   Walker to Okyenhene, 3 August 1944, AASA 3/297.
39   J.B. Danquah to Okyenhene, 7 August 1944, AASA 3/297.
40   The law required that remands in custody should not exceed seven days. These men were defendants and not convicted men. Therefore Crown applications for further remands in custody and defence requests for bail were heard, *de novo*, every week until the murder trial began.
41   J.B. Danquah to Okyenhene, 27 September 1944, AASA 3/297.

CHAPTER FIVE

The Trial and the Sentence

The accused came to trial in Accra on 3 November 1944 in Accra's sombre Assize Court buildings. The prosecution was represented by the Assistant Attorney General, J.S. Manyo-Plange.[1] A.E. Akuffo Addo and Nii Ollennu apeared for the defendants Opoku Afwenee, Asare Apietu, Kwame Kagya and Kwasi Pipim. Frans Dove and Sarkodee Addo appeared for Kweku Amoako Atta and A.E.B. Dankwa and Heward Mills[2] for Kwadjo Amoako and Owusu Akyem Tenteng. Bewigged, gowned and sweltering in a crowded court which had recently been fitted with rather ineffectual electric ceiling fans stood six of the highest-paid, best-known and most impressive figures at the Gold Coast Bar.[3]

In the dock sat the eight accused men in the civilian clothes worn by unconvicted, remand prisoners. As if to underline their distinction[4] they wore expensive cloth.[5] The judge was Mohammed Fuad, Justice of the Gold Coast Supreme Court and a Cypriot.[6] He had served for many

---

1 The scion of an immensely distinguished coastal family, he had begun his career as Senior Superintendent of Police at the age of twenty-three in 1924. He was called to the Bar in 1932 and served in the Solicitor General's Department from 1942. By 1951 he was a Puisne Judge.

2 A lawyer who had, ironically, been an adversary of Ofori Atta I in the 1930s, being 'unduly concerned . . . with political agitation against the Chiefs . . .' (Ofori Atta to DC, 26 September 1932, AASA 4/69). Dove had also acted for Akwatia stool in its litigation against Ofori Atta I in the 1930s. DC to Provincial Commissioner, 21 August 1940, NAG ADM 32/1/29.

3 The background of these senior figures at the Gold Coast Bar can be followed up in Bjorn M. Edsman's *Lawyers in Gold Coast Politics c.1900–1945* (Uppsala, 1979).

4 They constituted, as J.S. Lambert in the Colonial Office minuted on 29 November 1944, 'an impressive list'; PRO CO 95/783/1.

5 In the Colonial Office O.G.R. Williams observed on the eve of the trial: 'This promises to be a cause celebre which will throw other controversies in the shade for a time.' 16 October 1944, PRO CO 96/783/1.

6 A bitter, unhappy man. A letter of resignation to the Colonial Office shows that he felt his failure to become a colonial Chief Justice owed everything to 'prejudice against my name and religion'. The letter also touches on his ill health and the long periods of separation from his wife and family who remained in Cyprus. Fuad to Secretary of State, 27 April 1945, NAG 12/532.

81

years in the Gold Coast and at sixty-two was coming to the end of a long career.[7]

The jury were sworn in. Jury trial had been instituted in the Gold Coast as early as 1853 in the Supreme Court Ordinance[8] and was retained in capital and other grave cases under the Criminal Procedure Ordinance of 1876 (no. 5). Under the Criminal Procedure Amendment Ordinance of 1898 (no. 2), the number of jurors was reduced from twelve to seven. Although the system was tinkered with by the Criminal Procedure Amendment Ordinance of 1916 (no. 12) and the Criminal Procedure Code of 1935 (no. 10), it remained in operation in the colony, the south of the colonial state, although the Governor-in-Council could stipulate jury trial in individual cases in other regions. It was common ground in all of this legislation that African defendants had to be tried by a jury at least half of whom had to be African.[9]

None of the jurymen was challenged although the defence had the right of peremptory challenge.[10] Six of the jurors were African, drawn from the ranks of literate rate-payers in the Accra area and, ethnically, were Ga people. The seventh juryman was a European bank clerk.[11] As English and Twi were to be the languages used by witnesses, lawyers and defendants, court interpreters were also sworn in. On this first appearance the judge heard applications from the defence for remands in custody so that the defence case could be further prepared; these were granted and the prisoners returned to court for the hearing on 8 November.[12]

7   This chapter is based on two trial transcripts. One is a manuscript record in Fuad's hand, NAG SCT 28/8/20. Gold Coast judges were required to keep a verbatim record of serious trials. These notes are slightly more extensive than the shorthand writer's record in PRO CO 96/783/2. The judge's record, for example, notes who witnesses were addressing when giving evidence and records hesitations and non-verbal outbursts. There is no discrepancy of any evidential significance between the two.

8   No. 1, s.6.

9   See J.H. Jeary, 'Trial by Jury and Trial with the Aid of Assessors in the Superior Courts of British Africa', in the *Journal of African Law* IV (1960), pp. 133–46, V (1961), pp. 36–47 and 82–98.

10   Challenge was often used to change the composition of juries when the defence suspected that jurymen might be biased against the defendant.

11   During the trial the jury lived in the Accra Hotel, Rolyat Castle; NAG CSO 15/3, 0170, S.F.71. This was owned by Nii Bonne Taylor, who was to lead the boycott of European goods, one of the most significant preludes to the riots of 28 February 1948. Also known as Theodore Taylor, he had been a business partner of Nana Sir Ofori Atta I in the 1930s, who had been a shareholder and director of Theodore Taylor & Co (Accra), an import–export company. Amongst the other shareholders were T. Hutton-Mills and the Omanhene of Akwapim; AASA 5/41.

12   There was concern in the Colonial Office about press coverage. An indecipherable hand minuted on 6 November 1944: 'My personal view is that

Manyo-Plange outlined the prosecution case succinctly and called his first witness, Akyea Mensah's wife, or as he was attempting to prove, his widow. Ama Owuakyir gave her evidence quietly in Twi. She told the jury that she had seen him for the last time on 'that Sunday'. Akyea Mensah had 'a small bump' on the right side of his head, 'a sort of scar' which was visible when his head was shaved. It was to be alleged that this minor deformity was visible on the disinterred skull. Only Akuffo Addo sought to cross-examine. He established that Akyea Mensah's second wife, Ekua Waa-Waa, was the daughter of the defendant Kwame Kagya, one of his clients, and that relations between Kagya and Akyea Mensah had been 'happy and cordial', although not extending to visits to one another's houses.

Manyo-Plange next called Henry Ampomah, a Kyebi schoolteacher who had been a lodger in Akyea Mensah's Kyebi house.[13] He offered little in chief to the court. He had seen Akyea Mensah leaving the house between 6.00 and 8.00 am. Akuffo Addo, in a knowing cross-examination, was able to turn this prosecution witness into a defence asset. Ampomah agreed that on a previous occasion he had spoken with Akyea Mensah. The Odikro had told him that he was ready to abdicate.

> I had gathered from previous conversations that he was not happy because of the trouble he had been having with some of his subjects . . . he did tell me long before this occasion that he was going to abdicate to forestall his subjects . . . he was going to abdicate after the conclusion of the funeral ceremonies. . . . From what Mensah told me . . . part of his trouble was with the Mankrado of Apedwa.

Ampomah proved a poor witness for the prosecution, reinforcing as he did the defence argument that Mensah was disturbed and had motives for wanting to get out of Apedwa or even for taking his own life.

The third witness was of more help to Manyo Plange. Kwame Karikari was a cocoa farmer from Yirikyire and a brother-in-law of the late Okyenhene. He had seen Akyea Mensah in front of the Ahenfie on that Sunday. His account was anodyne but Heward Mills elected to cross-examine him. His first question scored in that it elicited Karikari's

no publicity is required or desirable during the trial but in the event of a conviction a small measure of publicity both in the UK and on the African Service [of the BBC] might be rather salutary to persons of a Fabian tendency.' PRO CO 96/783/1. This was a triumph of hope over experience.

13 Many notables had houses in Kyebi as well as in their home towns. The frequency of festivals and state occasions made this a cheaper option than renting accomodation. Having a 'second address' was also evidence of eminence. Kyebi's population expands greatly during festivals and other state occasions.

agreement that he was a member of the Amantoo Mmiensa. He also
agreed that as Captain of the Amanfrom Asafo company he had led the
search party which initially looked for Akyea Mensah. That might have
suggested to a juryman that his was partisan evidence. But Heward
Mills pressed him further. Was Akyea Mensah alone when he saw him?
Karikari agreed that he was alone when he saw him inside the gate of
the Ahenfie, 'but I saw two young men under a tree about six paces
from the gate'. Did he know them? 'Their names are Botwe and Fosu. I
knew one of them before that day but I did not know the other. . . .'
Unwittingly Heward Mills had allowed Karikari to establish that two of
the key Crown witnesses were in the Ahenfie at the relevant time. While
trying to get Karikari to physically distance his clients from Akyea
Mensah, he had helped Manyo-Plange establish a link in the chain of
eye-witness evidence.

Manyo-Plange presented his case chronologically. He had established
Akyea-Mensah's movements that Sunday and had now got him into the
Ofori Panin Fie. At the beginning of the second day he called the
divisional surveyor to explain the plans of the complex layout of the
palace. The jury were shown the drawings and were allowed to retain
copies as a kind of atlas of events. Manyo-Plange now called his fifth
witness. Samuel Opoku Botwe was a cocoa-buyer and farmer who came
from Apedwa. He and Kwaku Fosu had come to Kyebi with the Odikro
for the funeral. They met him outside the Ahenfie on the Sunday and
went in with him. They went as far as the third courtyard of the palace
and there saw the eight defendants. The Odikro greeted the defendants,
and they him. They asked him to sit with them, and A.E.B. Danquah
invited him to take a drink of palm wine. Whilst he was drinking,
Kwaku Amoako Atta got up and stood behind the seated Odikro. The
Odikro got to his feet but while rising was hit on the head with a
cudgel. He could not be sure who had wielded the cudgel. All eight
defendants then 'fell on' the Odikro. Botwe claimed that he and Fosu
chose this moment to beat a hasty retreat. He had tried to tell Police Inspector Gyampo about what had happened but the Inspector 'drove him
away'. Eight days later he wrote to the Assistant Superintendent of Police
at Koforidua but received no reply. No trace of that letter remains in
the police files today but that record is incomplete.[14] Had this letter
survived Manyo-Plange would certainly have sought to have used it.

14   What survives in the NAG is the CSO series which awaits classification and
     shelving. I consulted CSO 0170. SF.73, *Apedwa Murder Case*; Conf. DCS 465.
     SF.2, *Actions of Defending Solicitors*; Conf, 0170/S 117, *ibid.*; 4556, *Police and Privy
     Council Appeals*; 0170/SF.11, *Case of Akwa* [Akyea] *Mensah*; and 522/33, *IGP vs.
     Hayfron-Benjamin on Lenient Sentencing*. I am very grateful to J. Anim-Asante for
     brave efforts to extract this material from the repository. As they are stored in
     no logical order this proved to be very hard work.

Botwe was cross-examined but stood by his story. On the third day Manyo-Plange put in Kwaku Fosu, who Botwe claimed had accompanied him. Fosu corroborated Botwe's account in detail. He and his story stood up well to cross-examination. Like Botwe, he was quizzed on what he knew about the relationship between Akyea Mensah and the *Ahenemmaa*, the 'sons of the stool', the princes in the dock. He was asked if he knew of any disputes between any of them and the Odikro over women or land and denied that he did. There was no particular reason why either of these quite ordinary men should have had such knowledge.

Manyo-Plange adhered to his chronological plan of attack. He next called Yaw Gyekyi, a rubber-tapper and stool carrier for the late Okyenhene. He was a palace official and had no discernible connection with the missing Odikro, the Amantoo Mmiensa or Apedwa town. He confirmed that he had seen seven of the eight defendants in the third courtyard of the Ahenfie, the 'courtyard called Mpotokur'. After adjournment he continued with his account. He had seen Akyea Mensah in a sitting position with an executioner's dagger stuck through his cheeks and with blood flowing from both sides of his mouth. Akyea Mensah was, he thought, dead; but of course had he been dead the blood would have ceased flowing. At the grisly scene he saw his fellow stool carriers Opanin Atta, the head carrier, Kwame Buahin, Kofi Adjei, Kwame Agyapong, Kojo Ewua and Kofi Appiah. Another stool carrier, Kwasi Mireku, entered the courtyard. Opanin Atta handed Mireku a bowl and that bowl was full of blood. Each stool carrier then dipped his hand into the bowl and began to smear the stool. There were seven blackened stools in the courtyard and the eighth, on the floor of the courtyard and being 'washed', was the late Okyenhene's stool. This was a staggering piece of evidence and demanded a concentrated attack from the defence.

In cross-examination, Akuffo Addo damaged the overall story very little. Gyekyi agreed that he had never seen Wirempe performed since he had become a stool carrier. He had seen Apietu pour libations in the Stool House during the Akwasidae and Odwira festivals in the past. He agreed that circumcised people were not allowed to enter the Stool House or the yard outside it. Akuffo Addo was cleverly establishing the traditional prohibition which might cast doubt on the presence of one of his clients at the scene of the crime. But he was not really destroying Gyekyi's horrifying account. Heward Mills pursued the same course as had Akuffo Addo, securing only the admission that Gyekyi had not known that Amoako Atta had been *Sanahene*[15] to the Okyenhene and had been destooled eight years previously as he had been medically

15   In effect his Lord Chamberlain.

circumcised; any physical deformity, whether congenital, surgical or accidental, can be seized upon as just cause to prevent a candidate from being installed or to destool him later.[16] Gyekyi said that all the stool carriers had discussed what had happened afterwards and had wondered about how 'we should best get out'.

The court was not to sit again until 13 November. They had heard much which needed to be digested. When they reassembled Manyo-Plange was eager not to lose the force of Gyekyi's testimony. He called another stool carrier, Kwasi Mireku. Mireku agreed that he too had seen the Odikro with a *sepow* through his cheeks. He had seen Apietu, Pipim and Kagya standing behind the body of the Odikro. Cross-examination yielded nothing of use for the defence team.

The testimony of these four eye-witnesses was the core of the prosecution case. It was powerful evidence, and survived close but curiously unfocused cross-examination. From an advocate's point of view, two bodies of evidence given by pairs of witnesses is a gift in cross-examination. Picking away at the evidence permits a lawyer to open up discrepancies between the parallel accounts which in turn might serve to raise questions in the jury's minds about the reliability of the witnesses. From the verbatim accounts we have, this was tried but it largely failed.

The prosecution next called Bernard Kwaku Osei Tawia, a mechanical fitter but, more importantly, a priest of the 'fetish' Ebum or Aboom, 'the fetish of the Okyenhene and the people of Kyebi'. His story was that Pipim, 'Drummer of the Big Drum and Captain of the Asafo', had come to him to confess his part in the murder. Tawia said that Pipim offered to show him the remains if he would give him medicine to 'keep his [Mensah's] spirit down'. Pipim showed Tawia the remains in a shallow grave behind the royal mausoleum. Pipim had told him, 'We are thankful to God that we heard of the Police before and removed the thing from where it was . . . we have put it near a stream nearby.'

Once again the defence seem to have been unwilling to contest this damaging evidence beyond trying to suggest malice and hence unreliability on Tawia's part. It was put to him that he had argued with Opanyin Atta, who was both head stool carrier and his uterine brother. This he denied. When the court re-convened next day, Nii Ollennu suggested to Tawia that the Asafo company, who 'owned' the fetish and whose Captain was the defendant Pipim, had sacked Tawia for selling a *Matakari* or robe which had belonged to Pipim; this too he denied.

Addo Kwaku was next to testify. He claimed to be 'next man' to the priest of another shrine, that of Kwankamea at Kwabira near Kumase. Kwame Kagya had come to that town to see one of the Akyem royals,

16 The aversion to circumcision was explained to me as being tied up with apprehensions about sexual potency.

Kwame Manu,[17] and to 'take him away to Kibi' – an account which was to be confirmed in the course of the defence case. Kagya told Addo Kwaku that: 'After the funeral . . . the ghost of the Odikro of Apedwa has been disturbing me so I want some Sassaduro.'[18] Given that this was another reported, damaging confession, cross-examination was slight. Manyo-Plange filled the rest of the day with technical witnesses who, for example, identified photographs.

At the end of the day, the Senior Superintendent of Police, E.M. Berkley-Barton, confirmed that he had been present on the banks of the River Krensen when some remains were exhumed. He also gave evidence of visiting the Stool House in the company of the new Okyenhene and Dr Danquah, where he had seen seven blackened stools but had seen no trace of an eighth and recently blackened stool. His evidence was hardly crucial but Ollennu, again attempting to build the defence case through cross-examination, asked if Berkley-Barton had met the Adikro of Tetteh and Apapam, who along with the Odikro of Apedwa constituted the elders of the Amantoo Mmiensa. Berkley-Barton agreed that he had interviewed them. Ollennu was clearly trying to establish a linkage between the police and the Amantoo Mmiensa which would suggest conspiracy.

Constable John Kwame Kpogli then gave evidence of exhuming the remains which were then produced. After legal argument the judge ruled that they could not be exhibited as the relics of Akyea Mensah; the forensic evidence simply did not permit such an identification. They were only skeletal remains that might or might not have been those of the missing Odikro, and they remained formally unidentified and hence not exhibits throughout the process.

On 15 November, the prosecution called Yaw Owusu. He was, he said, the elder, *Opanyin*, of the *Asona abusua*[19] in Kyebi, the royal clan. He had seen Ofori Atta's stool after the Wirempe rites at the end of February. It was a black stool. He also thought he had seen it in the Stool House. Cross-examination sought to establish animus between him and the late king. This he denied. He also denied that the stool which had been produced in court and which the police had been told was Ofori Atta's stool was indeed the late King's stool. It was of a different design and was therefore an entirely different stool.

On 16 November, the prosecution put Baffuor Asante, the Odikro of Tetteh for the past thirty years, into the witness box. He described the nature and functions of the Amantoo Mmiensa. He stated that the

17 A candidate for the Kyebi stool who had been supported by Akyea Mensah and the Amantoo Mmiensa after the death of Ofori Atta I.
18 A herbal specific amongst whose functions was the laying of ghosts.
19 And the oldest of the surviving *Ahenemmaa*.

Wirempe ceremony was preceded by the blackening of the stool which was done by the head stool carrier and his men. On this occasion it had been 'done against custom', as the Amantoo Mmiensa elders should have been present during the blackening. Baffuor Asante said that Apietu had apologised to the elders for this omission. He too was insistent that there had been an eighth stool; the stool that had been shown to the police when they had visited the Stool House was that which the court had been shown, but it was not that of Ofori Atta I. The stool the Amantoo Mmiensa had carried out into the bush during the Wirempe ceremony had been a different stool.

Once again the defence attempts to shake this damaging account were lame. He agreed, without much prodding, that the Odikro of Apapam had been destooled after the Wirempe ceremony, but that evidence was capable of being read in more than one way. Later in the day Adgyei Kwabi, the Odikro of Afease, was called and corroborated Baffuor Asante's evidence. He, like Asante and Yaw Owusu, insisted that the stool in the courtroom was not that of the late Okyenhene.

Although the Crown's case was not to close until the afternoon of 18 November, the rest of Manyo-Plange's witnesses gave largely technical, identification evidence. It was a skilfully made and well organised presentation, given that no body had been discovered; and it had withstood the rather slight attacks made upon it in cross-examination. It had certainly established a *prima facie* case. The prosecution had presented the court with two eye-witness accounts of an assault on the missing man and two further witnesses who saw Akyea Mensah apparently dead in the vicinity of the Stool House. It must have been clear to Manyo-Plange at this stage that the defence would rest on different arguments and evidence which would try to establish both the improbability of much of the Crown's evidence but also the impossibility of each of the defendants' having taken part in any such activities.[20] On reading the account today it cannot be said that the defence lawyers had seriously damaged the core of Manyo-Plange's case.

On 20 November the defence case opened with Nii Ollennu and Akuffo Addo putting their client Apietu in as first witness. His carefully led evidence suggested that the overall account of the washing of the stool which the court had heard over the preceding days was wide of the mark. The story they had heard was an impossible, contrived invention. The late Omanhene's stool had been placed on the grave where it was to remain for at least a year, according to custom. This was the stool

---

20 The defence had prior knowledge of the prosecution case from the committal proceedings in Koforidua but the defence were not obliged to serve the prosecution with advance notice of their case other than warning them of any intention to rely on alibi arguments.

which had been surrendered to the police during their visit to the Stool House and which was now produced as an exhibit. It had not been consecrated by February 1944 and, because it had been impounded, remained un-washed. He denied that there was any linkage between the blackening of the stool or *epun* and the Wirempe ceremonies, and ended by saying that he had nothing whatever to do with any murder.

He was cross-examined by Frans Dove who asked if either of his clients, Kweku Amoako Atta or A.E.B. Dankwa, were allowed near the Stool House. Apietu said that although they were *Ahenemmaa*, they were both circumcised and thus barred from entering the Stool House. Heward Mills rose to his feet and secured from Apietu that while he knew his clients Amoako and Tenteng, he had seen neither of them on the Sunday on which the alleged events had taken place.

It was now Manyo-Plange's turn to cross-examine Apietu. This was, from his point of view, unsatisfactory. Apietu's profound knowledge of the contents of the Stool House allowed him to deluge Manyo-Plange with detail. He named the stools in the Stool House, but denied that there was an extra, eighth blackened stool which had now disappeared. He agreed that human sacrifice had taken place in the past, but it had always taken place on the day of the Omanhene's death. In any case human blood was not used to wash stools. He denied knowing either Botwe or Fosu. Less plausibly he denied knowing what a *sepow* dagger was.[21] Re-examined by Akuffo Addo about human sacrifice he denied that anyone above the status of slave was ever killed in such a manner in Akyem.

Akuffo Addo then put Opanyin Atta, the head stool carrier, into the witness box. His evidence was important. He had been in hospital and had discharged himself at 9.00 am on the Sunday in question. He went to the Stool House with Apietu, the Abontendomhene. There they found the Sanahene, Kofi Appiah, and Kojo Awua. There were also two stool carriers in attendance. He selected the stool called Boakye Nkyira[22] which was to be carried during the Wirempe ceremony. This was an old stool. Any blackened stool, he said, could be carried during the Wirempe ceremonies. Although it had been agreed that a stool would be blackened for Ofori Atta I, this had not yet occurred. That stool stood in court as exhibit 2 and would have been blackened about a year after Ofori Atta's death in normal circumstances. He denied that any stool was blackened on that Sunday and that he had seen the two

---

21 Just such a dagger is one of the ornaments on the royal drums at festival times. I have yet to meet an Akan who did not know what a *sepow* was.

22 All consecrated stools bear the names of their incumbents. This would have been named for the seventh king, who ruled in the Adanse period of the kingdom and most probably in the opening decade of the seventeenth century.

stool carriers who had earlier given evidence for the Crown, Gyekye and Mireku, on that day. He supported Apietu in saying that Wirempe had nothing to do with blackening stools. In some slight details he contradicted Apietu but there was little Manyo-Plange could get his teeth into.

On the following day the defence case began to look rather more ragged. Kojo Awua, a senior stool carrier, differed from Opanyin Atta as to who was in the stool house that Sunday but like Atta denied that he had seen either Gyekyi or Mireku. He had played no part in the blackening of any stool and rather oddly insisted that he had visited the Opanyin in hospital at noon on that Sunday when the Opanyin had earlier said that he had discharged himself earlier in the morning. Kwame Buohene, another stool carrier, then gave evidence. He too had taken no part in any blackening ceremony. Less plausibly he denied going to the Wirempe ceremony and said that he did not know what the Wirempe custom was, a denial which did not ring true.

The slightly shaky quality of the evidence of these men was underlined when a further stool carrier, Kofi Awua, gave his account which began with a denial of being in the Stool House at all on that Sunday. Under cross-examination he agreed that he had made a mistake and had indeed been there although he denied that blackening had taken place. Kwame Agyepong, also a stool carrier, denied being in the Stool House and that he had ever told Botwe that the stool carriers had each been offered £10 by the defence to come and give evidence.

Akuffo Addo then put in Police Inspector James William Gyampo to contradict part of Botwe's evidence. He denied that Botwe had come to him to tell him what had happened or that he had sent him packing. Manyo-Plange cross-examined him skilfully. Gyampo agreed that his wife's father was Omanhene of Akropong. He also accepted that the new Okyenhene of Akyem Abuakwa's father was also from Akropong. Pressing him still harder, Manyo-Plange secured Gyampo's agreement that his wife and the senior wife of the new Okyenhene were first cousins. Manyo-Plange abruptly sat down having managed to insinuate that Gyampo was too close to the royal family for his evidence to be heard without some suspicion clinging to it. It also suggested that Botwe's account of having gone to him might have been true.

Things got no easier for the defence when they called Korankye Ampaw, the Adontenhene of Akyem Abuakwa, the state's most senior divisional chief. He confirmed the temporal separation of Wirempe and Epun and said that no stool had been blackened for the late king; no stool had been removed from the Stool House. Under cross-examination he changed his mind. The Bamunhene[23] had removed the stools before

23   The custodian of the royal mausoleum in Kyebi.

the police had arrived; he did not know if all of them had been returned: 'When I said first that the stool is not taken anywhere ... I made a mistake.' Even more confusingly for the jury and irritatingly for the defence he denied knowledge of the stool called Boakye Nkyira, which only the day before Opanyin Atta had insisted was the stool used in Wirempe, an odd denial from this extremely highly placed state official.

On 22 November the Gyaasehene of Akyem Abuakwa, Ofusu Pem gave evidence. As with previous witnesses, much of his evidence in chief chimed in nicely with the defence case. Under cross-examination, however, he too was to muddy the waters. On the issue of sacrifice he contradicted Apietu: '... In ancient times ... servants, wives and even court officials were sacrificed.' This was damaging, as Akyea Mensah as *quondam* registrar of the Akyem Abuakwa Native Tribunal and more recently as member of both Okyeman and the state's Finance Board had of course been a 'court official'. The argument that no one of Akyea Mensah's eminence had traditionally 'qualified' for ritual death was eroded. But while he agreed with Opanyin Atta's evidence that the stool taken off in the Wirempe ceremony was not that of the late Omanhene, he also denied knowledge of the custom of putting a late king's stool on his grave.

These disagreements about whose stool went where and when accumulated when Asuman Adu, the Omanhene of Oseawuo, another divisional chief, gave evidence. He agreed that there were only seven stools in the Stool House and that no stool had yet been blackened for Ofori Atta. But he insisted that the stool destined for blackening, that upon which he the late Okyenhene had sat, was traditionally a different stool from that which reposed on the dead king's grave. That stool '... should never be removed. It should remain there to rot.' The jury could only have been confused by what was and what was not 'custom'.

Little can be inferred from this evidence about orchestration by the defence. If such an attempt had been made,[24] it had been done without sufficient attention to detail. But it is entirely reasonable to suggest that these immensely distinguished men's confusion owed a great deal to the fact that there were so many versions of what was customary. That confusion was aggravated by the extremely long gap of thirty-two years between the last royal funeral, that of Amoako Atta II, and the death of Ofori Atta in August 1943. The ritual experts who had supervised the procedures in 1911 were all dead by this time; ritual expertise was almost definitionally the domain of the old.

Akyem Abuakwa's traditions had not been transcribed in anything like the detail that was available for Asante. The period running up to

24 It seems clear that just such an attempt had been made so far as the number of stools in the Stool House was concerned, for example.

the restoration of the Asante Confederacy had generated intense debates amongst Asante experts seeking to come up with consensual views about what would be presented as 'customary'. Although Dr Danquah's work had provided a useful transcription of and gloss on the Palace view of tradition, his writings went into much less detail than had, for example, Rattray's on Asante or the many official histories written in Twi which are kept in the Asantehene's palace. At any event the present proceedings had the royal family literally in the dock. Accordingly what was or was not 'right' was being struggled over in the courtroom itself. Beyond the instrumental uses to which tradition was being put, there was genuine disagreement about what had happened in the past. Tradition was being constructed, forgotten and re-made in the courtroom itself.

The defence next called the destooled Odikro of Apapam, Duro Sei. Until his destoolment he had been head of the Amantoo Mmiensa. His evidence in chief began disastrously. He denied going to the Ahenfie on that Sunday morning, then corrected himself and said that he had been there. It was hardly an occasion that anyone would have forgotten. When asked why he had been destooled he said, implausibly, that it was because he 'was not helping to search for the Odikro'. A witness who looked as though he might throw real light on the case from within the ranks of Amantoo Mmiensa proved to be very disappointing for the defence.

The lack of uniformity over what and what was not custom was amplified by the evidence of the Bamunhene of Kyebi, Kofi Mpong. He insisted that the stool to be blackened was that which was had been placed on the grave. In his evidence he contradicted both the accounts of the state's Gyaasehene and the Omanhene of Osweawuo. He denied, for example, that stools were left to rot on royal graves. Even more damagingly for the defence, who were clearly attempting to show that the prosecution allegations could not have happened because the alleged events contravened custom, was the evidence of the Gyaasehene of Akuapem, Kwatia II, given on 23 November. He claimed that Akuapem and Akyem customs were identical but contradicted earlier defence witnesses when he claimed that the blackened stool was that on which a king's body was placed for washing after death. The jury's understanding of custom had not been greatly advanced in the course of these two days, nor had they any clearer a picture of where Apietu was or what he was up to on the day in question.

On 23 November, Kwasi Pipim gave evidence. He said he was a state drummer and Captain of the Kyeren Asafo of Kyebi.[25] Pipim denied seeing Akyea Mensah or going to the Stool House on that morning. He

25   Unlike Asante or Fante practice, Kyebi had only one Asafo company.

sought to discredit the evidence of Osei Tawia which was, after all, evidence of his confession to murder. He said that Tawia was a member of the Kyeren Asafo company and agreed that there was indeed a fetish called Ebun which whose shrine was in Pipim's mother's house. But its priest was called Kwasi Bowom and 'Osei Tawia has nothing to do with it.' He denied going to Tawia for medicine and confessing anything to him. Why should Tawia have said all this? 'He hates me', said Pipim; in any case Tawia was both a thief and wife-beater and because of that had been dismissd from being a servant of the shrine three years previously by the Asafo. This evidence was somewhat qualified on the following day when the Ebun fetish's guardian, Kofi Kuma, Pipim's uncle, told the court that Tawia had in fact retained his position as *Siripi* or Lieutenant of the Asafo company.

In cross-examination Pipim agreed that he was in the Ahenfie that morning. He denied that his house was near the Krensen River where the remains had been found but agreed that he had to cross that river to get from his home to Kyebi. He said that a European policeman had offered him £100 in Koforidua if he 'told the truth about the Odikro'. Other drummers were called to give evidence. The head drummer, the *Asokwaahene*, said that Pipim arrived at the palace early in the morning and 'was there the whole time'. This was also the testimony of Kwasi Amoako, another drummer. Under cross-examination Amoako agreed that Pipim was his cousin and that the Asokwaahene was also related to them both. Just as the defence had sought to impute conspiracy, the prosecution in cross-examination strove to get the jury to believe that defence evidence emerged more from family loyalties than from real memories of real events.

The defence now sought to show that Akyea Mensah was alive after he had been allegedly murdered. This argument rested on the evidence of Yaw Adu, a cook from Adadientem who said he had seen Akyea Mensah at 8.00 am on the Kyebi–Adadientem road. The fact that Adadientem was Dr Danquah's home town was pressed by Manyo-Plange when asking Adu if it had been Danquah who had taken Adu to the police station 'to say that he had seen Akyea Mensah alive'. This he denied. Manyo-Plange had better luck with the defence evidence when a nurse, Kate Eshun, was recalled. Her statement evidence had been used to confirm Opanyin Atta's claim that he had discharged himself from the hospital at 9.00 on the relevant Sunday. In cross-examination her account did considerable damage to the way the defence was seen to have marshalled their case. It is worth setting this out at some length.

On Monday this week a man came to see me . . . and asked for a statement from me. . . . He asked me to sign a statement and I signed it without reading it. On the next day I received a subpoena. I went at once to William Ofori Atta who had asked me to make that statement ... I said to him: 'I want to see what you have got in my statement.' ... When I read it I discovered that it contained what I had not said and I asked for the original and he would not give it to me. ... In this statement William Ofori Atta wanted me to fix a date. I told him I did not remember the day. He said 'was it on the last Sunday of the funeral?' I said that there were many Sundays and I did not remember. ... Some parts of this statement is not what I said. I never stated any date ... nor did I fix the time. ...

Manyo-Plange had succeeded in adding suspicion about defence methods to the confusion which was emerging amongst the defence witnesses.

The third accused, Kwame Kagya, went into the witness box on 24 November. He had been ill throughout that weekend and took no active part in any of the 'custom'. He did not go to the Ahenfie at all on that Sunday. Akyea Mensah was his son-in-law. He agreed that three weeks later he had been sent to Kwabira to bring Kwame Manu back to Kyebi. He had gone with his nephew Kwame Danquah but they had not visited the Crown witness Addo Kwaku, whose evidence was accordingly a fabrication. This was supported later in the day by the evidence of Kwame Danquah who denied that they had visited Addo Kwaku in Kwabira. Kagya denied being Ahenemmaa. He was merely the great-grandson of an Omanhene of Akyem Abuakwa, he said; it is possible that the interpreter erred here for we know, as did most people in the court that day, that he was the grandson of Amoako Atta I. He also agreed that his sister Akosua Ahyia was one of the new Okyenhene's wives.

Late in the afternoon of 24 November Opoku Afwenee went into the witness box. He had left his wife's house as about noon on that Sunday and had gone out with Aaron Ofori Atta. He denied meeting or being with the other defendants that day or seeing Akyea Mensah. Continuing his evidence on 25 November, he said he knew some of the witnesses but had never had any trouble with any of them before. Three witnesses were called to support his alibi, his wife and two people staying in her house. This evidence was of mixed value for Afwenee. One of the witnesses, Ofei Darko, said for example that Afweenee left home between 10.30 and 11.00.[26]

---

26 One must have intense sympathy with witnesses asked to give evidence on times of events. Almost none of them would have owned watches. During the trial many of them were guessing times on the basis of the sun's position, although the Presbyterian church clock chimes the hours. Running an alibi defence in a situation in which few have access to reliable time information was accordingly difficult.

On the same day, evidence was given by Kwaku Amoako Atta. There were two elements to this. First he had been made Sanahene in 1934 but had to resign following clinical circumcision in July 1936. This, it was being claimed, should have prohibited him from going into or even near the Stool House. He had subsequently been appointed head of the Local Authority Police by Nana Sir Ofori Atta. He had not been to the Ahenfie of that Sunday. He was, rather, helping construct the shed opposite the Ahenfie which was to house the statuette of the late king which had been made by Mr Meyerowitz, a friend of the late king and director of the art department at Achimota School. He did this betwen 10.00 and noon. With him were his older brother Kwasi Young, Aaron Ofori Atta, William Ofori Atta and Kwabena Busompra, another stool son. He did not see Akyea Mensah. He stressed that he was a Christian and suggested that of the accused, only Kwadjo Amoako was not.

He said that the church held a memorial service for the late Omanhene on the Sunday. He accused Inspector Berkley-Barton of fabricating parts of the statement he took from him and which was used in court. He objected particularly to the sentence which said 'I heard about a stool being made on the night of 27th February, 1944,' which he denied saying. 'I suspect the police. I had no trouble with the police but judging from what Berkley-Barton has got in my statement, I suspect them.' Asked what else he objected to in that statement he specified elements in it which related to custom and what had happened on that Sunday. The jury asked the judge if they could verify his claim that he was circumcised, an application which was resisted by the judge!

On 27 November Aaron Eugene Boakye Danquah gave his evidence. He was the son of the late king but not a son of the stool, in that he was born before his father became king.[27] He had been circumcised in 1931. It had been alleged by the Crown that he had shown others a *sepow* knife whilst his father's body was being washed and denied ever owning one. This was not in any case the kind of occasion at which one would be wielded. It was a regal and proper occasion. 'A lot of literate brothers-in-law of mine including Mr Akuffo Addo[28] came there while my father was lying in state.' As the local press had made a great deal of the wealth, status and privilege of the accused it is doubtful whether the defence team were delighted by this public reminder of privileged personal ties being placed before the jury.

27 Who is or is not Ahenemmaa, sons of the stool, remains unclear and I heard as many definitions as the court did. There is much evidence in the palace archives which suggests that his father thought of him as a particularly favoured son of the stool.

28 Who was married to Ofori Atta's daughter Yeboah Akua.

The case reopened on 27 November with William Ofori Atta in the witness box. A Cambridge graduate, he was by this time the Akyem Abuakwa State Treasurer and had served as a schoolmaster at the prestigious school at Achimota. His evidence was designed to suggest the unreliability of the Crown witnesses and to explain why the Amantoo Mmiensa should have 'cooked up' this case. He sought first of all to discredit Yaw Owusu's evidence. He was not the head of the Asona clan as he had claimed, as there was no such person.[29] He then moved on to suggest a motive for the Amantoo Mmiensa. When the State Council upbraided the Amantoo Mmiensa for proceeding with the Wirempe ceremonies in the absence of Akyea Mensah: '... their attitude ... was definitely hostile to Kibi'. In cross-examination he said,

> I heard the Amantoo Mmiensa singing insulting songs with particular reference to stool sons. I don't know why. The State Council invited them several times but they would not come ... they were accusing in these songs the stool sons and sometimes the Kibi Elders of having killed the Apedwa odikro. It was after the meeting of the State Council on the 1st March that they started to sing these songs. . . .

Under questioning he returned to his attack on Yaw Owusu. He suggested that Owusu had been a 'fetish priest' but had given his fetish away. Owusu's dislike of the Palace and the State Council was perhaps explained by the fact that his allowance as a State Councillor was withdrawn in June or July of 1944 for 'not doing his duty. . . . I did hear that Yaw Owusu had allied himself with the Amantoo Mmiensa in his accusations against the Kibi people.'

On the following day the defence called five witnesses who confirmed the alibi evidence of the building of the shed on that Sunday morning. Under cross-examination each insisted that differing lists of participants had been there all morning and, unsurprisingly, their chronology was internally contradictory. Both Kwadjo Amoako and Owusu Akyem Tenteng were heard later that day. Both denied all the accusations. The evidence supporting their claims that they were elsewhere on the morning in question was made to look thin when presented; each of their alibi witnesses was close family and each gave somewhat contradictory accounts.

In closing the defence lawyers[30] said that they had demonstrated inconsistencies in the Crown's case. In some instances the accused

29   Denial that there was an Asona abusua Panin was incorrect.
30   The British justice system debars the prosecution from addressing the court at the end of the case unless it can be shown to answer points of law raised in the defence's final address. Manyo-Plange made no final address at the end of the prosecution case although entitled to do so.

could not have been in the alleged place of the murder because of the ritual prohibition against circumcised men; in other instances they had established alibis which had not been shaken. They had shown that there was malice against the sons of the stool on the part of the Amantoo Mmiensa, who had made matters look bad for the accused. And Akyea Mensah's death was not established fact, and a witness had said that he had seen him leaving town on that morning.

On 1 December Judge Fuad summed up. His directions to the jury were not partisan and no imputation of misdirection was ever seriously levelled against him.[31] He pointed out that the human remains were not material. He also insisted that the jury were to build nothing on what they had heard on the subject of what was customary or not customary: '... my experience in this country', he said, 'has shown me that it is difficult to get two witnesses to agree on what native custom in a particular case is. Native custom is a tool in the hands of the people here which they turn and twist as it suits their purpose.'

Although he never expressed his opinion in his summing up, it was the case that the judge felt the jury's unanimous conclusion after a relatively short retirement, that all the defendants were guilty, correct. Using his Bench notes for a report on the case for a later appeal he wrote on 20 November 1945:

> ... the Prosecution by the evidence of their own witnesses and by the cross-examination of the witnesses for the defence suggested, as motive for this crime ... blackening the stool ... no precautions were taken by the prisoners to conceal this crime. ... In this awe-inspiring exhibition suggestive of human sacrifice ... lay their safety. I saw the prisoners in the dock for over three and half weeks and watched them in the witness box while they were giving their evidence and I find it difficult to believe that the sole object of all them in committing this murder was human sacrifice ... some of the prisoners might have been prompted by some sinister and ulterior motive to get rid of him. ... This was a premeditated murder committed in cold blood and I have nothing to put forward on behalf of the prisoners.[32]

Closing the case, Mr Fuad put upon his wig the square of black cloth often called the 'black cap' and sentenced all eight men to death.

---

31 But his being a Muslim Cypriot was part of the lawyer Bryden's argument about the propriety of the proceedings. Fuad, Bryden wrote in his memorandum *A Gold Coast Mystery*, 'had spent the greater part of his life in Cyprus ... did not understand the language of the accused or of the Ga jury and as appears from his own remarks at the trial was woefully ignorant of African customs. ...' See PRO CO 96/783/5.

32 PRO LCO2/3231.

Analysing these proceedings presents immediate difficulties. The regularity of the transcripts belies the nature of court cases; indeed their relative brevity does not suggest the three weeks that the case took. The court at the time was in possession of far more information than we ever can be; they heard and saw things which were never part of the formal court report which is all we can see. They could study the demeanour of the witnesses and the accused men and doubtless played amateur psychologists in the retiring room. Anyone who has served on a jury will know that guilt or innocence are not entirely settled by the jurymen's command of rules of evidence. Juries impute and deduce and it is this commonsensical approach that commends jury trial over trial by judges alone to enthusiasts for juries. The jury saw whether witnesses were agitated, whether they avoided the eyes of others, whether they were embarrassed or blustering. None of this finds it way into the record.[33]

In brusque fashion one can say that the jury found these men guilty on the facts; they were explicitly asked to consider only the facts by the trial judge. They were to disregard what they had read about the case, to shrug off innuendo and to forget allegations; which had not been proved. But they were human and it is most unlikely that they were able to remain untouched by the surrounding circumstances. This is, however, mere speculation. There is no record of the deliberations in this jury's retiring room just as there are no records of jury discussion in any case under the British system. What happens in such rooms remains a mystery, and their conclusions will invariably seem bizarre and absurd to the one side which must be aggrieved in any legal proceeding.

At the same time there is little doubt that the prosecution presented an immediately more comprehensible case than the defence. The prosecution case was undeniably a strong one. Danquah, who watched the inquest proceedings which usefully rehearsed the prosecution evidence for the defence as they were also implicitly commital proceedings, wrote to the Okyenhene on 27 September 1944: 'The evidence against the accused is very strong particularly the evidence of Botwe, Fosu, Gyekye and Mireku. . . . But I feel certain that very conclusive evidence is available both at Kibi and in Ashanti against all these . . . witnesses.' As the lawyer most actively involved in instructing the defence team, it was clearly Danquah's plan to discredit prosecution witnesses. The trial record suggests that he was largely unsuccessful in presenting the defence lawyers with the evidence which would do that.[34]

33   Although as suggested earlier, Fuad's notes, sometimes hard to decipher, indicate which part of the court witnesses were addressing; thus one can reconstruct something of the choreography, as it were, of the proceedings.

34   AASA 3/297.

The defence were additionally hampered by having agreed to all the men's being tried jointly. This gave them presentational problems which possibly inhibited the flow of rebuttal. Each lawyer was striving to secure a not guilty verdict on his clients rather than for all eight of the defendants. It is clear from the way the case was fought and even clearer from subsequent events that they were trying to act in concert; all of them were, for example, being instructed by the same lawyer. But each lawyer, dealing with the prosecution witnesses, cross-examined in turn. And each had to use that cross-examination to the maximum benefit of his client or clients. Similarly the division of the defence into three 'teams' denied the defence the chance of presenting their case in the ordered, sequential fashion which Manyo-Plange was able to deploy. Such structural constraint was not imposed upon the defence. They had the inherent right to demand seperate trials. They had rejected that right, perhaps because such an election might have suggested that some defendants were, so to speak, less 'not guilty' than others.[35]

They were moreover retained by the Akyem Abuakwa royal family, but not the Akyem Abuakwa State, to defend not only the lives of eight relatives but also family honour which was impugned by the charges. This they clearly felt could be best done by challenging the prosecution case with the largest collection of legal artillery they could muster. That battery would, they hoped, present if not a total refutation of all charges against all men then at least a strong suspicion of reasonable doubt. This they manifestly did not or could not do at the trial.

Subsequent appeals, as we will learn, sought to show that this was both an unfair and an improper process. The latter objections mainly concerned points of law and procedure and were rehearsed endlessly before superior courts. But the unfairness or fairness of the procedure is not an entirely objective matter. Inevitably those on the losing side of any legal process will regard a trial as 'unfair'. How unfair was this case?

To begin with, defence counsel had received the witnesses' depositions, the 'informations' on which the prosecution would rely, in advance. They had moreover seen all the witnesses give evidence at the Coroner's Inquest in Koforidua between 12 and 23 September. They knew what was likely to be said in chief in court. Rather than accept statement evidence they insisted that the authors of each of those statements should appear in court; were such witnesses to refuse to attend they could have applied for witness summonses to force their attendance. They therefore could and did cross-examine live witnesses with a good deal of foreknowledge of what they would say and with

35   As it might suggest 'conflict of interests' in the matter.

absolute knowledge of what they had told the police. They were additionally free to make their own inquiries into the case and it is clear from some of the cross-examination that they had indeed done that.

The language issue, raised later in Bryden's[36] memorandum, was something of a red herring, albeit a large and noisome one. He wrote that the trial circumstances were like an English person having committed a crime in England being 'tried in Copenhagen by French law before a French judge who was a French speaking Moor, a Mohammedan who had spent the greater part of his life in Morocco, assisted by a jury of six French-speaking Danes and one Frenchman, none of whom, whether judge or jurymen, understood the English language . . .'.[37] This reads persuasively until the implications sink in. The Gold Coast was, and Ghana still is, a multi-cultural, multi-lingual society. Opinions differ even today about how many languages are spoken there. Leaving aside the Northern Territories in which the largest number of languages are spoken, inhabitants of the southern half of the Gold Coast spoke at least four distinct languages as mother tongues – English, Ewe, Ga and Twi.[38]

In minor matters local courts dealt with offenders in the vernacular and very often without the benefit of professional legal representation. But the major courts of the country were sited, as they are in most countries, in the capital and other major cities. Here the language of the courts was the language of the laws under which people were charged and tried, namely English. The legal system was in large measure a national system when it came to serious cases. Since the nineteenth century the language problem had been met, without previous objections that have been recorded, by interpretation and by the fact that many of the Gold Coast's lawyers were bi- or even trilingual.[39] So far as the criminal courts were concerned, a disproportionate number of defendants in serious matters were from the Northern Territories and even from outside the Gold Coast; to explain this one need only remember that northerners formed the poorest and most deprived communities in the southern towns. Almost without exception the Bar and the Bench

---

36   The British Privy Council lawyer who handled the appeals to the Judicial Committee of the Privy Council on behalf of the defence.

37   *A Gold Coast Mystery*, written in May 1946 but n.d., PRO CO 96/783/5.

38   And the Akan language Twi comes in a variety of distinct regional dialects. While I was in Kyebi one of the local 'born-again' churches had a popular preacher from neighbouring Kwahu who, despite speaking Twi, was forced to preach in English because Akyemfo found his Twi difficult to understand.

39   Some spoke only English as was the case with Frans Dove, a Sierra Leonean. As he had been in the Gold Coast for nearly fifty years it is likely that he spoke some Twi and Ga, the language of Accra, but I have not come across a case in which he used either of those languages.

were entirely dependent upon interpreters in such cases, for at this time none of them spoke any of the numerous northern languages.

The trial was conducted in English and Twi. Not all of the witnesses were mother-tongue Twi speakers.[40] No less importantly, nor were all the lawyers briefed by the defence Twi speakers. Frans Dove was a Sierra Leonean and Nii Ollennu a Ga mother-tongue speaker. That is to say that the interpretation into and out of English was constantly monitored and open to objection from either side. Manyo-Plange spoke both Twi and English. Defence counsel were, no less obviously, as capable of hearing mis-translations as Akuffo Addo and Sarkoddee Addo who were mother-tongue Twi speakers.[41] No objections were recorded as being raised over translation at any stage of this trial and none of the few who were present during the trial and are still alive recall any disputes over meanings. Had defence counsel been convinced that their clients neither understood what was being said or were being misunderstood, it would have been their absolute duty to have made this known.

To argue, as the defence was to do nearly a year after the findings of guilt, that the judge[42] and jury had no comprehension of what was going on is no more compelling an argument. Judges are fair game and are frequently accused of being 'out of touch'.[43] But Fuad's summing up reads as decidedly non-directive.[44] He did not suggest a finding to the

---

40   The Crown police witness, John Kpogli, was for example an Ewe speaker. Moreover something like a third of the witnesses, African as well as European, chose to give their evidence in English.

41   A point made in an Amantoo Mmiensa petition (6 September 1946) to the Governor. They objected, *inter alia*, to an article by George Padmore in the *Gold Coast Observer* (23 August 1946) headlined 'Sacco-Vanzetti case of West Africa. Chiefs sons to hang on framed-up charges says British M.P. Lawyer.' Padmore quoted Sidney Silverman MP who, clearly quoting from Bryden's memorandum, used the language issue prominently in his attack.

42   The sneer about Fuad being a Moslem was repeated in the House of Commons and in the press, and justifiably angered Governor Burns. 'Fuad is a British subject and a well-educated and cultured gentleman. In my opinion he was [he had since retired] and extremely efficient judge . . . reference to his Turkish origin and Muhammadan religion is a disgusting example of racial prejudice and religious intolerance for which I have utter contempt. I am amazed that British Members of Parliament should advance such an argument.' Burns to Secretary of State, 8 August 1946, PRO CO 96/783/5.

43   In most societies middle-class judges judge the poorest members of society and this inevitably must be to some extent true. Thus advocates of jury systems insist that ordinary people are best trusted with the all-important matter of deciding on guilt or innocence.

44   But it is right to note that the shorthand record of Fuad's three-and-a-half-hour summing up is not entirely satisfactory. During the appeal before the West African Court of Appeal (5 February 1945), the shorthand writer Kwaku

jury. He assembled the facts they had all heard over a period of three weeks and instructed them, very properly, to dismiss from their minds those things which they had heard which were imputations rather than facts. It reads as a very neutral summary.[45]

The jury, it was true, were Ga with the addition of one Englishman. It is highly unlikely that the latter spoke any Twi. It is much more likely that some of the African jurymen did understand Twi. While Accra was and is a Ga town, many of its population then as now were also Twi speakers and most inhabitants of Accra speak both or more languages. In any event the entire proceedings were translated and this fact accounts in part for the length of time it took to hear the case. In effect all the testimony was given twice.[46] It is also the case that while jury challenge was permitted under the rules of procedure, and was very commonly practised, no such peremptory challenges were made by the defence team.

The men were charged with murder and it was implicit that the act was alleged by the Crown to have been a 'joint enterprise'. Reading and re-reading the transcript this seems to have been the weakest aspect of the case. None of the defendants was clearly shown to have murdered Akyea Mensah although the eye-witness accounts suggest that A.E.B. Danquah was the wielder of the cudgel; but the evidence does not demonstrate beyond reasonable doubt that this was a lethal blow or blows. The assumption of the charges was that all the men had conspired to take Akyea Mensah's life and that was implicit in the mere fact of their presence at the murder site whilst it was being carried out. Conspiracy to murder was not, I believe, really shown to have occurred. Given the circumstances of the case and the way in which the defence

Addison was called. He could not swear that his account was a full and verbatim record. He admitted that he 'got muddled' towards the end of the session. This was a very long spell for a single shorthand writer and the Judges of Appeal felt that he was blameless. This court consulted Fuad's notes for the summing up as well as his Bench notes and concluded that Addison's records 'differ little in any material particular . . .'. This accords with my own reading of the two transcripts. The judgement (15 February 1945) is in PRO CO 96/783/2.

45 Any local expression of doubt about Fuad's competence was new. The *Gold Coast Observer*, whose editor Charles Deller was a close friend of Danquah's and frequently published pieces by Danquah and his wife Mabel Dove, daughter of Frans Dove, had been strong supporters of Fuad. On 17 July 1942, Fuad was applauded in the *Observer* for his 'strenuous and efficient labour', and on 9 October 1942 was praised for having 'discharged his onerous duties with scrupulous care, energy, ability and candour'.

46 Burns commented reasonably that the logical implication of any objection to the empanelling of jurymen who were not of the 'same tribe' as the accused was 'the abolition of all juries here'. Burns to Secretary of State, 8 August 1946, PRO CO 96/783/5.

team had chosen to contest it, it would have been difficult for any of the accused to claim that he had tried to oppose the actions of others for example; such a defence would have implicated others. This must be the lingering and reasonable doubt any reader of the case is left with. The evidence certainly suggests that the prosecution's case was a strong one. A murder had taken place. But can we feel quite so content that each of the eight indicted men had an equal share in its commission?

CHAPTER SIX

Appeals and Confusions

Following sentencing, the convicted men gave notice of appeal. This was heard promptly.[1] The Bench heard the same counsel who had acted for the defendants during the trial. The appeal rested on the contention that confusion had been created during the case which had misled the jury. That confusion had been added to, they argued, by a judge who had misdirected the jury in these matters. They centred their attention on what was authentic 'custom' and argued that the defence witnesses were more senior than those tendered by the prosecution and therefore had given the 'right' version. The Bench were against the appellants on this. They concluded that the jury 'apparently believed that ... many irregularities in custom had taken place with regard to the blackening of the stool ...'. Nor were the judges sympathetic to the idea that seniority conferred correctness. They based this on the 'obvious fact that the higher in position a witness might be the more interested might he be in averting the stigma that the conviction of the accused would bring on the State'. The crucial point was whether the jury, in possession of the evidence before the court, had properly convicted the men. The Bench were unanimous that there 'was ample evidence if believed by the jury upon which they could convict the appellants'. The appeal was dismissed.[2]

At this stage the Governor, Sir Alan Burns, was formally drawn into the matter. It was to prove an involvement that all but destroyed his career. What had begun as a local and family tragedy was now to engulf the colonial regime of the Gold Coast and, later, the Colonial Office and British Parliament in its intricacies. The Royal Instructions, the rules under which governors operated, demanded that the Governor take capital sentences to his Executive Council for review. The Governor had to wait as the defence declared that they would appeal to the Privy Council; on 20 February Frans Dove formally announced that they intended to petition the Privy Council's Judicial Committee for special leave to appeal. Burns telegrammed the Secretary of State that 'Every

1 Before Sir Walter Harragin, the Gold Coast's Chief Justice, and Judges Alfred Doorly and Leslie M'Carthy on 30 January 1945.
2 The appeal transcript is to be found in PRO CO/96/783/2.

5 Sir Alan Burns KCMG in 1946.

effort will be made here to expedite transmission of records and notes and [I] . . . trust that a quick decision will be made in London.'[3] As the case was once again in the air, Burns was forced to respite execution of sentence until the Privy Council had made their decision. It is clear that in March he was not utterly committed to executions of the eight condemned men. A letter to the Colonial Office says that he would take the matter to his Executive Council 'for advice on whether to commute the sentences or not'.[4]

Although intention to apply to the Privy Council was signalled in February, the petition was not forthcoming. The defence had secured the services of a London-based, specialist Privy Council lawyer, A.L. Bryden, by April. The Colonial Office briefed the lawyers Burchells who handled their court work. In August, Kenneth Roberts-Wray, one of the Colonial Office's senior legal advisers,[5] wrote to Burchells that 'We are becoming increasingly concerned at the delay on the part of . . . Bryden in dealing with this matter. . . . I think that a preliminary

3 Sent 20 February 1945, PRO CO 96/783/2.
4 Burns to Gerald Creasy, 10 March 1945, PRO CO 96/783/1.
5 And, ironically, part-author of *The Law of Collisions on Land* (London, 1944)!

warning should be given. . . .'[6] Burchells and Bryden agreed that the petition must be lodged by 20 September. Bryden reneged on this, arguing that 30 September suited him better as he was moving house from Maidstone to London, a bizarre excuse when the lives of men were at stake. The new deadline was again broken by Bryden who wrote to Burchells on 3 October begging for 'further indulgence'. The Secretary of State wrote to Bryden insisting on an absolutely final deadline of 26 October. The petition was eventually lodged on 23 October 1945, heard on 5 November 1945 and rejected.[7] It was almost exactly a year since the men had first come to court and twenty months since the murder. Delays of this sort were soon to be stopped by new regulations which stipulated time limits between the delivery of notice of appeal and the actual lodging of petitions with the Privy Council Office.[8]

Recourse to the Judicial Committee of the Privy Council was not the only iron the defence had in the fire. In the Gold Coast, lawyers were hastily seeking material which might provide grounds for further appeal. The political administration were aware of these inquiries, were apprehensive about further delays and were making their own inquiries. Burns was worried that the defence were using the many avenues the law presented to sidestep the implications of a crime which he believed was even more extensive than that tried at the end of 1944. At a private meeting with the distinguished African jurists Henley Coussey and Arku Korsah they discussed their conviction that 'other much less important people had also been sacrificed but that witnesses had not been forthcoming'.[9]

6   Roberts-Wray to Burchells, 22 August 1945, PRO CO 96/783/1.
7   Before Lords Porter and Thankerton and Sir John Beaumont.
8   These rules post-dated the notice of intention sent by the defence in this case. The regulations were drafted 'as a result of the concern by the S of S in consultation with the Lord Chancellor, of [sic] the question of the long delays which are apt to occur between sentence and execution in cases in which prisoners under sentence of death in the Colonial Empire apply for special leave to appeal to H.M. in Council. Governors in whom . . . the power of respite of . . . execution . . . pending appeal is vested were asked to draw up rules (which are not in any sense of a legislative nature) to be followed . . . For this purpose rules which have already been made in India . . . were sent to all Colonial Governors for guidance. . . .' Colonial Office to A. Cartwright (editor of *West Africa* magazine), 6 April 1945, PRO CO/96/784/1. This reform was not initiated by the Gold Coast. The circular referred to was sent on 18 July 1944 and the Indian regulations were those amended on 14 March 1944. The main thrust of the rules was to set a three-week limit between notification of intention to go to Privy Council appeal and the furnishing of proof that papers had been mailed to the lawyers who would plead before the Judicial Committee: see PRO LCO 2/3231; see also D.B. Swinfen, *Imperial Appeal* (Manchester, 1987).
9   Notes of a meeting held between Burns, Coussey and Korsah on 26 June 1945, PRO CO 96/783/1.

The main line of the new defence initiative rested on the identity of the skull and bones which were seen by the jury at the murder trial. Some time in October, Akuffo Addo wrote to Bryden that:

... there are rumours that the skull ... and bones ... discovered ... at Kibi ... were ... those of a woman who had died about $2\frac{1}{2}$ years before, that these were exhumed and planted ... by interested parties ... two men claim to be relatives of the deceased woman ... have sworn affidavits in support of a complaint made to the Authorities here for what they naturally consider to be a desecration. ... It was absolutely impossible for the defence to obtain expert pathological evidence to meet that of the Government Pathologist.[10]

The collection of this new evidence was not all that it appeared. However contested the accounts of the judge's summing up might have been, all sides were agreed that he had instructed the jury to ignore the extremely limited evidence of the unidentified skeletal remains.[11] But the affidavits[12] explicitly alleged that the Amantoo Mmiensa were malign conspirators. The first of these, that of Kwaku Dua, suggested that his mother's grave had been disturbed. His cousin, Kwasi Boadi, had told him that he had been one of a party led by Odikro Agyei Kwabi which had disinterred a body from her grave at an unspecified date in 1944. Agyei Kwabi was the Odikro of Afiesa and hence one of the elders of the Amantoo Mmiensa. He had also been a witness for the prosecution at the murder trial.[13] Kwaku Dua had a sworn statement from an Okomfo (priest) who had been with the digging party; this said that he had prepared 'medicine' for the Odikro and the rest of the party to 'wash' with before the digging commenced. Kwaku Dua said he was present 'at the digging for the bones and a skull'.[14]

Kwasi Boadi's affidavit was no less interesting. Whilst travelling from Afwenesse to Apam he had met the Odikro of Afiesa holding a lantern and a bottle of kerosene. 'The Odikro is the head of my family ... he asked me to accompany him to town'. Once there the Odikro took him to a house where he saw a man with 'bushy fetish hair', a reference to

10 Akuffo Addo to Bryden, n.d., PRO CO 96/783/1.
11 This is acknowledged in J.B. Danquah's letter to the Speaker of the House of Commons of 4 July 1946 (paragraph 19), PRO CO 96/783/5.
12 In PRO CO 96/783/1.
13 A point underlined in a letter which accompanied the affidavits to London, signed by Frans Dove, Heward Mills and Sarkodee Addo and dated 22 October 1945; PRO CO 96/783/1.
14 That he referred to 'bones and a skull' raises suspicions. The affidavit begins with a reference to the removal of 'a corpse' from a grave. It then uses the 'skull and bones' terminology which, perhaps too neatly, accords with that used for the grisly remains taken from the banks of the Krensen River.

the uncut and sometimes unkempt locks which can be affected by Akan priests and priestesses. There were three others present. The Odikro gave £4 to the priest. They then went out to where 'the bodies of our families are buried. The Okomfo carried some medicinal preparations in a gourd ... and this he placed near the grave, spraying some of the liquid on himself. The Odikro and the others then stripped themselves to the waist and washed in the medicine. I too washed in it.' They then started to dig.

> I got frightened and went off.... I later returned.... They had brought out some human bones ... the Odikro received the bones into a long box ... the box in which our family stools are kept ... we ... came to the village of Afiesa. The Odikro asked me to accompany him and two others to Akwedum,[15] between the Krensen River and the Birim River on the Suhum-Kibi Road [the main Accra-Kumasi road] but I told him that I ... could not go.[16]

The third and last affidavit was an altogether thinner piece. It was that of Kwabena Boaten, the priest named in the second affidavit who gave his address as 'Abijan [sic], Ivory Coast'.[17] Boaten said that he had been asked by his brother Kwabena Agyeman to prepare 'medicine' to exhume a body buried at Afiesa for a fee of £30. 'I enquired what the body was required for and Odikro Kwasi Agyei replied that it was required for use in court in a case.'[18]

These affidavits were to be made a great deal of in the months and years to come. J.B. Danquah was to rehearse their substance in a petition to George VI from the 'educated and enlightened sons and daughters of Akim Abuakwa state' of 4 January 1946.[19] He was to stress their contents in his letter to the Speaker of the House of Commons of 4 July 1946[20] and in his unpublished letter to the London *Times* of 29 June 1947. Substantially the same case was made by Bryden in his memorandum *A Gold Coast Mystery*,[21] which was then taken up on numerous occasions by British Members of Parliament.

It was the first major red herring to be raised by the defence. Judge Fuad had expressly gone out of his way to point out to the jury that the

---

15 The village is actually called Akwadum and is close to the site where the skull and bones were dug up by the police.
16 Both affidavits are dated 20 October 1945; PRO CO 96/783/1.
17 This is less bizarre than it appears: the Akan language and cultural zone spills way into the modern state of Côte d'Ivoire and significant shrines on either side of the border lured pilgrims in either direction.
18 Affidavit also dated 20 October 1945; PRO CO 96/783/1.
19 Pp. 41–3; PRO CO 96/783/3.
20 Paragraphs 16–19, PRO CO 96/783/5.
21 See PRO CO 96/783/5.

pathologist's evidence did not identify the bones they had seen; any inference about whose bones or skull they had seen should accordingly be resisted by the jury. It was also the case that whilst the sovernment pathologist, Dr Reid, had remained professionally cautious about identification (deploying with great frequency the formulaic 'perhaps', 'might have been' and 'possibly' defences against the chance of future contradiction), the one thing he had been definite about was the age and gender of the remains. He said in open court that: 'My determination of sex from the bones I saw was not a mere guess. It is based on the facts I have given of the muscular markings and on the measurement of the humerus ... muscular development of the male is generally greater than that of females.' Earlier he had said that: 'Based on the dental evidence ... [it was] a male skull. That is to say that I formed the opinion that the skull belonged to a male. Certain bones, particularly the humerus, in measurement were that of a male. ...'[22]

The bones were moreover those of someone who had died between two and eight months before they were forensically examined. If the affidavit evidence suggested that the bones were those of Kwaku Duah's mother then there was an immediate problem. She had died and was buried in 1942, a full two years before the alleged disinterment. While it is certainly gruesome, Reid's evidence on dating the period of death and interment rested on the presence of 'cerebral matter' – fragments of brain – in the skull. Had the skull been buried for longer than the suggested period then all such material would have disappeared because of organic or animal activity and Kwaku Duah's mother had been buried for very much longer than eight months.

The defence lawyers were clearly being briefed to do anything they could to stay the executions. This is evident in a long letter Bryden sent to the Colonial Office's lawyers after hearing that the Privy Council Judicial Committee had rejected his petition.[23] 'We venture', he wrote,

> to suggest that it would be very dangerous to inflict the death penalties in case some or all of the accused are innocent. No one with knowledge of the animosity with which local political quarrels are carried out in the Gold Coast Colony and notoriously in the state of Akim Abuakwa and taken in connection with the status or relation-

22 On 18 September; NAG SCT 28/8/20, pp. 115–19. Some members of the royal family told me that the pathologist had made a report which identified the bones as being those of a female, which was thereafter suppressed. A careful reading of the police records in NAG CSO 15/3. 0170 SF 73 revealed no such report nor any evidence of an earlier report which had been withdrawn or the obvious corollary of alterations to other material in the case file which would have been necessary if important evidence had been altered.
23 Lords Thankerton, Porter and Sir John Beaumont had refused the appellants' special leave to appeal on 5 November 1945.

ships of the accused would put out of question the possibility and perhaps probability of a plot against the accused. . . . A detailed examination of the evidence does not remove such doubt.

He went on to mention the affidavits concerning the provenance of the skull and bones. 'This might be the subject of a further application for special leave to appeal. . . .'[24]

There is evidence which suggests growing nervousness in the Colonial Office at the turn of events. On 9 November, the Secretary of State, George Hall, telegrammed Burns and raised the question of the affidavits. 'I am not', he said, 'in a position to judge whether or not the allegations . . . carry sufficient weight to justify any further postponement of the carrying out of the death sentence. I am . . . placing these documents before you to enable you to decide this matter locally in consultation will your advisers.'[25] Burns responded: 'I have considered documents transmitted . . . but do not . . . consider allegations justify further delay. . . . I am therefore considering the case today in the Executive Council.'[26]

That meeting of the Executive Council yielded thin minutes. Burns' own telegram on the meeting is weightier. He said that the Executive Council members attending had insisted on the law taking its course 'in the case of each of eight condemned men but I found myself unable to accept that advice . . . as I consider that public vengeance . . . will be satisfied and that sufficient deterrent effect will be produced if a lesser number were executed'. Using his own 'deliberate judgement' he disagreed with his Executive Council and decided to commute sentence to life imprisonment in the case of Kwadjo Amoako because he was 'less intelligent and educated than any of the other murderers' and Owusu Tenteng 'on account of his comparative youth'.[27]

Burns' sense that the matter was drawing to a close was strengthened by 30 November 1945. The defence had taken a further matter to the Gold Coast's Supreme Court. Here they argued before Judge Henley Coussey that the decisions of the Coroner's Inquisition should be quashed as improper, which would have the effect of making all subsequent hearings, including the murder trial, null and void. Coussey heard argument for two days and ruled against the appellants. In doing so he uttered some of the very few foolish words he ever uttered in his long, distinguished career. 'In this matter', he said, 'the applicants have

24 Bryden to Messrs Burchells, 5 November 1945, PRO CO 96/783/1.
25 Hall to Burns, 9 November 1945, PRO CO 96/783/1.
26 Burns to the Secretary of State, coded telegram, 19 November 1945, CO 96/783/1.
27 Burns to the Secretary of State, coded telegram, 20 November 1945, PRO CO 96/783/2.

exhausted their right of appeal.'[28] He was totally wrong; the appellants were to discover ever more avenues of appeal and were to persist in doing so until 1947.

The crux of the applicants' argument was simple enough. The Coroner, Charles Hayfron-Benjamin, had committed the accused men for trial 'upon his inquisition' under section 35 of the Gold Coast Coroners' Ordinance. The defence argued that this transition had been broken as the men were ultimately tried on information presented by the Gold Coast's Attorney General. In the first place, they insisted, the inquisition was a nullity because it was not an inquisition on an actual body; it was not '*super visum corporis*' but, rather, an inquisition on a missing man. Moreover as the accused were tried upon information, that information had to be illegal as it had not been preceded by proper preliminary examination and consequent committal for trial upon information – which, they held, the Criminal Procedure Code of the Colony demanded.[29] This was a heady legal argument constructed in London by Bryden. But its legal strength, which was slight, was of less importance than its capacity to bring the matter once again before the Judicial Committee of the Privy Council.

Burns signed the writs for the execution of the six men for 23 and 24 November. He respited execution as a further matter was before the Supreme Court of the Gold Coast. He accordingly fixed execution dates for 4 and 5 December 1945. On 1 December he telegrammed the Secretary of State in a mood of great exasperation:

> ... I have now received further petition from Counsel praying for a further respite as they have cabled ... their solicitors in England to file petition to the King in Council[30] against the latest decision of the Supreme Court. I do not propose to grant this further respite as this is merely another attempt to delay executions and any further delay will make it appear to the public that these men are able to evade the law on account of their position and money.[31]

However strongly Burns might have felt, he was advocating a dangerous course with a further appeal in the offing. The Colonial Office immediately telegrammed, 'Please delay executions temporarily.... I will telegram again as soon as possible after I have been able to ascertain position regarding petition from Solicitors here.'[32]

28   See PRO CO 96/783/2.
29   This is economically set out in a letter from Bryden to W.L. Dale, a CO legal adviser, on 22 November 1945; PRO CO 96/783/1.
30   The correct form for an appeal to the Judicial Committee of the Privy Council.
31   Telegram to the Secretary of State, 1 December 1945, CO 96/783/1.
32   O.G.R. Williams, coded telegram to Burns, 3 December 1945, PRO CO 96/783/1.

The Colonial Office consulted their legal advisers and the condemned men's London solicitor. The latter confirmed that he had instructions from the Gold Coast to lodge a second petition for leave to appeal to the Privy Council. He was to appeal against the Gold Coast's Supreme Court decision. The legal advisers' view was blunt enough; Burns was told: '... executions should not, repeat not, be carried out until this matter has been disposed of'.[33] Burns could not resist this instruction; but he responded angrily:

> ... trust that decision in this matter will not be long delayed as the delay that has already occured has occasioned considerable comments and the Government is being accused of weakness in handling the situation. I am advised that petitioners had no grounds in law for ... this further application to the Privy Council and that these present manoeuvres which are no more than gross abuses of the judicial system. Judge on [previous] hearing ... in his written ruling intimated that the application to him was without basis. Apart from other considerations, it is my view unnecessarily cruel to the condemned men for their lawyers to raise their hopes and for those hopes to be encouraged by repeated delays.[34]

Defence strategy at this moment was complex and, given the large number of lawyers deployed, extremely expensive. In London, Bryden harried the Colonial Office. He clearly felt that eventual success lay not merely in legal process; he also believed that the legal establishment in the Gold Coast could be side-stepped by the Colonial Office itself. On 21 November he went to see Dale[35] and stressed that the case against the accused was weak. He wanted the Secretary of State to intervene above the heads of the Gold Coast administration. No executions should take place until the bones had been re-examined.

> He also expressed his personal conviction (which he did seem to hold fairly strongly) that there was some doubt whether all these men were guilty.... I told him that the Privy Council had had before it the evidence in the latest affidavit from him relating to the ... bones and that the Secretary of State could not purport to review the findings of the Privy Council. The prerogative of mercy was in the hands of the Governor and the Secretary of State would not intervene....[36]

33 Coded telegram, Dawe to Burns, 4 December 1945, PRO CO 96/783/1.
34 Burns to the Secretary of State, coded telegram, 4 December 1945, PRO CO 96/783/1.
35 An assistant Legal Adviser at the CO.
36 *Minute* by W.L. Dale, 21 November 1945, PRO CO 96/783/1.

Thus not only was there a petition pending but Bryden was constantly raising new issues and exerting pressure. On 29 November he wrote to Dale, suggesting that 'this is a case in which the local people [the local law officers] require some greater guidance than in an ordinary case'. He also came up with the totally new proposition that West African laws seemed out of kilter with those of India in that a murder case involving no *corpus delicti* in India would not result in an execution. A worried Dale wrote immediately to the India Office's Solicitors Department to inquire if this was true. He was reassured on 4 December: 'there is no such practice in India as is stated by Messrs A.L. Bryden ... nor could I imagine what authority they have for making such a statement'.[37]

Bryden also pressed for an extension of time within which the petition to the Privy Council had to be presented. This was agreed to, but the tension between the Colonial Office and Bryden is apparent in the tart exchange which followed this. Dale, on behalf of the Secretary of State, agreed to extend the submission date from 31 December to 7 January 1946, 'But I should inform you that the Secretary of State is strongly of the opinion that it is in the public interest and in the interest of the prisoners themselves that the interval between sentence and the final disposal of this matter should not be further prolonged.'[38] Bryden replied on the same day[39] that he needed more time and that he sought facilities for the bones and skull to be sent to London for examination. The legal advisers were in a cleft stick. They, and the lawyers acting for them, were strongly of the opinion that there would be no substance to the threatened petition and that the Judicial Committee would dismiss it, 'but of course it is impossible for the respondent to prevent a petition being lodged'.[40] The Colonial Office had been skilfully boxed in, not merely by the legal 'rules of the game' but also by the moral overtones. As Dale had minuted in October, 'It seems to me impossible to contemplate that men in the Gold Coast shall hang because a firm of solicitors in London is dilatory in getting on with its work....'[41]

Knowingly or unknowingly the defence had created tensions between the Legal Advisers and the permanent Colonial Office staff. The latter clearly shared Burns' sense of frustration and wished to cut through the legal red tape. O.G.R. Williams reported meeting the Police Superintendent most closely involved in the case whilst the latter was on

37 Oxley to Dale, PRO CO 96/783/1.
38 Dale to Bryden, 21 December 1945, PRO CO 96/783/1.
39 It was common for letters to be sent and received on the same day within London in the days before automation slowed everything down.
40 Burchells to Dale, 13 December 1945, PRO CO 96/783/1.
41 *Minute* by W.L. Dale, 10 October 1945, PRO CO 96/783/1.

leave. Berkley-Barton had suggested that more evidence might come in following the conviction.

> It might be possible to establish a case against the new Omanhene as accessory before the fact . . . and . . . there are some indications that there had been many more 'sacrifices' . . . about 100 perhaps. It w'd make the Gold Coast a happier place if this custom could be really stamped out. Various officers have told me of the dreadful states of fear in which people live in the neighbourhood after the death of a chief. . . .[42]

There was then a growing conflict between the perceived imperatives of 'good government' and those of legal propriety. Bryden was succeeding in calling attention to the case. He had lobbied some Members of Parliament[43] and they in turn were informally asking the Secretary of State what was going on. In an unusual step, George Hall asked Dale for a formal minute on the background to the case and the subsequent appeals.[44]

The new petition for leave to appeal to the Privy Council was lodged on 7 January 1946. In an accompanying letter, Bryden announced that there was an intention to take 'other proceedings to set aside the convictions' if the petition were to fail.[45] The committee heard the King's Counsel Bryden had briefed, J.D. Casswell, at length. Without calling on the counsel briefed for the Colonial Office, they refused leave to appeal. Casswell's case was a technical one.[46] In brief it was that the Coroner's Inquest was null and void and accordingly all process which

---

42   *Minute* by Williams, 8 October 1945, PRO CO 96/783/1. Generalisations about 'ritual murder' were being made in parts of the Gold Coast press at the time. Berkley-Barton is hard to evaluate as a witness. He was formally censured by the Secretary of State for a major error some time in 1944; what that fault was is unascertainable as the archival material on 'personnel' matters is withheld, but see NAG ADM 12/1/131 and ADM 12/3/83. These files suggest that he recovered his reputation and had 'eradicated past failings'. This on its own does not cast great doubt upon his reliability. However W.H. Beeton's diary entry for 11 June 1951 (Mss Afr S 1517, Rhodes House Library, Oxford) records that Norton-Jones and Branigan 'say that there is only conflicting evidence of Berkley-Barton being concerned in burglary at K'si Licensing Office . . . [he] is being allowed to retire' is more worrying; but it is impossible to resolve if it is correct. For safety's sake Berkley-Barton's long account of the trial (in Rhodes House, Oxford) has not been used here when not substantiated by other evidence.

43   The most persistent of these was Platts Mills, who was a lawyer as well as an anti-hanging Labour MP.

44   On 6 December 1945; PRO CO 96/783/1.

45   The petition was heard on 21 January before the Lords Macmillan and Simons and Sir John Beaumont.

46   Full counsel's opinion can be read in PRO CO 96/783/4.

led from that inquest must also be null and void. It was an illegal inquest in that it was not held upon a body but on a collection of bones and a skull: 'that it was not held upon a view of the body of Akyea Mensah'. The committal proceedings were also *ultra vires* in that the Coroner's Court was not a court under the Gold Coast Courts Ordinance and hence had no power to commit for trial. Lastly, and less technically, the applicants held that their clients were victims of a criminal conspiracy.

The Judicial Committee had done their homework. They had spotted that the British distinction between coroners' and magistrates' courts did not apply under the Gold Coast Courts Ordinance. Hayfron-Benjamin was a magistrate and was quite legally sitting in both that capacity and as coroner during that hearing. They also held that the inquest was properly held. Casswell asked finally that the Judicial Committee order a stay of execution whilst further proceedings were taken in the Gold Coast. This they refused to do.

This last decision mattered little. On 4 January 1946 J.B. Danquah had, in the name of the 'enlightened sons and daughters of Akim Abuakwa', petitioned George VI. Whilst this was being considered, no executions could take place.[47] This was not the only step the defence was taking. In a letter to the Colonial Office on the day after the petition was rejected by the Privy Council, Bryden wrote, 'we are advised by Counsel that this is a case in which a Writ of Error can and should be issued . . .'.[48] Alongside this set of legal initiatives, Burns received a 'prayer' from the defence lawyers in the Gold Coast for an extension of the respite so that *habeas corpus* applications could be made and heard.[49] The defence were cleverly creating such a tangle of legal process that further delay was unavoidable whilst legal experts sought their way through the thicket.

Although the Colonial Office was now as convinced as Burns that these steps were 'merely another manoeuvre to delay execution of sentence',[50] they were obliged to treat each with respect. The Colonial

---

47   Burns was so instructed. 'Order for execution should not (repeat not) be given until the petition . . . to His Majesty has been received and considered here. Solicitors for petitioners have also intimated that they propose to take further action. . . . It is not known how they can show any grounds on which further proceedings could be based.' Secretary of State, coded telegram to Burns, 29 January 1946, PRO CO 96/783/2.
48   Bryden to CO, 22 January 1946, PRO CO 96/783/3.
49   Letter from Frans Dove, A. Heward-Mills, N. Ollennu and A. Akuffo Addo, 25 January 1946, PRO CO 96/783/3.
50   Burns to the Secretary of State, 23 January 1946, CO 96/783/3. For example J.K.Thompson in a minute of 4 February 1946 on the sons and daughters' petition wrote, '. . . this petition is, I suggest, not only an effort to spare the lives of the petitioners but also an attempt to discredit Crown Counsel'; *ibid.*

Office first pressed Bryden for an early intimation of what he next proposed to do.[51] But they also sought Burns' clarification of the issues raised in the petition sent to the King.[52] Burns replied but insisted that 'there is every indication of conspiracy on the part of Danquah and his friends to pervert or at least delay the course of justice. Investigations . . . seem likely to establish the falsity of affidavits as to exhumation of bones. . . .'[53] At the same time the Colonial Office's Legal Advisers were, with the assistance of Counsel, trying to advise the local law officers on the applications for *habeas corpus* and the issue of Writ of Error. On the first matter Sir Sidney Abrahams concluded that 'An application for a writ of *habeas corpus* may be made to every judge of the Supreme Court . . . such an application would be hopeless.'[54]

The institution of the Writ of Error caused more head-scratching and perusal of precedent than a workaday application for *habeas corpus*. Writ of Error was an antique procedure which had been abolished in the courts of England, Wales and Northern Ireland by the comprehensive extension of the right to appeal against decisions and sentences in 1907. Previously, specific errors in procedure and jurisdiction which were apparent on the record of process could be used in a writ which could then have the power to quash previous steps in the process. The drawing up of such a writ demanded the *fiat* of the responsible law officer who, in the case of the Gold Coast, was the Attorney General.

The last point referred to the personal animus between the prosecutor J.S. Manyo-Plange and J.B. Danquah, which was well known on the Gold Coast.

51 'Unless a letter is received on or before the 11th February which satisfies the Secretary of State that there is a substantial case for further proceedings on some issue not previously disposed of, the Secretary of State will be unable to agree to any further postponement of the executions.' Dale to Bryden, 6 February 1946, PRO CO 96/783/3.

52 CO to Burns, 6 February 1946. These concerned detailed assertions in the petition: 1. that the Odikro of Apapam was willing to reveal 'true facts', and 2. that there was evidence that Akyea Mensah had been seen alive since his 'disappearance'. Burns wrote on 16 February that the Odikro of Apapam had disappeared but that '. . . information as to his unwillingness to say more comes from a fetish priest to whom he is said to have confided that he was an eye-witness of the murder but he had been bribed by Danquah to withold this evidence'. The two witnesses of a 'live' Akyea Mensah had also proved untraceable. Their statements were not used by the defence at the trial although they 'are said' to have been made prior to that trial; PRO CO 96/783/3.

53 Burns to the Secretary of State, 16 February 1946, PRO CO 96/783/3.

54 *Minute* by Sir S. Abrahams, 10 April 1946. He added: '. . . if the application is made it means a further lease of life for the condemned men. I have no doubt whatever that these continued resorts to ineffective technical points are purely tactical in the hope that the Governor will eventually commute the death sentences on the ground that after so long a period they ought not to be executed'; PRO CO 96/783/3.

Neither he nor the legal advisers in the Colonial Office, helped by counsel's opinion, were sure that procedure by Writ of Error had ever been legal in the Gold Coast. It was a procedure which had never been invoked in its legal history. The defence team said that the right was enshrined in section 70 of the Gold Coast Courts Ordinance of 1935. It certainly was not spelled out there. The inauguration of the West African Court of Appeal and the surrounding legislation embodied in the Gold Coast Courts Ordinances between 1928 and 1935 which extended rights to the Gold Coast very similar to those in the appeals jurisdiction in the metropole, did not however formally repeal the Writ of Error procedure. The Colonial Office was on thin ice. Had Writ of Error not been removed from the statute book because it had never existed in the Gold Coast? They were not able to answer that question; could it be presumed to have been lapsed because of the introduction of new appeals procedures which amongst other things met and improved upon the rarely used and clumsy redressive function entailed in Writ of Error?

The Gold Coast Attorney General was stretched to breaking point.[55] His law library was not up to all of this and the uncharitable might have suggested that his legal mind was also out of its depth. But he had the sense to hear the application for his *fiat*, an application resisted on 29 April 1946. Burns reached for his telegram pad and fired off a curt message to the Secretary of State. In this he agreed that if *habeas corpus* proceedings began, or if the defence went to the Gold Coast Supreme Court to try to force the Attorney General to grant his *fiat* by the *mandamus* procedure, he would again have to defer executions. But if nothing else happened he would sign the death warrants for 3 and 4 May.[56]

Whilst Burns urged action, the Colonial Office was becoming re-signed to the inevitable. It could not act illegally and the rules per-mitted lawyers to exhaust all the legal opportunities open to them to save their clients. Abrahams wrote that, whilst he sympathised with Burns, 'so long as any proceedings are actually pending ... it would be undesirable to proceed with the excutions'. O.G.R. Williams' following minute complained that 'This may mean that it will be some years before all further legal devices have been exhausted; and the longer the delay the more difficulty may be felt in some quarters about execution. This is ... what ... Brydens ... are hoping for.'[57]

55 See his plaintive letter to Roberts-Wray on 13 April 1946, where he complains that 'in the end it will be I who will have to hold the baby. I am taking each step very cautiously. . . .' See PRO CO 96/783/4.
56 Burns to the Secretary of State, 30 April 1946, PRO CO 96/783/4.
57 CO *Minute* sequence, 1 May 1946. Williams goes on to say, 'If these men can be executed eventually despite these tactics all may be well, though even so, the

These predictions of more to come from the defence were immediately realised. Bryden's tactics are clear from a stern letter sent to Dale on 1 May following the Gold Coast Attorney General's refusal to grant his *fiat*:

> ... the Colonial Office as the trustee of the rights of His Majesty's colonial subjects ought to facilitate our clients ascertaining and establishing whatever rights they may have affecting their lives and liberties and to ensure that the local representatives ... acted accordingly. This it seems the latter are not doing. ... It is not for [the Attorney General], but for the Courts to decide whether error exists ... these ... points were dealt with by the House of Lords. ... We enclose an extract from the Journals of the House of Lords for the year 1704 ... a Writ of Error is a writ of right and not of grace. We trust that ... the Secretary of State will intimate to the local representatives of the Crown ... that the fiat should be given unless it should be decided ... that the proper course is to grant a free pardon to all the prisoners. ...[58]

This heavy emphasis on the need for the Colonial Office to press the legal system to comply with defence wishes was either very knowing or very naive. Had Colonial Office officials been able to control the legal process, the convicted men would have been hanged by then. On the other hand Bryden was well aware that using pressure in London created difficulties in Whitehall and in Accra. The suggestion that the Secretary of State should intervene seems likely to have been made in the knowledge that relationships between Secretaries of State and governors were inherently uncomfortable. Governors were appointed by the monarch although the Colonial Office obviously played a major part in their nomination. Governors exercised authority through Royal Instructions and Letters Patent and not through a direct line of command whose head was the Secretary of State. Legal process, moreover, enjoyed a much-vaunted independence of the executive, even if there were many examples of its having being pressured.

But Bryden was dealing with a Labour government, whose commitment to Empire was still unsteady. No less importantly, many on the Labour benches were opposed to capital punishment. There was a long debate about the future of both corporal and capital punishment raging within the Labour Party at this time which led to the eventual publication of the Criminal Justice Bill in 1947. There is much evidence

tardiness of execution is likely to spoil any deterrent effect. ... So the wretched people of the Gold Coast will-if they live in lonely places ... continue to go in fear ... whenever a chief dies!'; PRO CO 96/783/3.

58   Bryden to Dale, 1 May 1946, PRO CO 96/783/4.

which suggests that the government's original intention had been to abolish the death penalty; but they backed away from this by the time the bill was published.[59] Bryden certainly saw these cracks and used his legal crowbar wherever he could.

Bryden continued to batter at the doors of the Colonial Office. On 2 May he ventured 'to remind the Secretary of State that [Writ of Error] . . . was passed in consequence of just such a breach of the rights of British subjects during the Jacobean tyranny. . . . We may add that the Attorney General . . . was expelled from the House of Commons for his part in this act of tyranny . . . It is inauspicious for the future of the British Commonwealth and Empire. . . .'[60] and so on. Bryden was no stranger to the Colonial Office. In 1941, Sir Sidney Abrahams had minuted that '. . . petitions against convictions are by no means rare and Mr Bryden is a most persistent and contentious person. I have some acquaintance with him and I believe him to have a keen sense of justice which is strongly tinctured with partisanship leading him to give the impression that he believes his clients to be victimised by malice, prejudice, stupidity, incompetence or a mixture of all these. . . .'[61]

On balance this seems a fair judgement. Bryden was behaving in unorthodox fashion but he was acting on instructions and it is a poor lawyer who does not explore every avenue of the law in pursuit of his clients' liberty. But he does appear to have become increasingly personally involved. While some of that might be explained by a genuine belief in the innocence of his distant clients (whom he was never to meet), some of it was due to the chilly, condescending tone which the Colonial Office adopted towards him. In the dense correspondence he often complains of 'discourtesy'. At the same time he seems to have allocated to himself the romantic role of David against a Whitehall Goliath, and in pursuit of that was prepared to sail very close to the legal wind indeed.

His pressure paid dividends. In early May, Dale decided to try to calm matters by asking Bryden to a meeting at the Colonial Office on 3 May at which Sir Sidney Abrahams would be present. While no record exists of that meeting, it had two immediate results. The first

59 In the debate on the bill in April 1948, suspension of the death sentence for a five-year period was advocated by an amendment carried by 245 votes to 222, which gives some indication of feeling in the House in these post-war years. That amendment was overturned in the Lords by a large majority. The supporters of the amendment in the Commons withdrew it in June 1948 lest the entire thrust of a wide-ranging, reforming bill be lost when it returned to the Lords for second reading.
60 Bryden to Dale, 2 May 1946, PRO CO 96/783/4.
61 He was of course referring to another, earlier appeal; CO *Minute*, 31 March 1941, PRO CO 96/773/13.

was a telegram to Burns stressing that no execution should take place so long as there was any legal proceeding pending 'or if there is any notification on their behalf of intention to appeal to the Judicial Committee. . . . However regrettable these delays are, to execute any convict who has invoked the process of law would open the door to serious criticism.'[62] Second was a letter from Sir Sidney Abrahams to Bryden which signified that Bryden was now being dealt with by the most senior of the Colonial Office's Legal Advisers. In this Abrahams stressed that the Gold Coast Attorney General was advised by the Colonial Office. Although the decision to grant or refuse to grant his *fiat* was a matter for him alone, 'he has acted in conformity with that advice'.[63] Amongst other things Bryden had got the Colonial Office to concede that the local autonomy of the Gold Coast's law officers was subject to at least the 'advice' of Whitehall.

In the Gold Coast the defence took the matter to the Supreme Court to try to force the Attorney General to grant his *fiat* by way of a writ of *mandamus*. This hearing was before Leslie M'Carthy, the Gold Coast's Acting Chief Justice and a West Indian; his notes on that case are interesting. He resisted an application for an adjournment by Dove who wanted further counsel's opinion from London. 'Mr Dove', said M'Carthy,

> is a practitioner of considerable experience and the leader of the Bar. I cannot see why on points of law relating to Gold Coast practice he should place himself in a position of abject dependence on the opinion of English Counsel and confess that without such assistance he is unable to put his points before the Court. . . . If I thought that this motion could possibly succeed I might hesitate to strike it out. But I am satisfied that it is groundless, that there is no jurisdiction in error in this country and that if there were this Court could not make the order sought.[64]

The defence were not deterred. Dove sent a letter to Burns covering a lengthy petition signed by the convicted men praying for his intercession and asking that he 'direct the Attorney General to grant his *fiat* or . . . on behalf of the Crown, make a direct grant of *fiat*'.[65] Abrahams' advice to the Governor was that it would be 'improper to exercise any pressure on Attorney General' and approved the Governor's intention

62 Dale to Burns, 3 May 1946, PRO CO 96/783/4.
63 Abrahams to Bryden, 6 May 1946, PRO CO 96/783/4.
64 Bench notes on the application of a writ of *mandamus* in the matter of Rex *v.* Abontendomhene Asare Apietu and others; Supreme Court of the Gold Coast, Eastern Judicial Division, Victoriaborg, Accra, 7 May 1946, PRO CO 96/783/4.
65 Dove to the Colonial Secretary, Accra, 7 May 1946, PRO CO 96/783/4.

to refuse to intercede in the matter of the *fiat*.[66] But Dove's shotgun had two barrels. The other barrel was discharged and it signalled intention of a further petition for leave to appeal to the Privy Council against the refusal to grant *mandamus*. So habituated to start-and-stop procedure had the Gold Coast administration become, that the warrants for suspension of the death sentence were now drawn up *sine die*, which obviated the necessity of redrafting and withdrawing warrants on each occasion. Formal intention was received by the Gold Coast Law Officers on 10 May, and under the new rules about time limits for lodging such appeals[67] the applicants were required to furnish 'proof of further action' by 31 May. But Bryden was warning Sir Sidney Abrahams of his contemplation of an additional 'method of enabling the Courts to adjudicate upon the points under dispute'.[68] The Legal Advisers were left to guess what that might be. '*Habeas corpus*', minuted Sir Sidney Abrahams, 'would have about as much chance of success as would an action...for false imprisonment...nevertheless...this desperate measure might be attempted.'[69]

But the legal advisers were also clear that Bryden was likely to adopt tactics which lay outside the courts. 'I am certain', Abrahams wrote,

> that if he can raise no further points of law he will endeavour to persuade the Secretary of State to intervene...on the grounds that it would be inhumane...after so long a period....This line...was foreshadowed when we gave him that interview [on 3rd May]...this state of affairs has been brought about by the exercise of ingenuity and the possession of sufficient money to keep the game open in the hope that everybody will get tired of it and that public opinion... may be excited in favour of these men and so frustrate the ends of justice.[70]

Abrahams' assessment was astute. Part of this calculation drew on the fact that Bryden was playing to a weak Secretary of State for the Colonies, George Hall, who was shortly to be replaced by Arthur Creech Jones in the Cabinet re-shuffle of 1946. Hall, like his successor, was on record as a vociferous opponent of capital punishment. The matter was slipping out of the restricted arena of the courts and would become increasingly political.

The defence lawyers did not comply with the deadline of 31 May for showing that they meant business with the Privy Council. Bryden, and Dove in the Gold Coast, pleaded extenuating circumstances and the

66 Abrahams to the Governor, coded telegram, 9 May 1946, PRO CO 96/783/4.
67 Rules published in the *Government Gazette* of 16 June 1945, section 2(a), p. 298.
68 Bryden to Abrahams, 10 May 1946, PRO CO 96/783/4.
69 Abrahams *Minute* to O.G.R. Williams, 30 May 1946, PRO CO 96/783/4.
70 *Ibid.*

papers were eventually lodged with the Privy Council on 17 June. Essentially the new petition challenged M'Carthy's refusal to grant a writ of *mandamus* against Lewey on 7 May. It contained no new argument about the actual existence of Writ of Error in Gold Coast legislation.[71] The petition was rejected on 15 July 1946.[72]

There is no doubt that this is what Bryden expected. Shortly before the matter was heard, Bryden had circulated amongst those Members of Parliament who were also lawyers a memorandum entitled *A Gold Coast Mystery*. As J.K. Thompson observed when MPs' letters to the Secretary of State began to arrive at the Colonial Office, 'The expected campaign has begun.'[73] It was an inspired move by Bryden. The emotive yet technical memorandum emerged from a respected lawyer in a respected practice. Its potential constituency was large: a high proportion of MPs in the first post-war House of Commons were either solicitors or barristers. While it raised issues of legal precision, it also raised far more nebulous questions about 'natural justice'.[74] It was grist to the mill for many MPs. It appealed to Conservative lawyers who sought, as oppositions must, any opportunity to belabour the government of the day. It appealed to Labour opponents of colonialism, as here was chapter and verse about the rigid, unfeeling obduracy of colonial administration. It also appealed to the many opponents of capital punishment. These, and perhaps other reasons, meant that Bryden's undoubtedly partisan and, in many particulars, inaccurate memorandum was to be taken up by an unusually broad church.

Hall's 'in-tray' filled up rapidly. He was clearly rattled by it. His Private Secretary minuted 'The Secretary of State had a further short talk with Sir Sidney Abrahams about this case.... He is a little disturbed about it and may wish to mention it to his colleagues. He will be

71   Abrahams shared a splendid bit of *ex cathedra* opinion with Burchells before this hearing. He wrote that the defence had 'completely overlooked (and I do not think that they could have ignored it had they seen it) Section 157(1) of the Criminal Procedure Ordinance, 1876 which provided for proceedings in error and existed down to the time *I drafted* the West African Court of Appeal Ordinance, 1930, when of course it was repealed, as being, like its corresponding provision in England, of no further use...'. [my italics]. Abrahams to Burchells, 4 June 1946, PRO CO 96/783/4.

72   By a Judicial Committee composed of Lord Roche, Sir John Beaumont, Sir Madhavan Nair and M.R. Jayakar.

73   *Minute*, 27 June 1946, CO 96/783/4.

74   These were serious matters for the politicians of the period, who had scarcely absorbed the extremities of the negation of human rights under the Nazis, whose huge extent had been made apparent during the liberation process. The resulting war crimes trials at Nuremburg had similarly raised the absolute significance of the rule of law in the maintenance of civil liberties, for they had sometimes, however understandably, cut corners.

obliged if a short note summarising the facts could be drafted . . . as a basis for any statement which he may decide to make.'[75] On decoding this, it is clear that serious questions being raised on all sides of the House were the last thing any Minister wanted. Hall was less disturbed by the case itself than by the immediate prospect of being hauled in by his famously severe Prime Minister, Clement Attlee, and being asked what he proposed to do about it. The probability of this was enhanced by the uncomfortable interest one of Hall's Cabinet colleagues, Sir Hartley Shawcross, was beginning to take in the case. That the British Attorney General famous for his leading role as a prosecutor in the Nuremburg Trials should write '. . . the case is certainly one which causes a little misgiving and I cannot help feeling that, in any event, after the long lapse of time you may think that serious consideration should be given to the question of whether the death sentences should now be carried out . . .'[76] was more than simple comment. Shawcross, a senior if young Cabinet Minister, was clearly intruding into Hall's bailiwick and there is little doubt that Hall, a man of little formal education, was both affronted and frightened by the intervention of such a grand person. He instructed Abrahams to write an explanatory draft of the case for the British law officers which was completed on 8 July 1946.

Hall went to see Shawcross[77] and came back to the Colonial Office saying that the Attorney General continued to feel that execution of the six men would be wrong after such a protracted delay. Hall was palpably wavering. The Colonial Office permanent officials were indignant that mileage was being successfully made by Bryden's memorandum, which 'does not . . . give anything like the true picture . . . it is necessary to put the case on the other side . . .', Dale minuted to Hall's Private Secretary.[78]

Parliamentary interest now contributed to the delay. While the Privy Council had dismissed the application on 15 July, the Secretary of State telegrammed to Burns: 'Grateful . . . if no repeat no further steps are taken towards executions pending further communication from me as there are parliamentary representations which I must consider.'[79] In a fashion which reads rather cravenly today, Hall was now hiding behind his civil servants. He suggested that it was his Legal Advisers, rather than him personally, who were satisfied that no injustice had been done, although the record shows that he had been kept fully briefed on the

---

75   *Minute* by P. Rogers, 5 July 1946, PRO CO 96/783/4.
76   Shawcross to Hall, 8 July 1946, PRO CO 96/783/4.
77   That it was Hall who visited Shawcross and not the other way around suggests the force of the 'pecking order'.
78   11 July 1946, PRO CO 96/783/4.
79   Telegram, 15 July 1946, PRO CO 96/783/5.

case since December 1945.[80] Sensing Hall's loss of control, the parliamentary protest increasingly sought to put pressure on the British Law Officers[81] rather than on the Colonial Office.

In the midst of growing confusion in London, the defence team in Accra announced that they were contemplating civil actions for damages against the Gold Coast Attorney General. Writs were served on Lewey by each prisoner in which each claimed £200 damages for his 'wilful, malicious and wrongful refusal, contrary to law and due discharge of his office, of his *fiat* for grant of Writ of Error'. This matter came before the Gold Coast Supreme Court on 31 July and Dove lost no time in asking for an adjournment of two weeks, which he was granted.[82]

In the meantime Hall received a deputation of protesting MPs and failed utterly to turn their wrath. Instead he took minutes of their protest and promised to communicate these to the Governor, having made it clear that the prerogative of mercy lay with the Governor and not with him.[83] The Secretary of State accordingly resigned himself to acting as postman and put up no fight whatever despite the fact that he had been briefed on all the points raised by the MPs and could have corrected some of the many misapprehensions.

Burns deduced that support from his Secretary of State was at best equivocal. Hall was more interested in protecting his back than his civil servants, who he privately agreed were acting properly and utterly within the law.[84] Burns accordingly turned to the permanent staff before

80 That weakness left him open to persuasion. Leslie Hale, the most prominent of the Labour enthusiasts for Bryden's memorandum, wrote to Hall (17 July 1946) asking, 'Is this not a question where you would feel justified in enquiry yourself and making up your own mind?' (Hale to Hall, PRO CO 96/783/5). Given that he was getting officials to justify policy by point-by-point refutations of Bryden's memorandum for the British law officers at the time, this suggestion that he was not master in his own house must have hurt. That much was going on behind Hall's back which he nonetheless must have known about is obvious from Dale to Shawcross, 18 July 1946, CO 96/783/4, and Secretary of State to the Lord Chancellor, Lord Jowitt, 24 July 1946, CO 96/783/5.

81 Of the two law officers, Shawcross was the more content to get embroiled. Lord Chancellor Jowitt, whilst inquiring about it behind the scenes, insisted that 'the matter has nothing whatever to do with me. I should be usurping someone else's functions were I to express an opinion in this case . . . had I been sitting on the Judicial Committee of the Privy Council I should have felt bound to come to the same conclusions. . . . I must state quite definitely that it is not within my province to deal with the matter.' Jowitt to Leslie Hale, MP, 17 July 1946, PRO LCO 2/3231.

82 Acting Solicitor General, Gold Coast (J.S. Manyo-Plange), to Attorney General, Gold Coast (A. Lewey), 31 July 1946, PRO CO 96/783/5.

83 Secretary of State to Burns, 1 August 1946, PRO CO 96/783/5.

84 E.g. his letter to the Lord Chancellor, 1 August 1946, PRO CO 96/783/5.

telegramming Hall. In a terse telegram to Williams he stressed that 'the delay has become a public scandal and is being more freely discussed every day'.[85] He stressed his concern with the implications for 'good government' in a letter to Hall of the same date.[86]

There is no record of Hall's response to the substance of this letter. But his unwillingness to resolve the matter emerged quite clearly in an emergency meeting held between Hall, Sir George Gater, Roberts-Wray, O.G.R. Williams and J.K. Thompson. Here Hall's most radical intervention was the idea that the Governor should be asked to meet the protesting MPs, which he then insisted upon. This was Hall's position despite the fact that the civil matter had again been before the court in the Gold Goast. There the civil suits had been stayed on the grounds that they were 'frivolous, vexatious and abusive of the process of the courts'. Staying rather than dismissing the suits was almost certainly an attempt to prevent further appeals. Lewey was awarded £59 costs.[87]

The pressures on Hall mounted. On 4 July, Dr Danquah sent a nineteen-page letter to the Speaker of the House of Commons which recapitulated much of the earlier 'enlightened sons and daughters' petition but brought matters up to date. The Speaker was directly addressed because there was 'none in whom the intangible reality called British conscience is better embodied'.[88] Now the Colonial Office's officials were busy drafting replies for the Speaker as well as for what must have seemed like half the Cabinet.

Burns was due to come to Britain on leave on 29 August. Hall felt that the British MPs should be given the chance to put their case to Burns directly. Burns could hardly refuse to do this despite the implicit instruction from Hall that it was 'quite impracticable for sentence to be carried out before you have heard these representations'.[89] The 'impracticality' was probably no real impediment. The Secretary of State had been petitioned by a number of MPs, but the substance of

85   Burns to O.G.R. Williams, 1 August 1946, PRO CO 96/783/5.
86   'I am much disturbed by opinion which has long been widely held and is rapidly gaining ground . . . that delay in executions is due to financial and political standing of the condemned . . . the same law does not apply to the rich and to the poor . . . a public scandal. . . . Abuse of processes of Court . . . are bringing Courts and the law into contempt and . . . further delay would have unfortunate effect . . . execution is fully justified and . . . essential if worse things are not to follow.' Burns to Hall, PRO CO 96/783/5.
87   Heard before M'Carthy, whose judgement echoed Burns' concerns: 'The whole course of proceedings in this case is astonishing and I am gravely concerned lest the impression was created in this country . . . that there is one law for the rich and another for the poor. And that if a convicted person has sufficient means he can escape punishment for years by the institution of groundless proceedings.'
88   Danquah to D. Clifton Brown, 4 July 1946, PRO CO 96/783/5.
89   Hall to Burns, 12 August 1946, PRO CO 96/783/5.

that petition had already been conveyed to the Governor who had answered all the points raised. Hall was insisting on further delay to save his own political skin rather than because he was observing constitutional niceties. The upshot of this was that the executions were now respited until after Burns had met the MPs on 11 September 1946. It was now twenty-two months since the criminal trial had commenced and two years and seven months since the murder.

We have two accounts of Burns' meeting with the MPs.[90] The points raised were recapitulations of matters dealt with in the innumerable exchanges between the Secretary of State, Burns and interested MPs. Quintin Hogg took a rather different line from the others, the Colonial Office account says. He was not impressed with Bryden's argument but was unhappy about the law's allowing unlimited time between sentencing and execution. According to Bryden's informants, Burns was 'obdurate and did not budge an inch . . . a deaf adder. . . .' But Bryden wrote, the legal adviser was 'perhaps, considerably impressed with various points'. There is no confirmatory evidence in the Colonial Office minute that this was so. The only other major point raised concerned the question of where the prerogative of mercy lay.

In 1946 a new Secretary of State had been appointed to replace George Hall. In Arthur Creech Jones, the appellants must have sensed that the wind had definitively changed in their favour. He had been Secretary of the Fabian Colonial Bureau, and his earlier frequent criticisms of colonial policy made it likely that he would be happier than most incumbents to challenge permanent civil servants and their assumptions. He was also an outspoken advocate of the abolition of capital punishment.

If this was the appellants' legal advisers' calculation they were entirely correct. Eight days after the meeting, Creech Jones summoned Sir George Gater,[91] Dale and Williams to his rooms. The substance of the discussion was the new Secretary of State's strong interest in the possibility of his overriding the Governor's prerogative. He asked for precedents but there were none. The next gambit was to inquire if the representations made to Burns by the MPs could be regarded as an appeal to the king. If they could, might the Secretary of State then not

90 A five-page *Minute* drawn up by Williams on 11 September and a letter written by Bryden to Dove (12 September), PRO CO 96/783/5. How the Colonial Office got hold of this is unclear; Bryden writes, 'Please treat the contents of this letter as confidential. . . .' Bryden was not at the meeting but spoke on the telephone to two of the MPs present afterwards. The MPs who attended were Brigadier Medlicott (National Liberal), Quintin Hogg (Conservative), D. Rees Williams, J. Platts Mills and T. Paget (Labour). W.L. Dale and O.G.R. Williams represented the Colonial Office.
91 Permanent Under-Secretary of State for the Colonies.

advise the king to exercise his prerogative of mercy? The minute of this meeting noted that such a move 'would place the Governor in a most difficult position and it might be that he would not feel able to return to the Gold Coast'.[92]

Creech Jones had reached some of the MPs by 27 September. His own minutes of 20 and 27 September[93] make it clear that he was not defending Burns' position which was identical to that of the permanent civil servants in Whitehall. He had sided with the petitioners and was attempting to find legal avenues through which he could enforce commutation of the death sentences. He was virtually encouraging the MPs to petition the King so that he might be afforded the window of opportunity to intervene. This clearly alarmed the permanent staff. Dale minuted on 2 October 1946,

> ... there is no point in inviting the ... [MPs] to consider their next step (e.g. a petition to the King) unless the Secretary of State is going to intervene ... it is likely to be misleading if we invite further Petitions if the Secretary of State is not in fact going to advise His Majesty to intervene besides causing delay which ... will make the matter worse.... I do not see that the Secretary of State is likely to have any more material on which to consider this.... I suggest that the matter should now be decided and the decision communicated to the Members of Parliament....[94]

Creech Jones was still searching for a means to resolve the matter in his own way. Dale conceded that the King had a residuary power of pardon on which he could be advised by the Secretary of State. But was this a 'proper case' for the Secretary of State to seek to so advise the king? Dale felt that as there was no question of mistrial or unfair verdict, it was not.[95]

Things were no more placid in the Gold Coast. On 6 September, the Amantoo Mmiensa had sent off a petition of their own, protesting about the ways in which British MPs were presenting the case in the British press. It argued, *inter alia*, that the eighty-seven MPs who were up in arms were not 'conversant with the true facts.... "The voice might be Jacob's voice, but the hands are the hands of Esau."' The officer administering the government in the Gold Coast whilst Burns was on leave, T.R.O. Mangin, argued that the petition was 'an example of the public disgust in the Gold Coast at the actions designed to delay the

---

92 Note of discussion with the Secretary of State, 11.00 am, 19 September 1946, PRO CO 96/783/5.
93 In PRO CO 96/783/5.
94 PRO CO 96/783/5.
95 *Minute*, 10 October 1946, PRO CO 96/783/5.

executions . . . civil disturbance is to be expected in the Akim Abuakwa State if the murderers are not executed'.[96]

Overstated as it was, this kind of comment posed Creech Jones with a dilemma. He could present himself as a Secretary of State of great compassion and risk civil disturbance in one of the colonies for which he had responsibility, or he could take the bull by the horns. Characteristically, he dithered. While he dithered, the defence lawyers bent upon another tack. Now they were intending to take a case to the West African Court of Appeal. Here they would seek once again to get leave for appeal to the Privy Council against Chief Justice M'Carthy's decision staying civil actions against the Gold Coast's Attorney General. Every court decision, it seemed, could be appealed against, and there was not much that prevented that sequence going on into eternity.

Burns was at breaking point. On 18 October he telephoned the Colonial Office to find out where he stood. If Dale's notes of the conversation are accurate, Burns was little comforted. Dale had to tell him that while the Royal Instructions and Letters Patent did devolve the prerogative of mercy on the Governor, it remained legally possible for the King to exercise his prerogative. Burns pointed out that if the King were to be advised to intervene there would be a petition in each and every capital case in every part of the Empire, a prospect that the Legal Advisers to the Colonial Office must have thought about with some dread. Burns said he wanted 'the final word from here'. Dale promised to bring the matter again to the Secretary of State's attention.[97]

There is little doubt that the Colonial Office and its Legal Advisers were on the same 'side' as Burns. The joker in the pack remained the Secretary of State and minute after official minute expresses the civil servants' doubts about which way he would jump. Dove's warning of further appeal was, the legal advisers had decided, immaterial. It was an appeal in a civil matter and should not affect the outcome of the protracted criminal process. But towards the end of October they were still in the dark about Creech Jones' intentions: '. . . the next step must be for the S of S to decide whether to let the law take its course or whether to over-rule the Governor', wrote Williams on 23 October. The brutal language of this minute is evidence enough of where he stood in the matter.[98] Dale reinforced the pressure on the Secretary of State in a

96   Telegram to the Secretary of State, 12 October 1946, PRO CO 96/783/5. Mangin was an excitable correspondent much given to premature cries of havoc.

97   *Minute* by W.L. Dale, 19 October 1946, PRO CO 96/783/5.

98   The *Minute* continues, 'Even if . . . commutation . . . does not result in the "very serious trouble" which Sir A. Burns expects, his position & reputation . . . would be seriously impaired. . . . The African has always been . . . impressed by . . . British justice. He cannot fail to misunderstand a

minute which is an almost word-for-word rendering of Burns' earlier telegram; in considering whether to advise the king to commute, Creech Jones 'ought to have in mind the point that if His Majesty does intervene . . . it is likely that every condemned person throughout the Empire will petition the King . . .'.[99]

This campaign in the corridors of the Colonial Office reached its climax with the magisterial voice of Sir George Gater telling the Secretary of State that 'I think that the time has now come for a decision to be taken. Do you wish for further discussion?'[100] Creech Jones wanted none but waited a full four days before minuting his decision both to continue dithering and, whilst dithering, to wash his hands of the whole messy business. He wrote, 'I do not appreciate that this is a case in which I have to come to a decision'; this was an extraordinary comment given that the Colonial Office had been mulling over little else since Burns had met the Parliamentarians.

> The matter is within the province of the Governor. . . . The position [quite what he meant by that is uncertain from the text; Creech Jones' position? The legal position?] . . . has unofficially & privately been put to the Governor for I have no official standing in the case . . . whatever decision he . . . makes, I should have thought it right for the condemned men to be allowed to exhaust their legal rights. . . .[101]

It would be hard to avoid the Pilate-like sense of Creech Jones' reactions at this juncture.

decision to commute . . . as either favouritism, impotence or cowardice on the part of HMG. It would be a bad thing if this happened just now when we need so much that stabilising influences sh'd prevail.' As this was for Creech Jones' eyes, it was forthright, not least in reminding him of the pressure for 'colonial development' being exerted on the Colonial Office by the Cabinet at that time. PRO CO 96/783/5.

99   *Minute* by W.L. Dale, 24 October 1946, PRO CO 96/783/5. Again this *Minute* would be seen by Creech Jones and was intended to put pressure on him not to intervene. It mentions that Shawcross had now said that he was convinced that the men should hang. 'The agitation . . . amongst Members of Parliament has been caused by the misleading memorandum . . . every time we see Members of Parliament . . . they are impressed and (if not convinced) appear to drop the matter. On the 7th October we sent out copies of the telegrams . . . answering most of the points and there is not . . . a single reply from any Member of Parliament . . . except for Mr Hale's letter. . . .' The strong signal was that Creech Jones need no longer fear a political storm.

100 *Minute* by Gater to the Secretary of State, 24 October 1946, PRO CO 96/783/5. These were strong words indeed, and I have never encountered such a firm *Minute* from an official to a Minister in years of research in these archives.

101 *Minute* by Creech Jones, 28 October 1946, PRO CO 96/783/5.

On 4 November, Creech Jones asked for a letter to be drafted by Dale to the protesting MPs. This stressed that he was in no position to advise the king to commute sentence. This he could do only if there was a miscarriage of justice. 'I am satisfied that there has been no miscarriage of justice.' The Governor was, moreover, not only statutorily the man who enjoyed the prerogative; he was also 'in the best position to decide the case, knowing all the circumstances . . . the matter will therefore be left to the decision of the Governor . . .'.[102] On 6 November, Creech Jones spoke to Gater, saying that his inclination was now to send no further letter to the MPs. His inactivity was, of course, to maintain the protest as a live issue; as a colonial official was to minute, 'we are under no obligation to inform MPs of the final decision . . . but . . . it would be courteous to inform them, as in the draft . . .'.[103]

A further petition for special leave to appeal came before the Privy Council on 15 November and was, like its predecessors, dismissed. Creech Jones' unwillingness to send a blunt letter to the MPs resulted in a further flood of letters following the Privy Council decision demanding that sentences should be commuted on compassionate grounds. Dale suggested once again to Lloyd[104] that a letter should be sent to MPs and reminded him that the words of the original draft, which still lay on file, 'have been most carefully chosen'.[105] Lloyd agreed and minuted to Gater on 18 November that the 'S of S sh'd be advised to write to MPs', which was about as close a senior civil servant would come to saying, on the record, that Creech Jones should be told to do this.

Willingly or unintentionally Creech Jones was putty in the hands of a diminishing number of protesting MPs. He decided to send no letter and instead chose to speak personally to one of the most prominent leaders of the protest, Leslie Hale. That meeting, on 27 November, allowed Hale to worry him that 'another legal process was in train. . . . I said I would hold my hand should the Governor telegraph on the matter. . . .'[106] In some irritation Gater minuted that 'I know nothing of any further legal process being in train. . . .'.[107]

Creech Jones' inaction and the consequent encouragement of the protesters bore fruit towards the end of the year. On 20 December, Sidney Silverman[108] and Hale wrote to Creech Jones saying that

102 Draft letter from the Secretary of State to eighty-seven Members of Parliament, 4 November 1947, PRO CO 96/783/5.
103 *Minute* by Lambert to Sir Thomas Lloyd, 15 November 1946, CO 96/783/5.
104 (Sir) Thomas Lloyd, Assistant Under-Secretary of State for the Colonies.
105 *Minute* by Dale to Lloyd, 18 November 1946, PRO CO 96/783/5.
106 *Minute* by Creech Jones, 27 November 1946, PRO CO 96/783/5.
107 *Minute* by Gater to Lloyd, 28 November 1946, PRO CO 96/783/5.
108 The most prominent of the Labour Party opponents of the death penalty.

they would draw up a 'short memorial praying that clemency may be shown . . .'.[109] The letter went on to remind him that Parliament was about to rise for the Christmas recess, 'and it will take us some time to collect the signatures of legal members of the House. We urge . . . that . . . nothing shall be done until we can present our memorial and discuss it with you. . . .' Creech Jones replied that he wanted to see the memorial 'within the next three weeks'.[110] In turn he wrote to Burns that 'I feel I have no option but to agree to defer further action until memorial has been received . . . I fully appreciate the embarrassment which this delay will cause you. . . .'[111] Burns' anger was muted in his response the following day; he regretted the delay 'but realise it is inevitable. . . . I have been more than ever convinced that public opinion in this colony would be outraged if murderers escaped full penalty of their crime. I fear also that disorder and even bloodshed would occur owing to strong feelings of Apedwa people.'[112]

The procrastination of the Secretary of State had ensured that nothing further could happen before the date on which he demanded that the promised memorial should be on his desk; that was 15 January, a full two months after the last vestige of the legal battle had been thrown out by the Judicial Committee of the Privy Council.

109   Silverman and Hale to Creech Jones, 20 December 1946, CO 96/783/5.
110   Creech Jones to Silverman, 23 December 1946, CO 96/783/5.
111   'Secret and Personal' to Burns, 23 December 1946, CO 96/783/5.
112   Burns to Creech Jones, 24 December 1946, PRO CO 96/783/5. This more conservative appraisal than Mangin's earlier warning was undoubtedly well-founded. As noted below, tempers were high in Akyem Abuakwa.

CHAPTER SEVEN

Travesties and Tragedies

The competing interests continued to perform a grisly minuet with imprecise choreography. Creech Jones wished to be all good things to all men – conscientious Minister of the Crown in control of his department, high-minded guardian of justice and uncompromised opponent of capital punishment. His and his predecessors' inability to give priority to any of these internally contradictory imperatives had conduced at an avoidable impasse in which humanitarian issues had become slogans. In the process Creech Jones had seriously alienated his officials in Whitehall, whose internal minuting betrays a growing lack of confidence in his judgement. He was soon to provoke one of the most able and in many ways the most progressive Governor in British Africa to a pitch of righteous indignation which was to lead to the almost unknown step of his offering his resignation. In addition Creech Jones had by now attracted the unwelcome attention of the Prime Minister; a more incisive Cabinet Minister would have headed off the furore in the Commons and in the press. Attlee had enough on his plate without having to concern himself with, from his point of view, peripheral departmental matters.

Creech Jones was under fire from a Tory front bench always alert when they detected signs of weakness and indecision in the government. He was besieged by a group of Labour MPs, to some of whom he had been close as a back-bencher and who were using the murder case as a stalking horse in a more comprehensive attack on the unacceptable authoritarianism of colonial rulers and on the iniquity of capital punishment. By the end of 1946 Creech Jones was seriously embattled.

The defence lawyers had succeeded beyond their wildest dreams. The seven surviving Ahenemmaa[1] were still alive, even if they had had to suffer the heart-stopping process of being conveyed on several occasions to the prison where they expected to be hanged.[2] But in the protracted

---

1 Asare Apietu died, in his late sixties and of natural causes, in hospital on 28 November. Burns to Secretary of State, 2 December 1946, PRO CO 96/783/5.
2 Some British MPs suggested that the men saw the gallows on a number of occasions. The Director of Prisons' records show that they were transferred from the Ussher Fort gaol to James Fort gaol (where death sentences were carried

process Akyem Abuakwa's ruling family had become, to put it mildly, estranged from the colonial establishment. Given that the stool had been under strong internal attack for many years, this was a high price to pay; on many occasions in the inter-war years Nana Ofori Atta I had been grateful for the assistance of the colonial state in outfacing his increasingly vociferous, numerous and powerful local critics. The colonial establishment was no longer a resource the Okyenhene could count upon.

The defence lawyers had alienated the local law officers and in the process created an uncomfortable cleavage in the small and once reasonably cohesive Gold Coast Bar. The usually constructive relationship between advocates and the Bench had been poisoned. The legal profession was now seriously divided by personal bitterness, a situation which almost certainly helps to explain some of the weakness of 'moderate' nationalism by the late 1940s.

The Amantoo Mmiensa had become increasingly militant. The new Okyenhene's tenancy of the stool was uncomfortable. He and his court were frequently threatened by vocal opposition and threats of violence.[3] On occasions, and to his great embarrassment, government police were drafted into the area to prevent disturbances. The Amantoo Mmiensa continued to boycott the Okyeman Council and refused to render traditional homage to the new Okyenhene.[4] They demanded apologies from Ofori Atta II and compensation of £1,500 for the death of Akyea Mensah.[5] Nor were the Amantoo Mmiensa alone in their anger. Signs of dissent were reported amongst the Kyebi elders and in 1947 the Okyenhene's previously most vocal supporter, the Gyaasehene, resigned partly as a protest against the paramount's conduct of the case.[6] The situation in Kyebi and the surrounding area was volatile, and the Okyenhene could hardly claim that he ruled a united and contented population.

In London, officials got as close as safety and propriety permitted to outright criticism of their Secretary of State. Creech Jones was ignoring the time-hallowed customs of the Colonial Office in seemingly denying the Governor of the Gold Coast the customary and statutorily defined

out) on 20 November 1945, 1 May 1946, 31 May 1946 and 3 February 1947. They were taken back to Ussher Fort on 22 November 1945, 15 May 1946, 21 June 1946 and 6 February 1947. Only one ever entered a condemned cell (on 4 February 1947), and his hanging was postponed seven minutes before execution was due. None of the prisoners ever entered the gallows yard, let alone saw the gallows.

3 See e.g. *Quarterly Report* of the District Commissioner for the area based at Birrim, M.M. Miln, dated 9 January 1947, PRO CO 96/802/5.
4 See *Kibi District Book*, December 1946, NAG ADM 32/4/100.
5 And by March 1948 were pressing for Ofori Atta II's destoolment. See *Kibi District Book*, June 1949, NAG ADM 32/4/100.
6 See *Kibi District Book*, March 1948, NAG ADM 32/4/100.

6 British press interest provides some of the few extant photographs of the condemned men. *Clockwise from top left*: A.E.B. Dankwa, Kwasi Pipim, Opoku Afwenee.

areas of autonomy which governors enjoyed.[7] The stand-off resulted in a formal meeting between officials and the Secretary of State some time between 17 and 24 January 1947, in which some broad principles were agreed and minuted. The result reads uncommonly like a contract drawn up between warring factions and is worth reproducing *in extenso*.

'The Secretary of State considers that certain broad principles may be laid down. The first is that the Continental principle of "administrative justice" is not one which can be recognised; a decision of a Court of Law ... must be respected by this Department. ... The Secretary of State is not a revising authority for the finding of Colonial Courts.' This is evidence of victory for the overwhelming view of the officials, and especially the legal advisers, over the preceding year. If they were

7 E.g. the testy minute of the young Assistant Secretary K. Robinson to the Permanent Under-Secretary (4 January 1947): 'I feel bound to urge that full weight should be given to his [Burns'] assessment of local opinion. All the evidence available here supports his view...'; PRO CO 96/783/5. The implication was that Creech Jones was choosing to ignore the evidence and the advice of civil servants in Accra and in Whitehall.

7 *Left*: Kwasi Pipim, *top right*: Kwaku Amoako-Atta and *bottom right*: Opoku Afwenee.

allowed 'first blood' then the rules of engagement insisted that Creech Jones be allowed to score too. The second point stated that '... it must be admitted that in some cases the administration of justice in the Colonies leaves something to be desired'. This general suggestion added little to the particular debate but bowed to the dignity of the Minister. Thirdly it was agreed that

the Secretary of State is responsible ... for the efficiency of the machinery of justice ... and is entitled to intervene upon general questions such as the policy adopted by a Governor in relation to the reprieve of prisoners ... it is incumbent upon him to investigate and ... intervene in individual cases ... where there seems to have been a miscarriage of justice. Such intervention must not be regarded as in any way removing the Governor's general responsibility for the exercise of the prerogative ... [and] must not be regarded as a regular procedure.

That is to say that while the Secretary of State determined policy, intervention in individual cases was only merited where a miscarriage came to light. Creech Jones had to concede that there had been no miscarriage in the Akyem case.[8]

But even if the Secretary of State were to be, in certain circumstances, moved to intervene, the minute goes on to say, 'the normal method ... would be to address the Governor semi-officially conveying the doubts which have arisen and suggesting a reconsideration of the question. ... This would go out independently of any official despatch. ...'[9] The Governor's views, arrived at after statutorily consulting his Executive Council and therefore not merely his own, remained paramount. There can be no doubt that Creech Jones had been reined in. He had been told, and the suggestion in the formality of the minute is that he was told firmly, that he had no real *locus standi* in the case; his attempts to negotiate with Members of Parliament over the decisions of courts of law, and with a prerogative which lay not with him but with the Governor, were breaking the rules. Creech Jones clearly gave way. With this freshly drafted set of rules in mind he reported to Burns that he had not received the promised memorial from the MPs[10] and 'The decision therefore rests with you.'[11]

Burns formally knew little of the combat in Whitehall but was almost certainly in receipt of unrecorded private correspondence from some of those involved.[12] But he felt that the worst was over. He had played host to a visiting delegation of British MPs in the early weeks of 1947

8   Those questions had been tried and tested on numerous occasions in courts at every level of the imperial legal system.
9   Undated record of discussion in the Colonial Office but generated between 17 and 24 January 1947, PRO CO 96/802/5.
10 The deadline was 15 January 1947, by agreement between Creech Jones, Hale and Silverman.
11 Creech Jones to Burns, 27 January 1947, PRO CO 96/802/5.
12 There is a suggestion of that in a personal letter sent to J.K. Thompson (17 March 1947) which thanks him for passing messages to Burns' family. He says that Kenneth Robinson, then visiting the Gold Coast on CO business, 'has told me of your efforts to educate the Press ... and I am grateful also for this and the other kinds of help you have found time to give in this unpleasant business. ... I am very fed up ... and anxious to escape to the haven of retirement, but I am not going until I have done all I can to save the reputation of British justice in this colony.' PRO CO 537/2099.

and by the end of the visit was convinced that '... most if not all would agree that executions should proceed'.[13] On legal advice from both his Law Officers and the CO Legal Advisers he felt that he should allow the defence one but only one attempt at securing *habeas corpus* writs on the men. His soundings amongst the judges[14] indicated that these applications would fail. The defence threatened further applications to the Privy Council for leave to appeal against the West African Court of Appeal's refusal to hear a further appeal on the civil suit against the Attorney General. But again, on advice, he felt that this threat constituted no barrier to carrying out the executions, which 'I propose now to carry out'.[15]

Creech Jones was told by the Legal Advisers that Burns need wait no further for the defence to exhaust all the legal possibilities,[16] information he passed on to Burns. But he did so on the same day as he sent him a telegram which, for those impressed by moral blackmail, was a fine piece of drafting. 'I feel... as I informed you in our private talk... that... my personal feelings are... very strong after all these respites and delays. I recognise... that you will exercise your responsibility in accordance with your conscience and firm convictions and your feelings of public duty and requirements.'[17] Creech Jones was determined to maintain his monopoly of the moral high ground; he wanted Burns to feel that his persistence in this matter was cruel. Despite this, Burns fixed the executions for 5 February.

In the meantime the evidence suggests that Creech Jones maintained contact of a rather covert sort with the protesting Members of Parliament.[18] Perhaps encouraged by these contacts, seven MPs addressed a memorial to the Secretary of State on 4 February urging him to prevent the executions. Creech Jones concluded that the memorial, which was no more than a private letter, raised no new matters and that despite his strong personal feelings, the matter rested with the Governor.[19] Quite literally at the eleventh hour, a further petition, this time signed by nine MPs, was received and this time it was addressed to

13 Burns to the Secretary of State, 24 January 1947, PRO CO 96/802/5.
14 His admission that he talked to them suggests unconstitutionality. There is no record of such discussions but there is no doubt that defence tactics had thrown the Bench and the Executive together in a way that the Gold Coast Bench might have resisted earlier.
15 Burns to the Secretary of State, 28 January 1947, PRO CO 96/802/5.
16 Secretary of State to Burns, 31 January 1947, PRO CO 96/802/5.
17 Creech Jones, 'Personal', to Burns, 31 January 1947, PRO 96/802/5.
18 See Hale's letter to Creech Jones and a note from Creech Jones' Private Secretary confirming that an appointment had been made with Silverman for a meeting in the House 'before or after lunch today', both dated 4 February, PRO CO 96/802/5.
19 Creech Jones to Burns, 19.00 hours, 4 February 1947, PRO CO 96/802/5.

the King. It is possible that Creech Jones had advised that this was the best course open to the protesters. Constitutionally this had to be duly considered, and Creech Jones accordingly telegrammed the Governor to stay the executions until 'I am able to advise His Majesty'.[20]

Burns seethed. In a stern telegram dated 5 February he pointed out that the insistence on a respite was received 'only shortly before the hour for which the first execution was timed'. He had proceeded to this point because he had been mandated by Creech Jones' earlier telegrams, informed as they were by legal advice, to act on his own discretion. He went on to say that he felt 'real regret that I am not able to agree with your personal feelings . . . the reprieve of these murderers would be wrong and a betrayal of the true interests of the people of this Colony. . . . I consider it my duty to warn you that feeling in this Colony is running high and if these men are reprieved, serious consequences may follow.' This was a pretty crude attempt to trump Creech Jones' moral blackmail with a higher card in the same suit. Could Creech Jones, as the Minister responsible, conduce at an outbreak of 'serious consequences' in the Gold Coast? Burns turned the knife: '. . . the Executive Council . . . expressed great satisfaction when I informed them that the executions would be proceeded with. One of them said that if they were not . . . executed, the result would be deplorable. I again urge that public opinion in this Colony is of supreme importance in this matter. . . .'[21]

Creech Jones was in deep water. Burns probably exaggerated the extent of reactions to a reprieve but none of Creech Jones' advisers was going to tell him that. Despite the recent correspondence with Burns, Creech Jones had not despaired of getting his own way. On the evening of 5 February, Creech Jones asked for and got an interview with Attlee. The upshot of this was that they would seek a legal loophole which would allow the Secretary of State to override the Governor. Creech Jones' Private Secretary told J.K. Thompson and Kenneth Roberts-Wray that 'the Prime Minister was anxious that the Attorney General should see the Instrument of Appointment of the Governor . . . first thing tomorrow morning'.[22] Midnight oil was burned in the Colonial Office that night. The Prime Minister's interest had very little to do with the particularities of the case and even less with the implicit humanitarian issue. With a small majority, he was concerned about rebellious back-benchers. At the private meeting on 5 February Attlee

20   Secretary of State to Burns, 'Most Immediate', 23.00 hours, 4 February 1947, PRO CO /96/802/5.
21   Burns to the Secretary of State, 5 February 1947, PRO CO 96/802/5.
22   *Minute* by Roberston to Thompson and Roberts Wray, 5 February 1947, PRO CO 96/802/5.

wanted to know which MPs had been connected with the protest and on 6 February Creech Jones furnished him with the names of those who had signed the petition to the King of 4 February, the letter to him of 24 January and the petition to George Hall on 10 July 1946.[23] Attlee almost certainly considered that this was a matter which the Whips' Office could handle better than Creech Jones.

Attorney General Shawcross read the Royal Instructions and the Letters Patent with care and concluded, just as the Legal Advisers had done months before, that the prerogative lay with the Governor. Any attempt to wrest that from him would require legislation. That delegation to the Governor of the Crown's prerogative of mercy should, he argued, also inform the advice the Secretary of State must now give the King in the light of the petition from the nine Members of Parliament.[24] Creech Jones was still in the mire. Thomas Lloyd rubbed this in with gusto; he suggested in a peremptory minute to Creech Jones that he must now 'guide himself' by the long-established practice that the Secretary of State does not intervene unless satisfied (as you are not satisfied here) that there has been a miscarriage of justice'. It followed that he could not advise the Councillors of State and hence the King that 'there should be any departure from that practice'. If Creech Jones thought otherwise, Lloyd begged him to speak to the members of the parliamentary delegation who had just returned from the Gold Coast who were, it was known, convinced that Burns was acting responsibly. Lloyd went on, 'If Sir A. Burns' views . . . are rejected, he will take it very hardly indeed. But his feelings will be even more embittered if that rejection is decided without even consulting, as he has so recently suggested, a section of Parliamentary opinion which has at least some qualification to advise than are possessed by those who have been so assiduously intervening from this end.'[25]

Creech Jones was panicked by the accumulation of advice and instruction which had piled up in so short a time. He produced, in manuscript, an almost penitential shopping-list of 'things to do' which recalls the manic distraction of the White Rabbit:

1) I must speak again to the Lord Chancellery, 2) I must speak again with the PM, 3) I must see the MPs back from the Gold Coast, 4) I will then draft a full telegram for Sir Alan Burns indicating that on public grounds it will be unfortunate for the S of S to intervene when there has been no miscarriage of justice, 5) Prepare the [unreadable] submitted [unreadable] then go to the Palace, 6) Reply given to the

23   Creech Jones to the Prime Minister, 6 February 1947, PRO CO 96/802/5.
24   Hartley Shawcross to W.L. Dale, 6 February 1947, PRO LCO 2/3231.
25   *Minute* by Sir Thomas Lloyd to Creech Jones, 7 February 1947, PRO CO 96/802/5.

petitioners, 7) The procedures in matters of this kind should be overhauled.[26]

By 10 February, Creech Jones had the benefit of the Lord Chancellor's opinion. In a splendidly doddery response in the best traditions of the semi-senile judges of comedy, Jowitt obviously thought this present matter was completely new and unrelated to an earlier approach on the same case made to him in July of 1946. In no less confusion, he also felt that his advice differed from that of the Attorney General, which it did not. But his eventual message was clear. Burns was the final authority. If Creech Jones were to give advice contrary to that of the Governor then 'you will have a complete crossing of the wires. . . . I think this undesirable and not in accordance with precedent.'[27] The advice to the King and his Council of State was duly drafted and sent in accordance with these views. There had been no miscarriage of justice and the Secretary of State did not feel 'that grounds exist in this case sufficiently strong [sic] to justify him in advising his Majesty that there should be any departure from that practice' of leaving it to the Governor's discretion.[28] In a note to the Prime Minister, Creech Jones said that he had consulted the British Law Officers and 'the Labour MPs who recently visited the Gold Coast and they also agreed that this was the right course for us to take'.[29] On 17 February, Attlee had endorsed that note with one of his habitually laconic minutes: 'I agree.'

While the Colonial Office and Burns might have felt that they were coming close to the end of this matter, the defence lawyers had other ideas. Bryden still insisted that the executions could not take place as the convictions were null and void.[30] In the Gold Coast, the defence team continued to press on with the possibility of seeking leave to appeal against the West African Court of Appeal's rejection of their application for *mandamus*. In addition Danquah addressed a petition to the Gold Coast's Legislative Council, of which he was a prominent member.

Burns again telegrammed, now suggesting that the Amantoo Mmiensa towns were so incensed by the endless delays that their faith in British

26 *Minute* by Creech Jones to Lloyd, 8 February 1947, PRO CO 96/802/5.
27 Lord Jowitt to Creech Jones, 10 February 1947, PRO LCO 2/3231.
28 Creech Jones to the Council of State, n.d. but 11 February 1947, PRO CO 96/802/5.
29 Creech Jones to the Prime Minister, 12 February 1947, PRO CO 96/802/5.
30 See e.g. Bryden to the Under-Secretary of State, 11 February 1947, Bryden to Burns, 3 March 1947, and Bryden to Creech Jones, also 3 March 1947, PRO CO 96/802/5. The telegram to Burns makes for the first time the threat that 'Most serious responsibility upon you and your advisers if lives taken when convictions nullities.' He was to return to this charge later.

justice was deeply shaken.[31] Burns wanted a firm go-ahead signal and that he seemed to get in a telegram from Creech Jones on 20 February, which suggested that he might now exercise his 'responsibility in accordance with your conscience and sense of public duty'.[32] The rejection of the petition by the King in Council, an inevitability in the light of Creech Jones' advice, was the signal for a letter to the petitioners from Creech Jones on 26 February underlining the constitutional point: without evidence of a miscarriage of justice, the Secretary of State could not and, in this case, would not intervene. Leslie Hale was not prepared to let matters rest and through the private notice procedure tabled a question on the matter for the Secretary of State in the House for 3 March. It noted 'the failure of the Secretary of State ... to give directions to the Governor ...' and asked 'what directions or advice he has sent or proposes to send to the Governor with reference to the proposed execution tomorrow ....'.[33]

The debate was a disaster for Creech Jones. Officials had thoroughly prepared him for the question on the assumption that a soft, constitutional word would turn away the wrath of the dissident MPs.[34] The Speaker ruled that the question was out of order but was powerless to stop a wide-ranging debate on the case which purported to be a discussion of a point of order. Creech Jones utterly failed to stem a rising tide of indignation, encouraged not least by his own indifferent interventions. There is no suggestion that he connived at this. His debating skills were never marked and his performances at question times were always fragile, creaking affairs in which he usually succeeded in prevailing only because of the marked lack of interest in colonial affairs in the House.

But he was able to turn this debacle to his own advantage. If the constitution and Colonial Office tradition were against him, he could at least parley the hostility of the House into something close to support for his own position. He telegrammed to Burns immediately after the debate conveying the House's 'great excitement' and the 'efforts in all quarters of the House to compel my intervention to over-rule your decision. ... Attack was led by Winston Churchill and supported by Sir John Anderson and Liberal leaders as well as by Labour Members.'

31 Burns to the Secretary of State, 14 February 1947, PRO CO 96/802/5.
32 Creech Jones to Burns, 20 February 1947, PRO CO 96/802/5. Creech Jones however noted that 'I am moved personally by the arguments on humane grounds but ... must on grounds of public duty refrain from doing more than make my personal views known to you. ...' Creech Jones' personal views were not only well known to Burns but inscribed on his heart by February 1947.
33 Hansard, *House of Commons Debates*, 3 March 1947, cols. 37–51.
34 Draft response to parliamentary question prepared by K.E. Robinson, 3 March 1947, PRO CO 96/802/5.

The message to Burns was clear: the Secretary of State had been right all along and he, the Governor, was on his own. Rather than pointing out to the House the clear reasons why the executions were still pending two years after conviction, Creech Jones buckled and, in his own words, was 'finally obliged to inform the House that I would submit to you the deep feeling of the House and again ask your reconsideration and make strongest suggestion to you to respite the condemned men and that they should be reprieved.' Such obligation he might have felt to the Commons was generated, not least, by his own manifest failure to share with the House some of the detail of the case. Perhaps the most craven aspect of his performance was his implicit refusal to alter the opinion in some sections of the House that Burns was some form of latter-day Governor Eyre, a cold-hearted and even sadistic brute. Creech Jones' final words to Burns read as a masterpiece of hypocrisy: 'You already know my own strong feeling . . . but I made it clear to the House that I could not do more than convey to you the feelings of the House'.[35]

Burns could do no other than persuade the Executive Council that the executions should be postponed. But in telling the Secretary of State that he had done so he did not forgo the chance of a tart response: '. . . You are aware of my own strong feeling . . . that reprieve would be a surrendering of the principle of justice to the powers of money and influence.[36] I believe the attitude of the House of Commons is based on complete misconception of the facts. Local feeling here will be strong. . . .'[37]

Local feeling was indeed strong and no stronger than in the Governor's residence, the stately Danish castle of Christiansborg. Burns was on the brink of resignation. The exact sequence of events is hard to reconstruct. It is obvious that he made his decision to tender his resignation as a result of the Secretary of State's telegram of 4 March. In the very small collection of his papers there is a splenetic few pages which are, in effect, a calendar of outrage. That calendar itemises, in the form of an aide-memoire, the course of the case. Some of it is in black typescript, some of it in choleric red. Internal evidence suggests that it was written between 4 and 7 March 1947. It ends, in red type,

> If the men are not executed respect in the Gold Coast for British law and justice will be destroyed. The people will consider that they have been let down. There will probably be bloodshed in the Kibi area. Probably the best thing is for me to resign as a protest against the

35   Creech Jones to Burns, 3 March 1947, PRO CO 96/802/5.
36   This was manipulative. Burns knew that thus expressed, this was not a practice that a rather puritanical Labour Minister could support.
37   Burns to the Secretary of State, 4 March 1947, PRO CO 96/802/5.
38   Rhodes House Library, Oxford, Mss Afr S 1822.

FIFTH TIME LUCKY

8 A contemporary cartoon by the *News Chronicle's* political cartoonist Vicky.

interference of politics in the administration of law and justice and to let some other Governor (or acting Governor) sign the warrant of commutation which I am not prepared to do.[38]

Burns had prepared his ground by 4 March. He had certainly told his family of his intention of resigning 'in certain circumstances' before 5 March. He had sent this message, *en clair*, through J.K. Thompson at the Colonial Office, as he was clearly no longer much interested in being discreet.[39] The formal notice was telegrammed to the Secretary of State on 4 March. It was terse and to the point.

39   Burns to Sir Thomas Lloyd, 'Personal', 5 March 1947, PRO CO 96/802/5.

In all the circumstances I feel I must ask you to obtain H.M's permission for me to relinquish my appointment before expiration of my term of office. I should be glad to have your permission to proceed to England urgently for taking leave which I am entitled to, to retire on pension . . . need hardly assure you that I deeply regret having to leave the Colonial Service after 42 years, but I cannot conscientiously make myself a party to what I consider to be a gross miscarriage of justice.[40]

Burns managed some judicious leaking of his intentions; inquiries from the British press flowed into the Colonial Office. The Gold Coast press almost universally expressed shock and regret at the leaked news. The drama of Burns' action pushed Creech Jones towards recognising the full significance of the events rather than the sloganising around them.[41] He telegrammed Burns on 4 March and followed it with a sensitive if rather evasive long letter which was brought out by hand by Ivor Thomas.[42]

The telegram asked Burns to stay his hand until he had read the hand-delivered letter. Burns respected that request. The letter was 'not an easy one to write', said Creech Jones,

but its real inspiration is the real distress which the offer of your resignation has caused me. I can say that in all sincerity, for, though we have not always seen eye to eye over this most regrettable business, I have never allowed myself to forget that for you this was, as it still is, a matter of conscience. I know that you will recognise that my dislike of the capital penalty has made it difficult for me too.

This was indeed heady, personal stuff and not the normal run of letters from Cabinet Ministers. He went on to say that if Burns were to resign, 'deplorable consequences . . . may and almost certainly will follow . . . [and] may well spread beyond the Gold Coast'. This was intended to flatter, as was a passing references to Burns' 'fine record of achievement . . .'.

40   Burns to Creech Jones, 'Secret and Personal' telegram, 4 March 1947.
41   In a *Minute* to Attlee on 5 March he said that Burns had offered his resignation. He went on, 'He is an able and enlightened Governor and his retirement in these circumstances may well have unfortunate effects in the Gold Coast and possibly repercussions in the Colonies and the Colonial Service'; PRO CO 537/2099. It seems clear that the possible ramifications of Burns' retirement now outweighed the problem of dealing with his conscience and with a much shrunken number of fractious Labour MPs.
42   Creech Jones to Burns, 'Secret and personal', 5 March 1947, PRO CO 537/2099 (copy in Rhodes House Library, Mss Afr S 1822). Thomas, Parliamentary Under-Secretary of State, had left for West Africa to preside over a meeting of the West African Council in Accra.

Creech Jones seems to have recognised for the first time that part of the issue was the failure of successive secretaries of state to stand behind the Governor as was traditional. Why for example had he not stood up for Burns in the shindig in the House of commons? 'Any contribution from me would have provoked further debate . . .', which must have seemed pretty limp to Burns. The end of the letter begs Burns to think about the immensity of the move before committing himself.

And it was an immense step. No Governor had resigned on such grounds before, and Creech Jones must have speculated about the impact such a drama might have had upon him and his career. Any inquiry it might provoke would reveal his weakness and vacillation. It may have been the clear fact that the moment for temporising had come and gone that enabled the permanent staff at the Colonial Office to have a strong draft of theirs accepted by Creech Jones as a statement he should make to the House. Given the situation, he also accepted the point raised in a telegram from Burns which urged Creech Jones to 'make it clear that I am no enthusiast for capital punishment but that I believe so long as it is the law it should be applied to rich and poor alike . . .'.[43]

The statement duly delivered to the House of Commons was the first full account of the sequence of events it had received. Clearly drafted and concise, it neatly put the role of the Governor and his advisers in proportion. As Creech Jones was to tell Burns, it 'was received by House with attentive interest, in striking contrast to emotion and uproar which marked Monday's proceedings. You will see from supplementaries . . . that atmosphere was very much changed and that appreciative cheers from all sides . . . greeted reference to yourself.'[44]

Quite why the atmosphere altered in this dramatic fashion in two days is open to many interpretations. While the clarity of the statement may have commanded attention, it is likely that some of the Members recognised that matters had got out of hand in the House on 3 March. The Tory members of the House must have realised that while further knife-turning might damage a member of the government front bench, in this case they had also sided with the anti-colonial lobby within the Labour ranks. The Tory benches were notably subdued on 5 March. It is even more likely that the entire House was more prepared to listen to a case being made by a Secretary of State who at last seemed to have a certain amount of knowledge and conviction behind his comments. The constitutional position he adopted had been approved by both the Lord Chancellor and the Attorney General, and hence implicitly the combined wisdom of the most senior ranks of the home civil service.

43 Burns to Creech Jones, 'Secret', 5 March 1947, PRO CO 96/802/5.
44 Creech Jones to Burns, 5 March 1947, PRO CO 96/802/5.

The British press showed a rare unanimity in its analysis of how the House had behaved. The *Tribune*, no supporter of colonialism or its managers, wrote: '. . . when members . . . began to acquire the facts not only of the murder itself but of the methods by which the long delay in the executions had been secured, many members began to wonder whether in fact the House had not made a fool of itself'.[45] From the other end of the political spectrum, *The Economist* suggested that the row in the House on the Monday was 'a classic case of parliamentary solicitude for the welfare of colonial peoples at its most belated, ill-informed and misdirected. . . . In matters of justice it is usually the best course to trust the juries, the judges and the executive authorities on the spot. If Members of Parliament are not prepared to do that they should at least inform themselves of the facts.'[46]

Awaiting the outcome of the debate, Burns had agreed with Creech Jones that he would delay submitting his resignation but shared this information with his Executive Council.[47] It seems clear that some of them then went on to share this information with the local press, which enjoyed speculating about the rumours. 'His Excellency will resign?' asked *The Spectator Daily*. 'Rumour of Governor's resignation', said *The Daily Echo*.[48] There is little doubt that Creech Jones' judgement in a letter to Burns about the proceedings in the House on 5 March was entirely correct: '. . . the rumours which spread throughout the House and the Press that you were considering resignation has [sic], in spite of its pain, had a most salutary effect'.[49] Perhaps the person upon whom it had the most 'salutary effect' was Creech Jones himself.

Burns was back in the saddle, the horse subdued. The Accra press was generally favourable to him and bridled at suggestions that Burns might retire. In an interesting way the local press seemed angered that ill-informed actions and reactions in London should threaten the career of 'their' Governor and that he might be forced to leave the Gold Coast by forces outside the control of the inhabitants of the colony.[50] This is not to say that all the Accra press felt that the men should hang: the editors of both *The Daily Echo* and *The Spectator Daily* were signatories of

45   7 March 1947.
46   8 March 1947.
47   Burns to Creech Jones, 'Personal', 5 March 1947, PRO CO 96/802/5.
48   Both from 6 March 1947.
49   Creech Jones to Burns, telegram, 6 March 1947, PRO CO 96/802/5.
50   Even *The Ashanti Pioneer* of 10 March referred to the Governor as 'Our Sir Alan Burns' in an editorial which spoke of him as 'our much respected Governor' and talked of his 'vast prestige among Africans' and 'unexampled service to the Gold Coast'. A columnist in the same paper, which had until then been somewhat sympathetic to the defence, wrote, 'Sir Alan, let us assure you that the whole Gold Coast public is solidly behind your actions. . . .'

a petition to the Legislative Council on behalf of the condemned men. At the same time *The Spectator Daily* carried an editorial on 14 March 1947 headed 'Pity Parliament and British Public'. The article continued: '. . . Knowing as we do the trend of opinion in this country over Akyea Mensah case, we hope people in this country will not be forced to wage a counter-offensive against the organised might of the British Houses of Parliament and the equally emotional British public. And they call their diversion of justice a defence against a miscarriage of justice.' The press generally adopted a nationalist line against the interference of the British Parliament in their own affairs; this position ironically tended to support the Governor's position.

But most of the Gold Coast press changed its mind from time to time. *The Ashanti Pioneer*, which had given space to the royal family's case, was by 15 March quoting Marie Corelli: 'The heavier purse may weigh down the scales of justice.' It seems fair to say that by March 1947, the Governor had won the propaganda battle. Burns received motions of support from the judges of the Gold Coast's Supreme Court[51] and the Provincial Councils of Chiefs in the Colony.[52] By 16 March the few potentially dissident members of the Legislative Council had decided to withdraw a threatened resolution begging the Governor to reprieve the condemned men. Only Danquah of the thirteen MLCs from the Colony failed to sign a resolution strongly supporting the Governor's policy *vis à vis* the executions. By the same date Burns had the overt support of both Provincial Councils, which meant that of the paramounts of sixty-two out of the sixty-three states in the colony.[53] Public opinion is impossible to recreate. George Padmore was almost certainly right in suggesting that: 'the country was divided. Some for hanging; other against.'[54] But it is far harder to discover any widespread doubt about the actual commission of the crime.

On 19 March, the House of Commons met to discuss the vote on the account, an occasion on which some Labour MPs had threatened to

51 7 March 1947. It ends, 'Judges know of no reason for supposing that there has been any miscarriage of justice. They are of the opinion that the prisoners have not only pursued the normal legal remedies . . . but indeed for long have been instituting proceedings which were baseless and foredoomed to failure and that this has tended to bring the law into disrepute.' PRO CO 96/802/6.

52 That from the Eastern Provincial Council which had been dominated by Ofori Atta I resolved 'That His Excellency the Governor be assured of the unanimous and strong support of this Council with regard to his actions fulfilling his Commission to uphold justice fully'. 7 March 1947, PRO CO 96/802/6. It was not unanimous: the Okyenhene of Akyem Abuakwa was a notable absentee.

53 Akyem Abuakwa being the sixty-third. See Burns to the Secretary of State, 16 March 1947, PRO CO 96/802/6.

54 *Gold Coast Observer*, 21 March 1947.

raise the matter once again. There was, however, no discussion. On 19 March, Creech Jones telegrammed to Burns: 'There is therefore now no, repeat no, reason from point of view why you should delay your decision. . . .'[55]

The Legislative Council heard a petition from Danquah on behalf of the condemned men without comment on 18 March. A long exchange between Burns and Danquah ensued but no other member spoke. Tactfully, a counter-motion in the name of Tsibu Darku condemning ritual murder and deploring attempts to influence the Governor in his exercise of the prerogative had been rather showily removed from the Order of Business signifying, perhaps, that its movers were satisfied that the matter now rested entirely with the Governor and his Executive Council. Danquah stood alone. Recalling this in 1968, the Reverend Christian Baeta[56] said: 'It was an embarrassing half an hour. None of those present had the slightest doubt that the murder had been committed. All of us knew that Danquah had to make this special plea for a petition which we knew he had drafted on behalf of his family and the Akyem Stool.' On 22 March the Executive Council met and unanimously agreed that the remaining five condemned men should be executed two days hence.[57]

On 24 March and eleven minutes before the first execution was scheduled to take place, the defence served a notice on the Director of Prisons that an application for writs of *habeas corpus* was being made. A further respite was granted whilst the applications were heard. The *ex-parte* applications were refused by Henley Coussey and shortly thereafter three of the condemned men were hanged in the gallows yard of James Fort Prison in Accra,[58] the only prison at which executions were carried out in the Gold Coast. Reuters[59] reported these events with obscene glee: ' "I will pray for you," said the ju-ju murder man to warders on the scaffold . . . one of the three hanged yesterday . . . said . . . to warders who tried to force his hands behind his back: "Don't be rough with me. I will place my hands at my back myself. It is not your fault. When I go I will pray for you and very soon you will know the truth." '[60]

55 PRO CO 96/802/6.
56 Sitting at the time as the second provincial member for Eastern Province.
57 Burns to the Secretary of State, 22 March 1947, PRO CO 96/802/6.
58 At 2.00 pm A.E.B. Danquah was executed and Kwame Kagya and Kwasi Pipim at 3.30 pm. This information was sent to Creech Jones on 31 March 1947, PRO CO 96/802/6.
59 Reuters' 'stringer', Wuta Ofei, who filed these reports, had been a recipient of small handouts from Nana Sir Ofori Atta following a number of suitably egregious begging letters sent in the 1930s. See AASA 8/33.
60 Reuter's report, n.d. but numbered 1803; PRO CO 96/825/5. How the reporter acquired this information is unclear but it as possible that warders were interviewed by the press.

After the execution of the third man, notice of intention to appeal to the Privy Council was received from the defence lawyers. Burns immediately agreed to postpone the further executions and then considered 'whether in view of this further delay, sentence on the two remaining men should be commuted'.[61] As news of the executions broke in London, a group of Labour MPs attempted to raise the matter in the House of Commons late at night on 24 March but were ruled out of order by the Speaker of the House.[62]

Burns took the matter again to his Executive Council, who considered it at length on 25 March. He reported to Creech Jones on the same day that the Council was 'strongly of the opinion that the sentences on the two remaining men should not (repeat not) be commuted. I have not yet reached a decision.'[63] Burns reflected and then drafted a long and careful statement for the Legislative Council which he delivered on 28 March. In this he announced that he had decided to commute sentence on the two surviving men because 'they must have anticipated a similar fate as those executed on 24 March and suffered mentally in anticipation'.[64] A motion was tabled by the elected members of the Legislative Council on the same day and was passed by all those present, which excluded J.B. Danquah. It read: 'That this Council does place on record its high appreciation of the work of His Excellency Sir Alan Burns as Governor and Commander in Chief of the Gold Coast 1941–47 and the First President of this Council 1946–1947 and pray that his health, prosperity and progress in life generally and in the service of the British Colonial Empire may be endued with divine blessing and guidance both for himself and his family'.[65]

Some of this was genuine affection for Burns, whose robust style and humour was widely appreciated. But in part it emerged from the pleasure some in the Gold Coast derived from this ultimate humiliation of the Akyem Abuakwa royal family. With the horror and grief of the gallows a raw, recent memory, few in Akyem Abuakwa would have misread the debate in the Legislative Council on 28 March. Edward Asafu-Adjaye praised the police who, in his eyes, had 'risen to great

61 Burns to Creech Jones, 19.20 hours, 24 March 1947, PRO CO 96/802/6.
62 Only three indignant communications were received by the Colonial Office about the executions. A telegram from Henry Maxwell from the Travellers Club in Pall Mall reads: 'Execution of five ignorant niggers three years after crime is negation of elementary human decency and reduces England to level of Germany and Japan [stop] Implore you reconsider decision [stop].' See PRO CO 96/802/6.
63 Burns to Creech Jones, 25 March 1947, PRO CO 96/802/6. Burns added, 'African members have repeated warning that bloodshed will be inevitable if all the men are not . . . executed.'
64 Burns to Creech Jones, 28 March 1947, PRO CO 96/802/6.
65 Legislative Council *Debates*, 28 March 1947, NAG. ADM 14/2/48.

esteem. In the opinion of the public he is a friend and for that . . . I give credit to the Commissioner of Police. . . .' More remarkably, one of the original defence team, Nii Ollennu, an MLC, concurred: 'every encouragement is given to him in the execution of his onerous duties; and I am sure that the Police authorities will be good enough to testify to the cooperation the Force enjoys from all sections of the Community'.[66] The timing of this endorsement of the Gold Coast police by two of the most eminent lawyers in the country was precise if cruel. Akyem Abuakwa had never stood in lower esteem in its long history, and regrettably there were many who were gladdened by that.

The hanged men, those destined to spend years in the Gold Coast's prisons and their relatives were not the only victims of this wretched sequence of events. Burns' victory was a hollow one. He left the Gold Coast in August 1947, and from then until 1956 was the UK's permanent representative on the United Nations Trusteeship Council before retirement. A pioneer of constitutional change in Africa and a prescient observer of nationalist development in Africa,[67] he might have expected better things, including perhaps a seat in the House of Lords. Sadly these events marked him for life, alienated him from the Colonial Office and haunted him until his death. While his pain was much slighter than that of the families of Akyea Mensah and of the hanged men, this case left a bitter personal harvest for all involved, as well as having a profound impact on the politics of colonial Ghana.

66   Leg. Co. *Debates*, 28 March 1947, NAG. ADM 14/2/48.
67   For more on this, see Richard Rathbone, 'British Documents on the End of Empire:' *Ghana*, vol. 1 (London, 1992).

CHAPTER EIGHT

Meanings, Motives and Probabilities

What had really happened and why had it happened? We have seen the Crown's evidence and a series of alternative, exculpatory explanations of the Odikro's disappearance mounted by the palace and its legal representatives. As must be clear by now, I conclude that the murder did take place. This was not my position at the outset.[1] Such a change of heart and head is based upon not merely the force of the evidence which supports the commission of the crime but also on the no less copious evidence and argument that denied it. In trying to understand what this crime might have been about, I have taken the defence arguments and evidence very seriously. What other readings can be imposed upon the evidence we have? Trying to understand what lay behind such counter-arguments, subjecting them to analysis, is revealing. Some of this has already been tackled; we have for example looked at the arguments about the skull and bones and the mystery of how many stools rested in the Stool House. But it is important to take on some of the other counter-propositions.

The defence case actually opened well before the trial. The first elements of an alternative explanation of the Odikro's disappearance emerged when the Okyeman Council met District Commissioner Walker on 14 March 1944. On that occasion Opanyin Twum Barima,[2] a member of the Okyeman Council as both a lineage head and a senior royal, told the District Commissioner: 'Some time ago the people of Apedwa ... brought the Odikro Akyea Mensah before the late Nana Sir Ofori Atta attempting to destool him. The Apedwa people were found guilty and since that time the people of Apedwa particularly the Elders are not in good terms with the Chief. He was always threatened with destoolment.' This accusation prefigured the evidence given by Akyea Mensah's schoolteacher lodger at the murder trial; it also ties in very neatly with part of the character assassination which forms the core of J.B. Danquah's long petition on behalf of 'The enlightened sons and

---

1 As is clear from my article in *The Journal of African History* (vol. 30, no. 3) and the longer *Politics and Murder: a West African Case*, Boston University African Studies Working Papers no. 164, 1992, which was written early in 1991.
2 Who died on 13 January 1945.

daughters of Akim Abuakwa'. It is clearly an extremely important allegation. But was it true?

While the records of the Okyeman Council, before whom such allegations would have been heard, are not entirely complete, there is no written evidence whatever which supports the idea that Akyea Mensah was unpopular, played-out and desperate. As importantly there is no memory which supports it in Apedwa today. It is a significant accusation because it was used to support an allegation that Akyea Mensah had been so threatened and depressed by his relationship with his subjects that he took his own life. This was insinuated at various times in the 1940s; and it resurfaces once again in the strong assertion made by one of Nana Sir Ofori Atta's sons, Fraser Ofori Atta, who served as Abontendomhene until his destoolment in the 1970s. He also claimed that the entire murder story was fabricated. This was, then, an element of the royal family's case.[3]

Another variant of this argument suggests that this same misery and alienation from his people led him to choose to turn his back on life's cruelties by disappearing into painless anonymity. Given the considerable notoriety of the case it was extremely unlikely that Akyea Mensah could have disappeared, without identification and ensuing gossip. Ghanaian societies are intimate, face-to-face communities in which strangers are immediately apparent and noted. But this explanation is the burden of three extraordinary, long articles by J.B. Danquah in the pages of the *Ashanti Pioneer* entitled 'The Psychology of the Human Mind; Sidelighting the Kibi Murder Case'. Here he argued that a man who could testify that Akyea Mensah was alive after the alleged murder was too afraid or selfish to come forward. The allegations in these pieces echo the insinuation of Opanin Twum Barima mentioned above. There is, however, no evidence whatever which supports them.[4]

The only historical trace of friction between the people of Apedwa and Akyea Mensah emerges in a bizarre case heard before the Okyenhene's tribunal on 13 January 1938. On that day the Native Authority Police accused one of Akyea Mensah's nephews, Kwaku Amoako, with using 'disrespectful or insulting language' against the Odikro. Amoako was said to have called Akyea Mensah a fool, to have said that his deceased mother, Adjoa Frempomah, had had 'her nose cut'[5] and to have alleged that Akyea Mensah's house was not his but

---

3   In Appendix 5B of his valuable BA dissertation (University of Ghana, 1978) entitled 'The Amantoo mmiensa in the Political and Administrative Set-up of Akyem Abuakwa'.

4   See *Ashanti Pioneer*, 29, 30 and 31 January 1947.

5   Possibly an implication of slave status.

belonged, rather, to someone called Kwasi Fa. He was also accused of saying that the elders of Apedwa were idiots for having enstooled someone as foolish as Akyea Mensah; and lastly he was alleged to have said that 'There is no suitable chair in the Odikro's house for you [Akyea Mensah] to sit on because you have not yet succeeded in claiming the Stool you are fighting for.'

It is difficult to decode this case. Some people in Apedwa, fifty-three years after the dispute, argued about whether Amoako was in fact a nephew of Akyea Mensah; others said that he was mad. Whatever his insults meant, Amoako was fined £10 on each count, with the alternative of two months' imprisonment with hard labour on each count.[6] Such cases of insult are frequent in these records and the language quoted in them often suggests that so far as motivation was concerned, palm wine was more important than protest.[7] This case, which dates from six years before the murder, is the only direct evidence which supports the notion that Akyea Mensah was at daggers drawn with anyone, let alone the people of Apedwa.

There is, then, no evidence which supports the idea that Akyea Mensah's state of mind or political position might have led him either to take his own life or to disappear. Fraser Ofori-Atta certainly argued that he had taken his life and did so because of personal and political despair. He writes: '. . . Kwaku Asante, Odikro of Tetteh . . . confessed according to eyewitness account before he died that Akyea Mensah died by hanging himself and that his body was discovered and thrown into a pit to seal any trace of it.'[8] While the author is both a good historian and a son of the stool and thus a receptor of 'local knowledge'[9] of the sort any outsider would find it hard to gain access to, it is must be recognised that this is hearsay about hearsay; it is moreover unsupported by any other evidence. There is no record or memory of human remains being discovered in the near-half-century which has passed since the murder, in what is a very heavily cultivated area.

If details about Akyea Mensah's disturbed state of mind are hard to come by, this might mean nothing. It is rare in the history of Africa to be able to get psychological insights about much greater men and women than Akyea Mensah. But it is more significant that the frequent

6 Okyenhene's *Tribunal Records*, 13 January 1938, NAG ADM 32/1/16.
7 Insult always translates badly. Some of these insults seem trivial but often carry deeper meanings. Insult is constructed socially. By analogy Twi speakers find it odd that northern hemisphere English speakers should be so angered when someone challenges the legitimacy of their birth. A sense of informed cultural relativism must accompany readings of these cases.
8 Fraser Ofori Atta, *op. cit.*, appendix 5B.
9 And especially the 'things that should be kept within the house', the secret matters one does not dilate upon with strangers.

defence suggestions that the missing Odikro's town was in ferment against him prove impossible to document. On the contrary, in the decade before Akyea Mensah's disappearance, Apedwa presented as an unusually successful town. At the end of 1936 it was one of the few towns granted its own Native Tribunal chaired by the Odikro.[10] By 1942 its revenue of £525 was the highest of the Amantoo Mmiensa towns and approached that of many of the much larger towns of Akyem Abuakwa, such as the seats of the divisional chiefs.[11] While its exact population can only be guessed at, it had just over one thousand rate-paying adult inhabitants in 1941. Its large Presbyterian school was divided into infants, juniors and seniors and it established a Standard VI class in 1944. It boasted eight teachers and three stout buildings which had been built by local people. Its Cocoa Producers' Cooperative was successful.[12] It was, moreover, a loyal and proud town, which had heeded Nana Sir Ofori Atta's call for its young people to enlist in the army after 1939; no less than 160 of Apedwa's men had joined the army. Compared with other areas of the Gold Coast a very high proportion of the volunteers passed the military's medical screening, suggesting relatively high standards of nutrition and health care. By any account it was a thriving town, and not one obviously in the midst of a power struggle.[13]

The allegation that Akyea Mensah was in only fragile control of that town is also questionable. He was extremely close to the Kyebi stool during Sir Ofori Atta's lifetime and he was to live only six months after the death of his great patron. Before accession to the Apedwa stool in August 1936 he was, as one of Okyenhene's senior literate civil servants, a Tribunal Registrar in Kyebi, a position of trust and a well-rewarded one. Whilst holding office in the palace all the evidence suggests that he was well regarded. Okyenhene's letter to Akyea Mensah on his election is warm: 'It gives me great pleasure that the services you so faithfully and loyally rendered to me ... should have this crowning success ... you have given me entire satisfaction in the discharge of your duties. As a little mark of my appreciation I send you a cheque for £20. ...'[14] When introduced to the Okyeman Council as Apedwa's new Odikro on 7 August 1936, Akyea Mensah thanked the Okyenhene 'for all that he did to me when I served him. ... It is the vast experience I gained under his tutelage that will stand me in good stead. ... Nana in what-

10 NAG ADM 32/4/100.
11 It was to fall, as was that of many Akyem Abuakwa towns, a matter that can be attributed to the impact of swollen shoot disease upon farmers' incomes.
12 But was devastated in 1944 when its Secretary, E.E. Akyeampong, ran off with its capital; NAG ADM 32/4/56.
13 AASA 8/39.
14 Ofori Atta to Akyea Mensah, 11 July 1936, AASA 3/10.

ever form he castigated or criticised me was doing me good. It is like a child suffering from yaws and being bathed by his mother. In dressing the disease the child . . . may think that the mother is cruel not realising the good she does. . . .'[15] The Okyenhene welcomed him warmly and commended his competence and merit to the State Councillors.

There is nothing recorded which suggests that Akyea Mensah fell out of favour with the Okyenhene as some of my earliest oral evidence insisted.[16] On the contrary, he continued to be a member of the Okyeman Council and sat regularly on both the Okyenhene's and Abontendomhene's tribunals. Even more significantly, he was so obviously trusted and approved in the palace that he sat, until his death, as one of the only four members of the Akyem Abuakwa Finance Board, the key executive of the Akyem Abuakwa State Treasury.[17]

It is just possible that one could be a key player in state administration and still be an enemy of the royal family. But again the evidence contradicts that. His personal esteem and intimacy with the Ahenfie was such that he was selected by the Okyeman Council to be one of the six members of the Funeral Committee which organised the obsequies for Sir Ofori Atta. This must imply closeness to and trust bestowed by the royal family: funerals are intimate processes, and neither an enemy nor a neurotic would have been appointed. By the time of his death he was, moreover, paid an annual allowance of £72, a higher sum than the rest of the Adikrofo and only slightly less than the allowances made to senior chiefly figures such as *Oseawuohene* (traditionally the commander of the rearguard in war) and Sanahene.[18] Such prominence was hardly likely to have been accorded to an unpopular or mentally sick local ruler in imminent risk of destoolment.

Those who insisted, and still insist, that the murder never took place also tend to rely on the negative portrayal of Akyea Mensah that eventually found its final and vituperative form in the petition J.B. Danquah was to draw up and sent to King George VI on 4 January 1946.[19] This insisted that:

---

15 Okyeman Council *Minutes*, 7 August 1936, AASA 8.1/25.
16 Some insisted that there had been a 'falling out' with the Okyenhene in the late 1930s, and because this made good sense, I accepted this. But there is no evidence which supports this and a great deal which contradicts it.
17 AASA 5/69.
18 AASA 5/75.
19 The full title of this is: *The Petition of the Undersigned Educated and Enlightened sons and daughters of the Akim Abuakwa State of the Gold Coast of West Africa, A 'Model State' in the Gold Coast of Late Governed and Ruled by Your Majesty's Most Beloved, Trusty and Faithful Servant the Honourable Nana Sir Ofori Atta, Knight Commander of the Most Excellent Order of the British Empire, Member of the Legislative Council, Member of the Executive Council, who Departed this Life on August the 20th, 1943*; PRO CO 96/783/3.

Akyea Mensah was known to be a hard drinker. He was suspected also of being subject to epileptic fits, a condition held to be so degrading in a Chief, that when known he was bound to be de-stooled.[20] It was generally believed therefore that Akyea Mensah had probably soaked himself with drink, that he had been seized in a fit and had probably sustained injuries in his fall. Under such circumstances his best friends would try to conceal him and conceal his disgraceful condition.[21]

There is no evidence which supports any of these allegations. Again, was it likely that a man of that description would have been invited into such close circles in the palace both before and after Ofori Atta I's death?

Why then was Dr J.B. Danquah so vehement? Well, he was the late king's half-brother and hence uncle of some of the accused; his family was fighting for its life. But J.B. Danquah's role in these events is not all that it appears. He was the Akyem Abuakwa state's solicitor, and as such briefed the defence lawyers. But in many respects his prominent role in these events signified his 'coming in out of the cold' in Akyem Abuakwa.

As is well known, Danquah had 'fallen out' with Ofori Atta in 1934.[22] Danquah subsequently claimed that the reasons for this breach were political. He had come to deplore what he saw as his half-brother's conservatism and willingness to collaborate with the colonial regime. Danquah joined the party of Ofori Atta's greatest enemies, the Aborigines' Rights Protection Society, led by Ofori Atta's most consistent critic, Kobina Sekyi.

The breach was certainly serious. But there was more to it than politics. Danquah resigned his membership of the Okyeman Council and his post of legal adviser to the stool in 1935.[23] Danquah remained in Britain from late 1934, not, he claimed, sulking in his tent, but because his half-brother failed to provide him with maintenance and then refused to fund his return to the Gold Coast.[24] It is clear from the evidence that pressure was applied to get Danquah to return home. This he refused to do until the State Council provided him with '... 1)

20 Suffering from fits – *Otware* – is only one of the many physical and psychological disabilities which can provide *prima facie* cases for destoolment.
21 'Petition of enlightened sons and daughters ...', *op. cit.*, paragraph 29, p. 10. There is no other record I have seen either of these drinking habits or of this physical condition.
22 See S. Rhodie, 'The Gold Coast Aborigines Abroad', in *The Journal of African History*, vol. VI, no. 3, 1965.
23 Danquah to the Okyeman Council, dated Jubilee Day, 1935, AASA 8/31.
24 Danquah to the Okyeman Council, 26 August 1936, *ibid.*

A freehold house ... in Accra, 2) ... £200 to be placed to my credit, 3) my debts slightly over £100 to be paid and that 4) ... a sum of £1.16 a week be paid to me for my rent and an additional sum be given to me to buy food and personal care ...' After some graceless negotiation carried on through Walter Austin, Danquah accepted Ofori Atta's 'revised terms', which fell short of his original demands.

Ofori Atta and the Okyeman Council were undoubtedly infuriated with Danquah but obviously wished to continue to use his legal skills as a draftsman and to do so on the cheap. Danquah returned on 14 October 1936. Okyeman and Ofori Atta demanded a report and an apology from him. That report, made orally on 23 October 1936, barely mentioned political differences between him and his half-brother. Instead it rehearsed a long series of financial claims followed by an abject apology. The Okyeman Council's judgement was against Danquah; he was heavily fined but was eventually reinstated as legal adviser.[25]

This was not the end of the matter. The relationship between Ofori Atta and his half-brother had previously been cordial. Ofori Atta, writing to Walter Austin who had been deeply involved in trying to get Danquah to return to the Gold Coast, said: 'personally I feel that I could not restore him to my confidence. He has frightened me a lot and has given me as much cause for suspicion and mistrust. He stays with his wife in Christiansborg. ... Rather interesting.'[26] Danquah had, before the breach, always signed his letters to the Okyenhene with the familiar 'Joe'. He was never to address him in this way again. Similarly Okyenhene's letters previously addressed to 'My dear brother' thenceforward began 'Dear Dr Danquah'. While the rift was partially healed before Ofori Atta's death, things were never the same again. Before Akyea Mensah's disappearance, Danquah's relationship with the Okyeman Council had been formal and businesslike, despite his blood relationship with many of them. What survives of the correspondence suggests that much of that generated by Dr Danquah was dominated by requests for money, as the Okyeman Council rewarded him poorly for his services. That mattered because it is clear that Danquah's legal practice was not entirely successful. Danquah continued to live in Accra and attended Okyeman meetings or came to the Ahenfie only when asked to do so.

Thus Danquah's central role in these matters represented a return to the fold. Following years of coldness, he had again become a vital member of the royal family, commanding as he did an understanding of the legal background to these dreadful events. It would be cynical to

25 Okyeman Council *Minutes*, 23 October 1936, AASA 8/31.
26 Okyenhene to Walter Austin, 14 November 1936, AASA 8/31.

suggest that he simply exploited their need for him. Some informants suggested to me that he was shaken by the fact that his half-brother died without a full reconciliation having taken place. His extraordinary energy in pressing the defence case to the farthest ends of legality obviously owed a great deal to his genuine personal conviction that family and state honour needed to be defended at all costs. But it is likely that there was personal expiation involved as well. The case certainly gave him prominence but it was not, as we shall see, to advance his career.

Returning to Dr Danquah's petition, this also painted Akyea Mensah as 'a miserable and unhappy man' and 'miserably poor . . . of a brooding and melancholic disposition . . .', who thus had 'every human reason to commit suicide'.[27] Danquah's account of how Akyea Mensah took his own life contrasts with his later story. In the *Ashanti Pioneer*,[28] Danquah was to claim that Akyea Mensah, rather than commiting suicide, walked away from responsibility into distant anonymity. Danquah's initial suicide story also clashes with Fraser Ofori Atta's later account of his hanging himself. In the petition, Danquah says that Akyea Mensah tried to buy Lysol but having failed, acquired M and B tablets to do the deed.[29]

There is no doubt that Akyea Mensah was a reflective and even taciturn man; such a personality could be read in any cultural context as symptomatic of being a misery. But Akyea Mensah's family remember his demeanour as gentle. No one in Apedwa remembered him as a heavy drinker or as an epileptic. The frequently repetitious and often internally self-contradictory attacks on Akyea Mensah's personality, political skills and mental state persist throughout Danquah's petition. At times Danquah's attack descends to real depths. For example, Akyea Mensah is described as 'a Chief who could not afford or had not the inclination to have a change of clothes over-night and, too, it was the condition of a Chief who would go out of an early morning without first having had his bath, an unwholesome habit not regarded as tasteful among the Akan people'.[30] Many of these insinuations and accusations are repeated in a further account written by a Kyebi royal in 1980, which contains no new evidence and draws entirely upon previously published material.[31] There is no evidence which supports the notion that the mystery begins and ends in Akyea Mensah's

27   'Petition of the enlightened sons and daughters . . .' *op. cit.*, paragraph 51, p. 19.
28   See footnote 4.
29   Paragraph 114, p. 48.
30   'Petition of enlightened sons and daughters . . .' *op. cit.*, paragraph 66, p. 26. This is based entirely upon his wife's evidence at the trial, when she said that he had left that day without having his customary morning bath.
31   Oheneba (Prince) Owusu Akyem, 'The Justice of Mistakes; an Exposition on the Kyebi Scandal', unpublished typescript (January, 1980), AASA 10/504.

personality and abilities as a ruler. On the contrary, the Akyem Abuakwa State Council's and hence the royal family's trust in him is documentable up to the moment of his death. Accordingly it is hard to find the arguments persuasive.

This malign, personalised vision contrasts interestingly with an equally shaky set of accusations from another direction which sought to explain why he was singled out for assassination. This school of thought alleged that Akyea Mensah was so important and close to the stool and the stool family that he 'knew too much'; he thus had to be removed before he could divulge the damaging information to which he was privy, information which, it was claimed, would have impugned the probity of the immediate royal family.[32] I have heard such accounts from people who, while they have no love for the Kyebi ruling family, are sincerely uncomfortable with any suggestion that ritual bloodletting could have occurred so recently.

The only written version of this particular argument I have come across is the extraordinary illustrated pamphlet called *Why Kibi Ritual murder. An Inside Story of a Sensational So-called Ritual Murder Case.*[33] It is an important account because it seems likely that it is the source of the many oral variants of the story. There is no doubt that it has been widely read in Akyem Abuakwa and many Akyemfo still own a copy. David Ofori's argument is an intriguing if poorly documented and ill-argued conspiracy case which goes so far as dramatically and literally to indict a guilty 'Mr X'. Ofori describes him as 'The master chess-man, the conspirator in chief who planned the death of Akyea Mensah and caused others to be accused of a crime they never committed . . .'. Mr X was 'wily, full of guile, reckless yet influential, sleek and confident . . .'.[34] No serious motives are advanced for 'Mr X's' actions, and the innuendo is so bizarre that his identity could fit almost everyone and yet nobody in Kyebi. Given the background of Ofori's dislike of the royal family, he could have been implying that J.B. Danquah was Mr X. This is, I think, suggested in Ofori's comment: '. . . The proof of Mr "X's" influence and ingenuity is shown in the protracted Murder Trial of the eight accused persons. Money, influence and Knavish tricks were brought into play to acquit the eight murderers of Akyea Mensah. . . .'[35]

---

32 Berkley-Barton's account in Rhodes House shows that he and probably other policemen shared this view of motive.

33 By David Ofori. First published in 1947 in Accra, it ran to two further impressions, the last being published as late as 1954. Oral evidence suggests that the final printing was done at the behest of the Akyem Abuakwa Convention Peoples' Party who were in the midst of a grim struggle with the Akyem Abuakwa stool.

34 *Ibid.*, p. 31.

35 *Ibid.*, p. 32. Everyone in the Gold Coast knew that J.B. Danquah was the orchestrator of that defence.

Ofori agrees that the murder had indeed taken place but argues that there were no ritual overtones to it. Ofori claims that he, as a member of the State Treasury staff, was aware that Akyea Mensah, who was 'in the know' as a member of the Finance Board, proposed to reveal irregularities in the conduct of that Treasury in public after Ofori Atta I's death. Amongst other reform projects, Akyea Mensah had told him that he proposed to 'do away with nepotism' in its future conduct.[36] Ofori argues that he therefore had to be killed before he could either 'spill the beans' or attempt any of his reforms.

David Ofori's motives for writing this pamphlet become a little clearer in the Akyem Abuakwa State Archives. He was not much loved in the bureaucracy of Ofori Panin Fie. His downfall appears to have begun with a request for five days' leave from 13 November 1943 from the Akyem Abuakwa Treasury where he worked as one of the junior treasurers. He overstayed that leave by five days and this attracted a severe minute in State Secretary K.T.A. Danquah's hand: 'This shows great insubordination.... I recommend his dismissal as from the end of January....'[37] As K.T.A. Danquah was an experienced, usually calm, deliberative administrator, this slight offence could not have been the sole cause of this outburst; there must have been previous if unrecorded acts which had attracted the displeasure of the State Secretary. Ofori retaliated soon afterwards by apparently circulating rumours about corrupt dealings in the Treasury which named the State Treasurer, Rex Otupiri, for whom both the senior staff of the Ahenfie and the District Commissioner had only praise.[38]

Otupiri was understandably infuriated and wrote to J.B. Danquah, in his capacity as Akyem Abuakwa State Solicitor, on 19 January 1944. The accusation of corruption, which he showed to be inaccurate, 'nettles me beyond endurance.... Of late someone has been hammering poisonous ideas into peoples' head [sic] about the question of Nana's grants of £1,500 payable to the State College and saying that I have misappropriated the funds.... I have every reason to believe that Mr Ofori is the source of this information....'[39] The accusations led, however, to a formal and very proper inquiry by the Okyenhene. This concluded that 'there was not a scintilla of evidence to prove any dishonest dealings in the Treasury.... Mr Otupiri's honour was thus vindicated.... Mr Ofori had carried out a most pernicious propaganda

36   *Ibid.*, p. 10.
37   AASA PF/20.
38   Otupiri had been seconded from the Colonial Administration to the Akim Abuakwa Native Administration in November 1940 to 'sort things out' in what was acknowledged to be a chaotic State Treasury.
39   Otupiri to J.B. Danquah 19:1:1944. AASA PF/20.

amongst the people especially some of the Elders. . . .[40] Apart from these intrigues by Mr Ofori he appears to have an exaggerated opinion of his ability . . . we do not need his vaunted talent in this Administration . . .'.[41] That Ofori was one of Akyea Mensah's brothers-in-law might tempt a reader to believe in some of the confidences the dead man was alleged to have shared with the author. But the history of his employment and the manner of his leaving it erodes his value as a dependable commentator on these matters.

The secret affairs to which Akyea Mensah was supposed to be privy centred around the late Nana Sir Ofori Atta's personal fortune and its origins in the dishonest handling of stool funds which were then used to advantage his kin. We have already seen that there was some substance to these suspicions. But at the heart of these allegations was the mystery of the trading concern Dua and Company. The Amantoo Mmiensa towns certainly believed that this firm's operations were the key to what was supposed to be the royal family's pork barrel. So frequently was this allegation hurled at the royal family that Danquah sought to rebut it in his unpublished letter to *The Times* in 1947. There certainly was such a company and its main trading store was in Akyem Abuakwa's main thoroughfare, to the right of the portals of Ofori Panin Fie. It was registered as a company in 1936. It was, in J.B. Danquah's words, 'established by the late Omanhene for his children'.[42]

Many rumours circulated about Nana Sir Ofori Atta's fortune in his lifetime; they continue to do so today. His lifestyle, as we have seen, suggested wealth beyond the dreams of the vast majority of his subjects. Rumour insisted that he had secretly left no less than £70,000[43] to his kin and that this had been channelled through the agency of Dua and Company. £70,000 was an extraordinarily large sum; for a variety of reasons an exact comparison of the purchasing power of a pound in the Gold Coast in 1943 with the present day is difficult to compute. But the fact that the Gold Coast's Puisne Judges earned less than £1,500 per annum and that the £70,000 exceeded the revenue and expenditure of a major town such as Kumase in 1943 gives some sense of its magnitude. Rumours are, however, by their very nature, subject to the exponential of hyperbole. When first looking into this case, such a set of allegations was immensely tempting, and became even more seductive as the State

40 This might be a reference to Amantoo Mmiensa elders.
41 Okyenhene to J.B. Danquah, 8 February 1944, AASA PF/14. Ofori was sacked on 1 February 1944, only weeks before the murder.
42 He describes the company on page 35 of the long unpublished letter he sent to *The Times* in July 1947.
43 This sum is repeated in the contemporary material and orally to this day. It was and is never qualified or expressed as an approximation. I cannot account for why this sum is so consistently presented.

Archives revealed the haphazard and, it must be admitted, somewhat devious nature of Ofori Atta I's personal finances.

Manifestly the royal family's argument, which is still repeated today, that Nana had left only £200, rings hollow. Between September 1944 and the final outcome of the case in mid-1947, the family supported a series of legal actions connected with the murder allegations which were conducted by a team of the highest-paid lawyers in the Gold Coast and expensive solicitors and counsel in London. Although it proves impossible accurately to cost these actions, there is no doubt that considerably more than £70,000 was spent on the defence and the subsequent appeals. This is a crude calculation based on the fact that in the 1930s the Kyebi stool spent at least £100,000 in its litigation against Asamankese and Akwatia.

Those earlier actions were sporadic and never involved the large numbers of lawyers who were to be deployed as the defence in the murder case. The costs of the cross-litigation in the Asamankese case were frequently aired at the time, and there was no denial that the total cost to all parties was not far short of £200,000. The raising of these huge sums of money in the mid-1940s remains a mystery, and mysteries invite rumour. Representation in the murder case was definitely not funded, as some of the royal family's detractors claimed, by the State Treasury. It was paid for by the private wealth of the family. Little of this was, it seems, formally 'banked' or invested, both of which processes would have left evidential traces. Some informants suggest that wealth was often hoarded in the time-honoured ways of many rural communities – under floors, in roof-spaces and in locked tin trunks. The Gold Coast had only just begun to suffer severe inflation, and such conservation of notes and coins and possibly gold and diamonds was cheaper than using the banking system.[44] What can be said however is that the evidence shows that Dua and Company was not the conduit for such funds.

Dua and Company was, in banal reality, something of a disaster. At its height at the end of the 1930s the company, described as 'General Importers' in the official records, had stores in Kyebi, Accra,[45] Suhum, Asamankese, Bawdua and Koforidua. But the record of its business life[46] suggests that it was virtually bankrupt for all of its existence. It was in spectacular debt for most of its recorded business career. That business was the importation and sale of a variety of mainly household goods. These goods were provided from Britain, wholesale, by Austin

44   The documentation retained in the Dabre of the royal palace might contain the answers to these questions.
45   On Knutsford Avenue.
46   Which is most clearly to be seen in AASA 5/77.

and Young, whose founder, Walter Austin, was, as we have seen, an intimate of Nana Sir Ofori Atta's and whose son Eric Austin handled the Dua and Company account. By the end of 1940 Eric Austin wrote to Okyenhene to explain that Dua and Co were indebted to Austin and Young to the tune of £5,723.[47] Nearly twenty percent of that sum seems to have been tied up in an item headed 'sundry debtors'. Virtually all of these debtors were family members who were permitted to buy goods on credit but who, in effect, seldom repaid these sums.

Dua's Managing Director, Ofori Atta I's son A.E.B. Danquah,[48] found it hard to resist such demands when they were made by kinsmen. Complaining about this to the Okyenhene on 20 August 1941 he wrote:

> ... K.T. Ampofo, at the time of his marriage asked me to place indent for two hand sewing machines for him.... He has failed to pay for the other one and the account standing in the books has given Mr Austin occasion to make certain remarks of which I feel despondingly shameful. He now demands immediate legal action to recover the amount. I therefore pass through you to demand Mr Ampofo to endeavour to redeem our good name which his action has ... threatened to soil.[49]

By 1942 Walter Austin complained to the Okyenhene that A.E.B. Danquah '... will sell goods to his brothers and sisters on a credit basis and the outcome will be that he will not always receive cash ... if they are unable to pay in cash then they must get your guarantee that you will pay for all goods supplied ...'.[50] In May 1942 Ofori Atta wrote reassuringly to Austin that: '... Things have changed and I think the credit system has come to an end ... everything will now be sold for cash.'[51]

But things continued to go badly for Dua and Company. The Suhum store was forced to close down and the balance sheet remained worryingly in the red. Eventually A.E.B. Danquah was to blame the complex wartime licensing regulations and the racialism of the customs service for preventing Dua and Company from bringing goods into the country

47 'Unless Dua can make substantial strides in the immediate future, I doubt our ability to continue on the present footing. After more than five years Dua should be showing signs of having built up a business. ... I fear that such signs are lacking.' Eric Austin to Okyenhene, 21 October 1940, AASA 5/77.
48 One of those convicted of murder.
49 AASA 5/77.
50 Walter Austin to Okyenhene, 18 March 1942, AASA 5/77. The letter continues, 'It is really distressing to me that Dankwa [sic] is such a fool as to advance money to people. ... Dankwa has made me despair many times and I only wish he had a little more business acumen.'
51 Okyenhene to Walter Austin, 4 May 1942, AASA 5/77.

and thus blocking the company's commercial recovery. Writing to his father he said: 'my failures will be due to the machinations of the very Europeans . . . because of your connections with the various Heads of Government Departments and their knowledge that I am your son, it would be better if I passed through you for the necessary connections and contacts to be made'.[52] This complaint led to a long letter's being sent by Okyenhene to the Customs Service on 5 September 1942. The Comptroller replied on 12 September pointing out that while Dua and Company continued to ship goods, they were doing so without having even having applied for, let alone having secured, import licences beforehand. As no application had been applied for, it followed that none could have been turned down.[53] There was little more that Okyenhene could do in this matter.

Whatever else, it is clear that Dua and Company was never the pork barrel and money-spinner which opponents of the royal family still claim it to have been. Certainly it gave some members of the royal family access to goods on credit and, in some cases, goods for free, for few of these debts were ever paid. But its accounts were relatively public accounts, and there is no evidence whatever of small, let alone large, sums of money being passed through it for the benefit of the young royals. It was simply an attempt by the Okyenhene to get his sons off to a flying start in trading, an attempt which failed. Above all there is no evidence whatever before the demise of the firm in 1945 that any sum of the size suggested by rumour ever entered its accounts. Yet this ramshackle little company was, and in some quarters still is, supposed to be the centre of Akyea Mensah's 'dangerous knowledge'. It seems very unlikely that he was killed to prevent his making this essentially sad little venture's affairs public.

The reasons for the selection of Akyea Mensah as a murder victim are more arcane and essentially much more interesting. To begin with no one in Akyem Abuakwa seriously denies the practice, in the past, of human sacrifice.[54] It was certainly an important aspect of Akan royal rituals.[55] But I had always assumed, on the basis of the ethnographic literature, that such a fate was 'traditionally' suffered by 'strangers', and most particularly criminals and slaves.[56] No one ever suggested

52   A.E.B. Danquah to Okyenhene, 15 May 1942, AASA 5/77.
53   AASA 5/77.
54   Some informants in Akyem Abuakwa, and Akyemfo living outside the area, said that it still happens, but some of this should certainly be read as teasing the credulous *oburoni* historian.
55   That is fully acknowledged by Danquah quoting Ofori Atta II: 'In ancient times we used to indulge in human sacrifice as part of our religious belief. . . .'; *Stalins in a Colony. A Letter to the Times*, p. 49.
56   For a recent exploration of this, see Akosua Perbi's 'The Abolition of Domestic Slavery by Britain: Asante's Dilemma', in *Legon Journal of the Humanities*, vol. 6,

that Akyea Mensah was of slave origin. But there is a particularity about Akyem Abuakwa's traditions of human sacrifice, and these seem to relate very directly to the circumstances of the murder in 1944.

Oral tradition, and written versions of oral tradition which date from as early as 1917, agree that in the past the Adikrofo of Apapam, Apedwa and Tetteh were collectively responsible for the furnishing of victims for sacrifice in the course of specified state ceremonials.[57] In some circumstances, one of the Adikrofo might offer himself or be required to offer himself personally for such sacrifice; a much celebrated case of this occurred in the reign of Queen Afua Dokua,[58] when the Odikro of Apapam 'gave himself' for sacrifice in an act of supreme courage which was rewarded by the subsequent primacy of Apapam amongst the Amantoo Mmiensa towns.

These roles are confirmed and further specified in the work of Fraser Ofori Atta.[59] But he apparently forgets the famous case in Queen Dokua's reign when he argues that this 'horrific ancient custom was abandoned since the time of Nana Asare Bediako Okyenhene in 1811'.[60] In the course of his thesis he makes far more specific the role of Apedwa and the Odikro of Apedwa in particular in these matters. He reminds his readers that the name of Apedwa[61] invokes its traditional role in sacrifice. Its Odikro, he writes, or 'nine people provided by him in his capacity as the Wirempehene were done to death during the funeral rites of an Okyenhene'.[62]

1992. But part of the ritual observed by royal widows mentioned above suggests that once they were expected to join their dead husbands.

57 See the report on the unsolved disappearance of two 'Hausa' traders on the Apedwa–Kyebi road in 1917, NAG ADM 32/4/100. This clearly draws on contemporary oral tradition in this very restricted geographical region of Akyem Abuakwa.

58 1817–35.

59 Fraser Ofori Atta, *op. cit.*, appendix 5B. He says that his sources were largely those of the many strands which comprise 'tradition' in Akyem Abuakwa. There is no evidence that he looked at the 1917 investigation in NAG ADM 32/4/100: his work is footnoted throughout with admirable scholarly rigour and there is no suggestion that those files were consulted. Consequently the 1917 evidence and that collected by Ofori Atta in the 1970s might be seen as corroborative.

60 Almost all Akans writing about human sacrifice insist on a nineteenth-century termination of such practices. The importance of the permeation of Christian ideas in constructing these accounts must be acknowledged.

61 Literally 'find sheep' in Twi. Sheep are frequently sacrificed in the course of ritual; tribunal fines and conciliation fees are often paid in sheep. Some suggest that sheep were gradually substituted for human beings in the course of the nineteenth century in rituals once involving human sacrifice.

62 Fraser Ofori Atta goes on to say, 'It appears probable that it was that obsolete and abandoned custom which, I guess, led people into believing the otherwise sensational but fabricated story of the so-called Kyebi ritual murder of 1943 [sic].'

Fraser Ofori Atta's account is based upon intense consultation with the conservators of the various strands of Akyem Abuakwa's traditions – drummers, horn-blowers, stool carriers. It is striking that his treatment of the murder case is underlined by a denial. As a son of the stool closely related to some of those convicted for the murder, this is hardly surprising. But as an historian, his fascination with the threads of the past appears to push aside elements of the royal family's case. In the quotation above he implictly questions a key aspect of the defence case. Even if one accepts his insistence that human sacrifice had ended in 1811, he does cite human sacrifice *within* the funeral process for the dead king, a conjuncture which was hotly denied during the trial.

He moreover specifically ties in the functions of Wirempe, a major function of the Amantoo Mmiensa, with human sacrifice. The timing of the murder and the involvement of the Odikro of Apedwa, albeit as victim, becomes less obviously 'against tradition', despite the defence's strong insistence that this was so during the murder trial. Fraser Ofori Atta's recent conclusion chimes in with further and older evidence of a connection between Wirempe and human sacrifice in the past at least. In 1914 the *Akuapemhene* sought government support for the suppression of the Wirempe custom. 'Wirempi is', he wrote, 'a Twi custom inseparably connected with the funeral of native potentates and members of their families. It consists in the seizing by the subjects of a deceased Chief of anything they come across including, in former times, bodies of persons who were usually sacrificed. . . .' Opposing Akuapemhene's proposal, Nana Ofori Atta I agreed that there was such an historical linkage but wrote: '. . . it is only proper to discard altogether from consideration the recollection of human sacrifices which the decease of a Native Chief, in the very old ancient times, entailed.'[63]

It must be made clear that no unequivocal evidence can be offered to support the suggestion that is being implicitly made here. Nor is there any evidence for any other explanation of Akyea Mensah's death or disappearance. To recapitulate, there is no evidence whatever which supports the suicide allegation. Nor do I believe that it was possible in the particular circumstances for Akyea Mensah simply to disappear into undemanding anonymity. There is no better evidence which supports the idea that Akyea Mensah was killed to keep him silent. He certainly knew a great deal about Akyem Abuakwa stool affairs, but so did many others. There is no evidence to suggest that he was a potential reformer whose zeal had to be prevented. The evidence suggests that he was well and happily integrated within the palace and with the royal family.

But his disappearance and, it seems, murder in the particular circumstances of Kyebi in the midst of the anguish of *ayie*, the last rites of

63   Ofori Atta to the DC Kibbi, 27 October 1914, NAG ADM 11/1/564.

Nana Sir Ofori Atta, coupled with the specific historical background of the office he held, is at least suggestively coincidental. That is reinforced to some extent by the presence amongst the accused of the Abontendomhene, Asare Apietu. As Danquah himself wrote in his unpublished letter to *The Times*, Asare Apietu was 'the high pontiff of the Chair House.[64] In ancient times no executions for sacrifice could be made without his sanction. . . .'[65] He is also remembered as a harsh tradionalist. One distinguished member of the royal family recalled him as 'a primitive, savage man; a man of the old times'.[66] Tying in the remaining accused men is more problematic, beyond the obvious observation of their close relationship to the late Okyenhene. For example, Opoku Afwenee's mother came from Nkronso, a village whose traditional obligations include the maintenance and repair of the royal mausoleum or Bamu, behind which the remains were alleged to have been briefly interred; on its own, that connection tells us nothing. The Native Administration Police Inspector Amoako Atta had a previous record for violence in a case brought before the Okyenhene concerning what was essentially rape of a young girl. While Ofori Atta I accepted his kinsman's version of events, a local tribunal at Achiasi, where the event took place, found him guilty.[67] But this is at best contextual and provides only thin circumstantial evidence of mood and motivation.

There is understandably serious ambivalence about the events in Akyem Abuakwa today. While some members of the royal family and people close to the palace feel significantly distant from the events to be able to agree that Akyea Mensah was murdered and probably by those indicted, there are those who deny it. But even informants who agreed that the Odikro was killed were of little assistance when I sought a motive for the murder.

On the basis of so little information about motive it is hard to reconstruct the feelings of eight accused individuals. What certainly united them was profound grief. In the particular way in which the Akan express the death of a king, Ofori Atta's death was the felling of a very great tree. The shade he had provided during the thirty years of his reign had undoubtedly sheltered all eight of the accused in relative comfort. Some of them, and especially his sons, must have felt great grief at the loss of a man who was, as we have seen, a warm if

64 Stool House.
65 *Op. cit.*, p. 37.
66 G. Ofori-Boakye, a nephew of J.B. Danquah, interviewed in Accra in July 1991.
67 The facts are hard to recapture, and the exoneration of the young man by his father/Okyenhene is muddied by the fact that Amoako Atta apologised to the girl's father in public. It is rendered even more tragic by the fact that the girl tried to commit suicide by drinking Lysol; see AASA 2/94.

demanding father. The other five, all kinsmen, must also have felt this loss, albeit in slightly different ways. Ofori Atta's death was literally devastating, and left a hole in the state as well as more specifically in Kyebi, the palace and the family.

But by the time the murder took place, a new Okyenhene was on the stool. While he too was a kinsman, did the eight feel insecure? Were they worried lest the considerable patronage that each of them had undoubtedly enjoyed from the dead king would dry up? Did Ofori Atta II have his own clients who would in time supplant these men? After all, each of them filled a post, traditional or modern, which lay in the gift of the Okyenhene. Moreover the encroaching formal bureaucratisation of the Akyem Abuakwa state, and especially the growing formalization of the State Treasury, exposed such recipients of favours to the threatening rigours of audit and inspection.

Such apprehensions might have served to exacerbate the profound sense of loss which I believe lay behind their violent act. But the materialist cast of this reasoning explains little beyond a state of mind. While seven of them regarded themselves as Christian, all of them are remembered as 'traditionalists', and some informants suggested that they collectively felt that the passing of a great king, a very great king, was being insufficiently commemorated. That Ofori Atta was recognised in palace circles as the greatest king since Ofori Panin, the founder of the state, is clear. But he was destined to join his ancestors accompanied by rituals which fell far short of those which had signified this transition for previous kings who were of much slighter status than Ofori Atta I. That is largely explained by the fact that the Okyeman Council had passed a bye-law which restricted funeral expenses to £500 for the paramount.[68]

His stool, possibly the first to be blackened in the twentieth century, was to join the others in the Stool House after a ritual cleansing which fell short of that used on the stools of predecessors. One informant suggested that the murder occurred because 'they did not want to let him [Ofori Atta I] down. They were frightened of his anger'. While it can only be surmise, this explanation is at least plausible. Eight insecure, grief-stricken men combined in an act which they felt to be appropriate to this staggering recent loss. By that act they would additionally protect themselves from the late king's ancestral wrath at being ill-served in death.

The fact that there was controversy about the 'traditional' rectitude of such an act at such a time suggests confusion and despair. This is

68   The Akyem Abuakwa Funeral Custom bye law, 1942. Wartime economies and austerity also helped make the funeral less lavish than it would have been twenty years earlier.

further suggested by the presumption that they had some, arguably naive, expectation that the act might remain undiscovered. There is no evidence which suggests animus between Akyea Mensah and his executioners. On the contrary, if the accounts are correct, he was content to join them for a drink in the palace in the moments before his death. If that is so why did his knowledge of the possibly life-threatening implications of being Odikro of Apedwa not make him very cautious indeed? Informants in Apedwa say that he was very careful in Kyebi at this time. Was he not accompanied by two retainers into the palace, who stayed with him until he reached the gateway of the courtyard in which he died? Why was he not worried about the intentions of the eight mourning Ahenemmaa? Again informants suggest that these were men he knew well and who, with the exception of the Abontendomhene, were, like Akyea Mensah, 'modern' men, Christian men. An Inspector of the Native Authority Police, a businessman, a freemason and an ex-Sergeant in the Royal West African Frontier Force were not the kind of people one would anticipate as one's executioners, they argue. But we can never know all the answers to such questions.

There is moreover no evidence which suggests that it was an act designed to intimidate the Amantoo Mmiensa, who had certainly been a thorn in the late Okyenhene's side earlier in his reign. If intimidation was the motive then they must have expected that the act would have been discovered, or at least widely talked about, and there is no evidence which suggests that this was the case. We are left with a explanation of grief and uncertainty, coupled with a sense of traditionally unfinished business leading up to this tragedy. While it is even more un-knowable, our knowledge of Nana Sir Ofori Atta I suggests that his shade was unlikely to have welcomed this valedictory act[69] and what followed it. His spirit would have been even more distressed as it watched the wretched consequences of the act undoing so much of creative state-building and family enhancement to which he had devoted his life.

69 For obvious reasons I am entirely sceptical about the idea that Ofori Atta I's ghost 'is supposed to have sent a message back to his family saying: "You have despatched me in the other world with some very inferior people – not my class or type. Send some one worthy of me...."' *Gold Coast Observer*, 21 March 1947.

CHAPTER NINE

The Aftermath

The awful finality of the hangings should have ended this dreadful, damaging sequence of events. But in Akyem Abuakwa, in Accra and in London this was not to be the case. The Amantoo Mmiensa felt unrevenged. They had worked themselves up into a mood of righteous indignation from which it was increasingly difficult to return. They had come together as never before over this case and were now formally organised, with a full-time secretary and a president. Throughout these events they held regular weekly meetings.[1] It was this new organisation which drafted an indignant petition to the Governor.[2] But this bureaucracy did more than drafting. In the course of a series of 'conferences' in October and November 1946, the young men were advised to have their firearms in readiness.[3] There were, the DC alleged, Amantoo Mmiensa plans to attack Kyebi by night from the Apedwa hills, although he sensed that tempers had cooled as the legal processes consistently favoured 'their interests'.[4]

The period of calm was shortlived. The death in Korle Bu hospital of Abontendomhene Asare Apietu in November 1946 further heightened passions. The news of the death quickly became known, as did the intention of the royal family to have his corpse brought back to Kyebi for burial. A small party of royal women went to Accra to wash the body according to ritual. William Ofori Atta headed a group of male royals, including Aaron Ofori Atta, to buy the coffin and to deal with the arrangements for transport back to Kyebi. The mourning party

1 *Quarterly Report*, Birim District, 31 December 1947, NAG ADM 32/1/136.
2 *The Humble Petition of the Amantoommiensa Council of Akim Abuakwa*, 6 September 1946. The DC, D.S.D. McWilliam, described it, off-handedly, as 'somewhat meaningless'. Quarterly Report, Birim District, 30 September 1946, NAG ADM 32/1/137.
3 *Quarterly Report*, Birim District, 9 January 1947, NAG ADM 32/1/136. 'Firearms' meant smooth-bored muzzle-loaders called 'Dane guns' since the coastal trade in weapons in the eighteenth and nineteenth centuries. Many were locally made, and legally owned if licensed with the district headquarters. Annual returns for licences and for the purchase of 'black powder' show that many thousand hunting guns were owned in the region. Guns also perform a social role and can be seen – and heard – at funerals and seasonal festivals.
4 *Ibid.*

which was to accompany the body were as apprehensive about the possibility of an Amantoo Mmiensa attack as were the police.[5]

By 29 November, Amantoo Mmiensa elders were at the District Comissioner's office demanding to be told what was intended and stressing that if the body returned to Kyebi a riot would occur. The Mankrado[6] of Apedwa and the Odikro of Tetteh ordered a band of young men to picket the crossroads at Apedwa to prevent the return of the body. The Inspector of Police at Suhum accordingly diverted the lorry through Mangoase, along the Koforidual–Tafo road through Tetteh to Kyebi. The DC reported that between one and two hundred men had to be turned back from the crossroads, a precaution he believed prevented further violence.

It was a nightmare journey. Fearing disorder the DC had also banned the local sale of liquor, drumming and the firing of guns, and had asked the Okyenhene to bury the body immediately.[7] The circuitous route and the other precautions were read as yet another insult to the royal family. J.B. Danquah fired off an angry letter to the Chief Commissioner:

> ... You will ... agree that for the traditionally law-abiding and loyal house of Akyem Abuakwa to be subjected to such indignities must be cause for much sorrow to the members and people of the State. For nearly three years we have been compelled to suffer these indignities ... how gravely we have been misjudged ... I realise ... that the baseless ... accusations against the sons of the Stool as having killed Akyea Mensah is at the bottom of the continuous persecution ... anything proceeding from any one from the Kyebi Ahenfie ... is treated with scant respect and credence.[8]

The Abontendomhene was buried on 30 November in Kyebi.[9] The ceremony was a royal funeral, but lower-key than his birth and status would normally have demanded; nothing can be deduced from this. Okyenhene was desperate to do nothing to inflame local feelings; it cannot be assumed that this funeral reflected any kind of judgement on the worthiness of the deceased.[10]

---

5 AASA 3/297. Report by William Ofori Atta to the Okyenhene on his mission to Accra, 5 December 1946.
6 The 'second-in-command' to the Odikro, and in his absence, acting Odikro.
7 AASA 3/297.
8 8 December 1946, AASA 3/297.
9 *Quarterly Report*, Birim District, 9 January 1947, NAG ADM 32/4/100.
10 I was unable to recover memories of the burials of those hanged. All the record allows is the Okyeman Council's telling the District Commissioner on 20 January 1948, 'Their relations ... have performed funeral custom for them which was quite proper'; AASA 3/297.

The greater matter remained live, and the subject of major contention within Akyem Abuakwa. On 26 May 1947 the much disputed remains of Akyea Mensah were returned to Apedwa to be interred. *The Ashanti Pioneer*'s account of the event evokes the atmosphere of heightened emotion and considerable tension:

> ... Akyea Mensah ... interred amidst deep inexpressible sorrow. Promptly at 9 am the Police lorry arrived from Accra with the ... remains and handed them over to Nana Boakye Yiadom, Mankrado of Apedwa. A pathetic atmosphere at once shrouded all hearts; all here – citizens, denizens and strangers alike burst into spontaneous tears. After certain customary performances the remains were laid in state in a beautiful coffin befitting the dignity of a Gold Coast Chief. The various singing bands from the neighbouring towns joined those here to render doleful songs and hymns. The schools in town which have lost a great education enthusiast demonstrated their love and grief by wearing black ribbons – both pupils and teachers and sang mournful hymns. The Amantoommiensa who were fully represented performed their respective customary rites. Volleys upon volleys of gunfire and dolorous drumming filled the solemn air. British sense of orderliness [a reference perhaps to the contingent of escort police who were on hand in case of trouble] and deep patience of the citizens prevented any unbecoming demonstration. The remains were peacefully laid to rest in a well cemented tomb in an open place on the southern end of town, a few yards away from the market on the Apedwa–Suhum road. It is learnt that a historic monument will be later erected to his memory.[11]

Things were not to rest here. On 10 June, the Amantoo Mmiensa Council sent a petition to the Okyeman Council. The petition again rehearsed the case and stressed that the dead Odikro had been a loyal servant of the paramount stool, that he died at the hands of kinsmen of the Okyenhene and, worst of all, whilst a guest of the royal family. It demanded financial restitution in the form of a single payment of £5,000. Such compensation was required because the Odikro's family had lost

---

11   30 May 1947. The burial did not satisfy all the family. In 1950 one of Akyea Mensah's sons, E.H. Ohemeng, wrote to the Okyenhene complaining that his father's tomb had not been properly cemented: E.H. Ohemeng to Okyenhene, 3 August 1950, AASA 8/48. Akyea Mensah's final funeral rites were not carried out until 1988. People in Amantoo Mmiensa towns insist that the Okyeman Council paid for the funeral expenses and claim that this amounts to a final admission of guilt. The royal family deny that this happened. Without any documentary proof the matter remains open.

... their strongest prop. The people of Apedwa have been robbed of an enlightened and loyal Chief in the prime of life. The Amantoomiensa Council have lost the Head of their Second County and the most senior educated chief on the council. Innocent Odikro Akyea Mensah has been forced all of a sudden to part company with, and so left unprovided for, his wives and children.

Further expenses had been incurred because important documents, including plans for a senior School in Apedwa, which had been drawn up by Akyea Mensah could not be found and had to be re-drafted. The Amantoo Mmiensa had, moreover, to bear the expense of searching for the missing Odikro; in addition many Amantoo Mmiensa Elders had pledged their cocoa farms to meet the costs of

1) the formal customary interment ... 2) The performance of funeral obsequies ... 3) the election and installation of new chief, 4) reimbursements of various sums of money borrowed to pay huge debts necessitated by this protracted case which debts were solely borne by the relatives of the late Odikro ... and the Amantoommiensa Council with great suffering. That for the promotion of peace and harmony and maintainence of cooperation and goodwill among all sections of the community, your humble petitioners deem it absolutely necessary that some compensation should be given us to redeem our farms and to pay off the debts. ...[12]

This demand fell within the 'normal run' of reparatory claims in Akan societies, although its scale was exceptional. It was widely agreed that compensation should be paid by perpetrators to victims and, in the case of death, to victims' surviving close kin. This claim was considered by the Okyeman Council and by 3 July 1947 they replied to the Amantoo Mmiensa. The claim was rejected in short, and peremptory, order. As the expenses for funerals of all Adikrofo had been limited by Akyem state bye-laws to an outlay not exceeding £25, the sum asked for was, they said, manifestly excessive; more extensive expenditure, of the sort the petition said had been spent, was illegal under this sumptuary law. So far as the election and installation of a new chief was concerned, the Okyeman pointed out that Apedwa was in the Benkum Division and '... neither the Benkumhene nor the Okyenhene was ever notified at any stage that a new chief was being elected or installed for Apedwa'. Their dispute with the fourth ground for damages was more contentious. The Okyenhene asked the petitioners to recall that the Council had decided at the inception of the case that 'the State was not to take part or sides. ... The cost of the Defence was therefore borne entirely by the accused persons. . . . At no stage did the Amantoomiensa appear as a party to the proceedings and the claim . . . is therefore rejected. . . .'[13]

This was less than a straight answer, although the demand was no more righteous. While the State may have sought to distance itself publicly from the case,[14] the Okyeman Council could not so neatly gloss over the obviously close relationship between the Okyenhene, his immediate family and the Okyeman Council itself. The fiscal basis of the State and kingship itself were, as we have seen, closely intertwined. It was disingenuous to claim that the funding of the defence case, which ran into hundreds of thousands of pounds, was met solely by the defendants' funds;[15] or rather, if such expenses were met by family funds, how certain could any Akyem citizen be about where family coffers ended and those of the State began? From the point of view of the elders of the Amantoo Mmiensa and many of their townspeople, the murderers were only the tip of the iceberg. The blame lay within the palace, with the living rulers of Akyem Abuakwa and not merely with the seven remaining condemned men.[16]

It seems clear that this apparently solid wall of Okyeman opposition to the Amantoo Mmiensa was more fragile than it seemed. The Amantoo Mmiensa continued to defy the Okyenhene and his State Council. The Akyem Abuakwa state's Gyaasehene resigned in 1947. Several informants suggested that this was in protest against the paramount's policy over the case but the ostensible reason was the charge of financial peculation that had been levelled against him by members of his *oman*. In June 1948 the Adontenhene was destooled, a devastating loss for the Okyenhene.[17] There were also signs of dissent amongst and against

---

13 Okyeman Council *Minutes*, 1 July 1947, AASA 8.2/42. The full text was also published by *The Ashanti Pioneer* on 3 July 1947.
14 'Not a penny from the State Treasury was voted or spent to assist or aid the eight men. . . .', Okyeman insisted in a letter to the District Commissioner on 20 January 1948, AASA 3/297. The available record suggests that this was so, although it is true that all the accused men remained on half-pay from the Native Authority or the Palace during the entirety of the proceedings.
15 The answers to this question probably lie in the un-released documentary material remaining in the Okyenhene's Dabre. At the same time the stool remained parsimonious in the extreme; for example J.B. Danquah not unreasonably asked Okyeman for an increase in his annual retainer on 26 January 1945. They had paid him £72 in 1944 and he now requested £250. They granted him an additional £50 'on the understanding that he is not entitled to consultation fee in respect of cases involving Stools in Akyem Abuakwa'. AASA 8/37. This was certainly legal advice on the cheap.
16 An aspersion still voiced today.
17 He had 'lost the Gyashene and Adontenhene who were the two principle advisers of . . . Sir Ofori Atta in purely Akim Abuakwa affairs and he is also left without a single literate Divisional [Wing] Chief who can deputise for him at

other Kyebi elders.[18] More obviously, there were attempts to destool both the Nifahene and Adontenhene of Akyem Abuakwa at the begining of 1947.[19]

There is no doubt that the confident *elan* of the Okyeman Council of the days of Ofori Atta I had gone, to be replaced by a more uncertain mood. The minutes of that Council are less full than they were; debate was less assured, less magisterial, perhaps because it was less structured by the guiding hand of a confident Okyenhene. Even more revealing was the frequent attendance, by invitation, of the District Commissioner at Okyeman meetings throughout 1947, a development which would not have occurred under Ofori Atta I. Other states with whom Akyem Abuakwa was in contention sensed the weakness in Kyebi. The Omanhene of Akuapem and the Konor of Manya Krobo both sought to revive their claims to superior jurisdiction over Akuapems and Krobos living in Akyem Abuakwa in 1946.[20]

Not all of this is explained by the tensions unleashed by the old king's death and then the murder. Akyem Abuakwa was now in poor shape economically. The incurable cocoa disease, swollen shoot, had been especially virulent in the area. By the end of the 1945 harvesting season it was estimated that about a hundred square miles of 'the best cocoa has been devastated and the life of Suhum as a cocoa centre threatened. In addition there is a threat on both flanks of the Atewa Range towards Asamankese and the Central Province on the south and through Osino (largely wiped out) towards Kwahu on [sic] the north...'.[21] The area had recently endured severe food shortages 'resulting from the increasing needs of Accra and the large towns.

meetings such as the Joint Provincial Council'; *District Record Book*, 30 June 1948, NAG ADM 32/4/100.

18 *Kibi District Record Books* of December 1945 and March 1948, NAG ADM 32/4/100. Close reading of the entire run of District Record Books suggests that the Okyenhene was also losing supporters amongst farmers and members of the newly founded United Gold Coast Convention.

19 So volatile had things become, that public meetings were banned in Kukurantumi, Osiem, Old Tafo, New Tafo, Ehokrone, Asiakwa, Maase and Anyinasin. Some of this volatility must certainly have been the result of the 'bigger' events in Ghana's history, and most notably the pivotal riots of February and early March 1948 in the bigger towns but not in Kyebi.

20 *District Record Book*, Birim District, 16 July 1946 and 31 March 1947, NAG 32/4/100. By 1946 Akuapemhene went as far to suggest the creation of a tribunal under his jurisdiction in Suhum, which has a large Akuapem population. An entry in the second of these sources by the DC suggests that 'for the present the Paramount Stool has lost face in the State and there is evidence to prove the unpopularity of the Omanhene and his immediate advisers in Kibi...'.

21 *Notes for Birim District*, 30 September 1945, NAG 32/1/119.

Prices . . . soared to an unprecedented level. . . .'[22] The area's plight was worsened by the persistence of drought. Reporting on the financial year 1946–7, the Agricultural Department noted that the colony had endured the fourth year in succession in which rainfall was well below the ten-year mean. This and more localised sources report drought 'such as has not before appeared in our records'.[23] These dry conditions were favourable to the vector of the swollen shoot virus, the amiably named but deeply threatening mealie-bug. In part this explains the edginess of farmers, some of whom were faced with imminent ruin. Undoubtedly these conditions contributed to a sense of decline and disorder since the old king's death.

Lastly some of the key organs of the Akyem Abuakwa state showed signs of atrophy. The Native Authority Police[24] were finding it hard to recruit suitable trainees.[25] More significantly, the management of the Akyem Abuakwa State Treasury began to fall apart. At the end of the financial year 1944–5, the DC reported that it had had 'a very disappointing year, the second in succession, so that the great promise shown in previous years has not materialised'.[26] There is evidence of conflict amongst Okyeman Councillors on financial matters. The weakness of the Treasury led to a proposal that wing-chiefs and palace notables should accept a reduction in salary.[27] The ensuing row led to the resignation of the Treasurer, William Ofori Atta, of whom the DC wrote, 'The treasury is greatly handicapped by having a highly qualified Treasurer who is not interested in his work and who spends the greater part of his time dealing with matters which do not really concern him. . . .'[28] A divisive stand-off between him and his uncle J.B. Danquah, who led the opposition to the salary cut, ensued. He was relieved of his duties as State Treasurer by the Okyenhene and appointed Principal of the Akyem Abuakwa State College in September 1947. This issue also created a serious division between Okyeman and the Kyebi Executive Council, resulting in the uncomfortable necessity of

22   *Ibid.*
23   *Report* of the Agriculture Department, 1946–7, NAG ADM 5/232.
24   Whose Inspector was one of those condemned for Akyea Mensah's murder.
25   *District Record Book*, Birim District, 16 July 1946.
26   *Quarterly Report*, Birim District, 31 March 1945, NAG ADM 321/1.119. The DC, R. Walker, commented that 'This is in very considerable extent due to the disrupting influence of the late Omanhene's death and . . . the regrettable Apedwa case which has set the State back many years. . . .'
27   Administrative costs and particularly wages and salaries accounted for little short of fifty percent of the State Treasury's expenditure.
28   W. Brian Smith in *District Record Book*, Kyebi, 30 June 1947, NAG 32/4/100. The 'matters' were of course nationalist politics. Willie Ofori Atta was one of the founders of the United Gold Coast Convention, which was launched two months after this comment was made.

the Okyenhene's making a ruling on behalf of the Kyebi Council, the vast majority of whom were his kinsmen, against his State Council.[29]

The crisis in the State Treasury led to the appointment by Okyeman of a committee to balance the books.[30] The DC's analysis of this situation was not the only possible reading. J.B. Danquah regarded it as further evidence of colonial pressure on the state. In a letter to the Okyenhene on 18 July 1947 he wrote: '. . . As you are aware the Government has been seeking for a long time to have an excuse to seize the Akim Abuakwa treasury. . . . During the progress of the Kibi case they tried in many ways to find an excuse for saying that the money for the defence had been obtained by the N.A. Treasury. You will remember yourself that Mr McWilliams stated that it would be better for the Akim Abuakwa Treasury to be under a white man as it was a big treasury!' Danquah went on to suggest that Okyenhene and Okyeman had been inept in not denouncing clear malpractices to the DC; that ommission had left it open for the DC to intervene and accuse the Okyenhene of being soft on irregularities.[31]

The new Treasury Committee recommended an increase in the local rate to bail out the Treasury; this was resisted by Okyeman fearful that a rate hike in the midst of economic decline and political volatility might prove fatal. By mid-1948 the State Treasury's books were in such disorder that the District Commissioner threatened to withold the government grant to the Treasury if things did not improve.[32] An impasse was reached when the Chief Commissioner refused to approve the estimates because of 'various irregularities and the chaotic state of certain accounts'.[33] By 19 October 1948 matters had become so threatening that the Okyeman elected the newly enstooled Adontenhene[34] rather than the Okyenhene as Chairman of the State's Financial Committee. The DC recorded that 'the Omanhene is not happy over his removal from office'.[35] Although matters improved somewhat, irregularities continued to emerge. The Audit Report of July 1949 found further irregularities, and successful criminal proceedings were instituted against the state's Assistant Treasurer and two senior clerks.[36]

29   *Quarterly Report*, Kyebi District, 9 October 1945.
30   AASA 3/40.
31   *Ibid.*
32   He did so, he said, after unearthing 'a grossly irregular payment of £1,240 which had been concealed as an entry under Revenue entitled "Return of book sales by Central [sic] . . .".' *District Record Book*, 30 June 1948, NAG ADM 32/4/100.
33   *District Record Book*, Kyebi District, 30 September 1948.
34   The very able A.O. Forster, previously Chief Registrar of Akyem Abuakwa. He adopted the stool name of Kwabena Kema II.
35   *District Record Book*, Kyebi District, NAG ADM 32/4/100.
36   *District Record Book*, Kyebi District, 31 July 1948, NAG ADM 32/4/100.

While much of this is detail, the toils of the Treasury were a further example of the ways in which everything seemed to be coming apart at the seams after the death of the late king.

What is more difficult to reconstruct is the morale, for lack of a better word, of the royal family at this time. They had suffered very much more than the formal indignities referred to by Danquah in his letter to the Chief Commissioner. Their personal and deep distress was made the more bitter by the colonial authorities' cold resolve.[37] One of the more dreadful relics of the whole grisly business is a series of letters on official paper from the condemned men to the Okyenhene. For some of these men these letters were their last written communications with the living. Their letters tell us that, at least initially,[38] they were regularly visited by members of the royal family within the limits of the regulations. They also indicate that all of them continued to insist on their innocence. Most of them appear to have become intensely religious, 'born again', in prison.[39] One of the most profoundly poignant of these letters was written in Opoku Afwenee's hand on behalf of Pipim, Kagya, Amoako Atta and A.E.B. Danquah on 24 March 1947, on the eve of what they had every reason to believe was their last day of life. Like most historians I have read many documents which have moved me deeply. Reading these letters, and perhaps this one most of all, was almost too much to bear. To understand both the anguish of the prisoners, and the agony of the royal family, it is worth repeating this in full:

> Our dear and illustrious Nana,
> In the name of God Almighty we thank you most heartily for all what you have done for us in this case.
> We are leaving this material and wild world this morning as innocent

37 Occasioned almost certainly by the widespread official belief that the new Okyenhene had been involved in some fashion with the murder.

38 Contact with the four gaoled men tailed off. In April 1949 Amoako Atta wrote to the Okyenhene, '... As matter of fact ... we have not been hearing from home for a very considerable time. ...' (AASA 10/236), a complaint that still rankles with the sole survivor of the eight accused.

39 Kwadjo Amoako Atta writing from James Fort Prison (19 January 1947) to the Okyenhene complained: 'When you last visited me I requested you to send me one Twi Bible and hymn book but up to the time of writing this letter I have not received them. ... I thank you very much for the visit. ... It assures me of your love towards me and therefore gives me much comfort. ...' Opoku Afwenee in a letter to the Okyenhene on 19 April 1949 thanking him for the gift of a Bible wrote: 'God is the greatest power. He is so merciful that He will not cast away anyone who calls on Him in time of need. ... The Lord is doing wonderful work in our small Assembly here in prison. I am referring to the Apostolic Assembly. ...' (AASA 3/297).

men. We will not be unconscious and we will ever remember the brave stand which you took on our part in fighting for our just cause. May God bless you. We have nothing to say at present than to commend you unto the hand of the Almighty and merciful Father who will keep and guide you against all odds. Again we thank you very sincerely and goodbye to you, Elders and Councillors.

> Till we meet again in Heaven,
> Cheerio Nana.[40]

It would take a very dispassionate reader to fail to find the insouciance of the final 'Cheerio' almost unendurably sad.

In this atmosphere of gloom and tragedy which haunted the palace, the Okyeman Council rejected the Amantoo Mmiensa's petition denying responsibility for what they called 'the alleged murder' and its repercussions. But Okyeman continued by not merely rejecting the Amantoo Mmiensa's claims but also by sternly upbraiding them: 'I am to remind you', wrote the Council's Secretary, K.T.A. Danquah,

> of the open hostility of the Amantoomiensa to certain members of the State Council, as an instance the recent unprovoked attack on the Adontenhene by certain elements at Tetteh and of the long and continued absence of the Amantoomiensa from the Council of State. For three years you have refused to take part in the administration of the State and to perform your customary duties. I am directed to invite you to appear before Okyeman and take immediate steps to bring an end to your present hostile attitude to the constituted authority in the state.[41]

There is no doubt that very serious tension reigned in and around Kyebi.[42] It was a period of considerable inter-personal violence and intimidation, only a proportion of which ever reached either the colonial or the Native Authority courts. There is strong evidence which suggests that both sides contributed their fair measure. The royal family 'leant on' witnesses and potential witnesses both before and after the murder trial.[43] Amantoo Mmiensa violence was no less obvious. Senior chiefs

---

40 Condemned men to Okyenhene, 24 March 1947, from Ussher Fort Prison, Accra, AASA 3/297.
41 *The Ashanti Pioneer*, 3 July 1947.
42 By definition the Amantoo Mmiensa towns are physically very close to Kyebi and dominate the roads and hence travellers going to and from the capital.
43 See e.g. the testimony of Kate Eshun at the trial on 24 November 1944, NAG SCT 2/80, p. 236. See also the case against Ernest Prempeh and others (amongst whom was another of Ofori Atta's sons, Eric), Kumasi Assizes, 29 December 1944. At this hearing and in the subsequent unsuccessful appeals, the courts heard good evidence that the accused had tried to persuade others to give perjured evidence that Akyea Mensah was still alive. One Crown witness,

were assaulted.[44] In May 1948 Amantoo Mmiensa youngmen armed with cudgels planned to ambush the Okyenhene on his way to the Empire Day ceremonies but were disarmed by the police and sent home.[45] In an even uglier case, some youths from three Amantoo Mmiensa towns[46] used the conflict as an excuse to abduct some Kyebi women to Apapam where, some while later, they were raped. The police were never able to assemble enough evidence to proceed to charge any offenders for this.[47] People living in Amantoo Mmiensa towns who had remained loyal to Kyebi were literally hounded out.[48] By April 1948 Okyeman claimed that there were at least fifty such refugees forced to live in Kyebi for their personal safety.[49] By October 1948 the new DC, Duncan, was impelled to write to the Adikrofo of Ahwenease, Adadientem and Apapam that: 'I . . . remind you that no party has any legal right to force any person to change his or her place of abode because of his or her interests or alternatively his or her lack of interest in a political dispute.'[50]

The final executions failed to satisfy the Amantoo Mmiensa's sense of outrage and perceived need for revenge. While the visible parts of Gold Coast public opinion seemed content with Burns' Solomonic judgement to mix executions with reprieves, the Amantoo Mmiensa felt they had been denied justice by an act of unwarranted clemency. In an angry telegram to Creech Jones, the Amantoo Mmiensa pointed out that the accused's 'mental agony' had been stated by Burns as a reason for mercy in his speech to Legislative Assembly.

> What mental agonies did Chief Akyea Mensah not suffer as for hours on end the murderers' cold dagger gagged him alive while his innocent blood gushed profusely on that wretched stool. . . . Psychologically these condemned murderers have no human feelings and

Osei Tawiah, was assaulted, arrested and denied bail by the Kyebi Native Authority Police in May 1945; DC to Okyenhene, 29 May 1945, AASA 10/248.

44　Including the very senior figure of the Adontenhene. See his anguished telegram to the Okyenhene about the stoning of his car on 26 March 1947, AASA 3/297.

45　*District Record Book*, 30 June 1948, NAG 32/4/100.

46　Apapam, Adadientem and Ahwenease.

47　*District Record Book*, Kyebi District, 30 September 1948.

48　Interestingly Apedwa seems to have been quiet during this violence.

49　This is apparent in exchanges between Okyeman and DC Walker, April 1948, AASA 3/297. There is no doubt about this claim as Walker investigated the matter and pressed the police to prosecute the offenders.

50　Duncan to the Adikrofo of Ahwenease, Adadientem and Apapam, 14 October 1948, AASA 3/297. The refugees slowly returned to their homes without further violence in the course of the following month.

rightly deserve none. . . . History has a long memory and therefore we appeal not to Caesar but to the Supreme Judge of the world.[51]

Manifestly the executions had not cleared the air but had, rather, paved the way for a continuation of the dispute. The perpetuation of the 'present hostile attitude' was not solely of the Amantoo Mmiensa's making. On 10 June 1947, the Amantoo Mmiensa elders visited the royal palace in Kyebi. From an account which clearly emanated from the Amantoo Mmiensa themselves published in *The Ashanti Pioneer*,[52] their intentions were formally to announce the death of Akyea Mensah; this was an occasion which would have demanded that they pour libations before the Okyenhene and some of his divisional chiefs of the Okyeman Council. They also told the reporter, rather sanctimoniously, that their business included 'composing every misunderstanding that would appear to have arisen as a result of the murder . . .'. The delegation reported to the senior *Okyeame* who in turn reported their presence to the Okyenhene and the council. They were asked to wait and were then told that the Okyenhene and those chiefs present had refused the conventional official vistors' gift of 'drinks', usually gin, on the flimsy grounds that such an announcement was a matter for the entire state and that it should be delivered before the full Okyeman Council which was not due to meet until 19 June and to which the delegation would be invited.

Despite this promise of an invitation, the Amantoo Mmiensa were not invited. The Amantoo Mmiensa Council accordingly met on 23 June and sent a message to the secretary of the Okyeman Council saying that they were coming to Kyebi with the same purpose in mind on 25 June. No acknowledgement of this was received by the Amantoo Mmiensa. None the less they left for Kyebi 'loaded with the customary drinks and money'. They again presented themselves to the senior Okyeame who told them that whilst the membership of the Okyeman Council was present in Kyebi, no meeting of the Council was scheduled for that day. The delegation quickly found out that the Benkumhene (in whose division Apedwa lay) and the Adontenhene were actually with the Okyenhene in his rooms at that moment, but Okyeame Adu told them that this private meeting did not constitute a meeting of the State

51 Telegram to the Secretary of State, 10 April 1947 from Kwadjo Asante for President (first county), Boakye Yiadom (acting Odikro of Apedwa, second county) and Okai Mireku, Mankrado of Tetteh (third county); PRO CO 96/802/6. Creech Jones asked Burns if he would tell them 'in suitable terms' that the prerogative was a matter for the Governor alone. Secretary of State to Burns, 18 April 1947, *ibid*.
52 8 July 1947.

Council.[53] The delegates then tried forcible entry but were turned back by the Native Authority Police, who said that even if they gained entrance to Nana's office there was, in any case, no Okyeame present to 'interpret' the delegates to the Okyenhene as custom demanded. The delegates then spotted two of the Akyeame (Adu and Asare). Adu slipped away down a corridor into the maze of the palace whilst a besieged Asare protested that he could do nothing without his senior, Adu, being present.

The delegates left Ofori Panin Fie and indignantly rambled around Kyebi desperately knocking on the doors of each divisional chief of the Okyeman Council. They met with no success and became 'disappointed but not discouraged'. They again visited Kyebi on 26 June. The heralds of the Amantoo Mmiensa announced their arrival at a full meeting of the Okyeman but the delegates were told to wait whilst council settled a dispute from Kwabeng before they could be heard. For twenty-five minutes they waited, standing 'calmly but soldierly on their feet at the State Council hall . . . No member of the Council spoke to or exchanged greetings with the delegates.' Noon arrived and the Okyeman, still grappling with the Kwabeng case, resolved to put off discussion of that case until 2.00 pm. Nothing was said to the delegates as the members of the Okyeman dispersed.

Before the sitting resumed the delegates asked to be allowed to greet the council members but 'were brushed aside with "WAIT"'. They did wait until 4.30, when they asked whether the Amantoo Mmiensa still formed part of Akyem Abuakwa and, if so, were they not entitled to a hearing? They were again told to wait. The newspaper account ends with the comment that the 'Amantoommiensa have been patient for three years . . .'.[54]

The article was partisan but there is no doubt that the executions had not provided either side with the space in which a dignified reconciliation could begin. In November 1947, an initial attempt at reconciliation was attempted. This, the DC reported, turned into a noisy demonstration by Amantoo Mmiensa youngmen who 'uttered wild imprecations against the Omanhene for his alleged part in the Akyea Mensah case'.[55] By March 1948, the Amantoo Mmiensa had drawn up charges for the destoolment of Ofori Atta II. They tried to force their way into the palace once again to present the charges but were forced back by Native Authority Police. Ofori Atta II, undoubtedly weary with

---

53   The reporter added a sly, populist note to this: 'Could they have accepted a Royalty or concession rent for the State?'
54   *The Ashanti Pioneer*, 8 July 1947.
55   *District Record Book*, Kibi District, December 1947, quoted by Simensen, *op. cit.*, p. 332.

the matter, asked that the Presbyterian Church officials in Kyebi should mediate. The mediators were met by an implacable Amantoo Mmiensa Council who insisted that they would only talk if £1,500 was forthcoming from the stool in partial reparation for the death of Akyea Mensah. On another occasion the Amantoo Mmiensa had forced their way into the palace with the intention of seizing the Okyenhene and marking him sufficiently seriously to warrant destoolment on the grounds of his physical incapacity. It took forty Native Authority Police to beat them back.

Reconciliation was not to take place, and even that was superficial in many senses, until 1949. By then an alliance of the Akyem Abuakwa Scholars' Union, the Presbyterian Church and the new Adontenhene effectively broke down some if not all of these very bitter resentments.[56]

Desultory skirmishing continued in London. A reduced core of dissident Labour Members of Parliament led by Sidney Silverman continued by private letter and at question time to ask for more details. Bryden maintained his pressure on Creech Jones and his Legal Advisers. There is no doubt that Bryden was briefing the politicians. At the same time Bryden's own campaign had become very personal. While his frequent letters raised genuine if arcane points of law, his manner had come close to being unpleasantly intimidatory. Twice in early March he had telegrammed Burns suggesting that if he were to carry out the executions he would render himself liable to trial in the Kings Bench Division for murder: 'Most serious responsibility upon you and your advisers if lives taken.'[57] This was followed up by a letter to the Colonial Secretary in Accra which again pointed out that as the convictions were nullities (an opinion shared by none of the tiers of appeal which had heard this matter), any executions 'will be murder, a point . . . we advised the Governor seriously to consider'.[58] Governors and Secretaries of State were used to veiled threats and imprecations, but it was rare for such to come from an eminent lawyer. Lloyd certainly regarded the telegrams as having gone beyond the bounds of normal propriety and agreed with Burns that they were intended to intimidate.[59]

---

56 *District Record Book*, June 1949, NAG ADM 32/4/100.
57 Telegram from Bryden to Burns, 3 March 1947, PRO 96/803/1.
58 Bryden to the Colonial Secretary, Accra, 12 March 1947, PRO CO 96/803/1. The day before he had written to the Colonial Office suggesting that the Governor, knowing that the convictions were nullities, might 'involve himself in a charge of murder upon which he can be put upon trial and that those who advise or counsel him . . . also charged as accessories'. Bryden to CO, 11 March 1947, *ibid.*
59 *Minute* by Lloyd to the Secretary of State, 19 March 1947, PRO CO 96/803/1.

Burns asked the Colonial Office if steps could be taken against Bryden. The Legal Advisers felt that nothing could be done. Roberts-Wray felt that a protest to the Law Society, Bryden's professional body, would only elicit the predictable comment that Bryden was expressing an opinion on a point of law. If that opinion was sound, he had a duty to convey it to the Governor. The Society could not be expected to adjudicate on whether the opinion was or was not sound; that was a matter for the courts. Everything had to be done to prevent any impression being given which implied that the Colonial Office wished to muzzle or even bully the defendants' legal representative. While Roberts-Wray felt that Bryden's threats were 'sheer nonsense' he advised that no action should be taken against him.[60] Lloyd counselled Creech Jones that whilst nothing could be done, full sympathy could be expressed to the Governor.[61] Lloyd's minute is notable in that it conveys a strong sense of 'mother knows best'. It certainly reminded Creech Jones of the need for proper and sensitive conduct toward Burns. 'I send this on', he minuted, 'because I feel that Sir A. Burns, knowing the close interest which you have taken in this matter, will certainly assume that the telegram now to go has been approved by you.'[62] It was implicit that Lloyd felt that there was fence-mending to be done.

The general concerns which had emerged about procedure in the course of the appeals surfaced in Cabinet the day after the men were hanged in Accra. The Lord Chancellor who had been unwillingly drawn into the case said that he felt that the administration of criminal justice would be brought into disrepute if these 'inordinate delays in executing the sentences of the courts were allowed to continue'; he and Creech Jones were to draft a Cabinet memorandum for consideration in the near future. At the same time some concern was raised over the Speaker's ruling that this was a matter which could not be discussed in the House of Commons. Was it right, an unnamed Cabinet member asked, that Parliament should be precluded from discussing questions affecting liberty of the subject in British territories overseas? The Home Secretary intervened to point out that it was long-established practice that the prerogative of mercy could not be called into question by Parliament. This matter was no different from one in which a murder had been committed in the United Kingdom. To shorten a developing discussion about ethics and procedure, Cabinet agreed that this ques-

60 *Minute* from Roberts-Wray to Sir Thomas Lloyd, 18 March 1947, PRO CO 96/803/1.
61 *Minute* by Sir Thomas Lloyd to the Secretary of State, 19 March 1947, PRO CO 96/803/1.
62 *Ibid*. The telegram of the same date simply endorsed Roberts-Wray's current view that no action against Bryden was feasible.

tion too would figure in the eventual memorandum produced by the Lord Chancellor and the Secretary of State for the Colonies.[63]

Creech Jones brought the matter back to Cabinet on 31 March. With the Lord Chancellor's agreement[64] he advocated the introduction of rules limiting the time within which petitions were to be lodged with the Privy Council's Judicial Committee. He also advocated the adoption of a new administrative rule which allowed the Privy Council to disregard a petition which was in the view of the relevant colonial governor 'intended only for the purpose of causing delay' or if the petition was 'clearly and completely without substance' or if it re-submitted on matters already decided by the Judicial Committee. Creech Jones proposed no alteration in the current system whereby the Governor retained the local prerogative of mercy. Lord Jowitt had resisted a Colonial Office suggestion that there should be a limit on the number of petitions for special leave to appeal.[65] Cabinet agreed to these proposals on 1 April.[66] In effect this decision merely expanded the instructions circulated by the Secretary of State for the Colonies on 18 July 1944 which stipulated that a convicted person must signal intention to petition the Privy Council within three weeks of conviction.[67]

The underlying concerns were further canvassed in public in a forthright letter to *The Times* by Lord Simon.[68] The timing of this leaves no doubt that Simon 'was put up to it', and that a letter from so distinguished a jurist would pave the way for wide agreement to the new rules. The letter is peppered with partisan comment. Bryden and those briefing him 'contrived' to secure delays by seeking leave to appeal 'at leisurely intervals'. The postponements of execution were 'deplorable'. In all of his forty years' experience Simon said he had never known 'so flagrant a breach of the principle . . . that punishment should rapidly

---

63 *Cabinet Minutes* (47) 32nd conclusions, 25 March 1947, PRO LCO 2/3231. The matters were discussed between Jowitt, J.D. Waters of the Privy Council Office and Creech Jones in late April 1947, largely through the circulation of letters and memoranda; see PRO LCO 2/3231.

64 Jowitt's grasp of the essentials of the case did not increase with the passing of time. In the midst of the discussions with the Privy Council's permanent officers and the Colonial Office he wrote to the Home Secretary: '. . . the matter became acute in connection with the five West Indians who having been sentenced to death were kept in uncertainty . . .'. Lord Chancellor to Chuter Ede, MP, 12 May 1947, PRO LCO 2/3231.

65 Lord Jowitt to J.D. Waters, Secretary to the Privy Council's Judicial Committee, 18 April 1947, PRO LCO 2/3231.

66 *Cabinet Minutes* 34(47) conclusions, 1 April 1947, PRO LCO 2/3231.

67 Circular from Oliver Stanley, Secretary of State for the Colonies, 18 July 1944, PRO LCO 2/3231. This and its appended instructions came into force, of course, after the initiation of the Kyebi case.

68 1 April 1947.

follow on conviction'. He felt that the law and rules on time limits should change to prevent 'a repetition of this misspent ingenuity of advisers who calculate that even if their efforts fail . . . yet there will be so much delay created as may make it seem improper for the full severity of the law to take its course'.

Bryden did not take this public caning lying down. He replied in robust fashion in *The Times* of the following day. The Gold Coast case was, he agreed, 'extraordinary', but did it provide 'a sufficient reason for restricting the present constitutional right of subjects to petition His Majesty in Council . . . without time limit?' Bryden suggested that the delays had, amongst other factors, 'arisen from the war-time and post-war difficulties under which legal business has been carried on . . .'. Bryden again rehearsed his argument that the proceedings were not valid and claimed that delay could have been obviated if Counsel had met 'to discuss . . . whether the trial and convictions were illegal and nullities . . . On the point of delay . . . it is the prisoners who have good grounds for complaint.'[69]

On 3 April 1947 Creech Jones made a statement to the House of Commons about the implications of the case. He agreed that most of the steps taken by the lawyers were open to defenders of any condemned man in the United Kingdom with the exception of appeal to the Judicial Committee of the Privy Council. But, he argued, 'practitioners in the Courts of this country would not lend themselves to the bringing of a series of fanciful applications to the Courts in which there is no substance'. He went on to speak of the defence's actions as 'an abuse of the process of law'. He gave notice of changes in procedure which would ensure that it would be more difficult to deploy 'repeated delaying tactics' to avoid execution of sentence in colonial cases. The new rules were elaborated to the House of Commons on 23 July 1947, and were broadly in line with the changes endorsed by the Cabinet in April. A three-week time limit was imposed, during which time the defence had to show proof to the relevant governor that they had sent the necessary instructions to solicitors in Britain for them to petition for special leave to appeal. The Secretary of State then had the executive power to fix a date 'usually one month after the arrival of the papers in this country', within which time the British solicitors had to lodge the petition with the Judicial Committee. Creech Jones added, 'I intend that these rules shall be strictly adhered to and if a petition is not lodged in time an execution will, normally, proceed.'

The government took the view, he said, that further legislation was

<hr />

69   *The Times*, 2 April 1947. Officials at the CO favoured a reply but Dale advised against it; there were pending appeals and the matter might be considered *sub judice*. Minute by N.J.B. Sabine to Sir Thomas Lloyd, 2 April 1947, PRO CO 96/802/6.

inadvisable and that the inherent right of subjects to appeal to the sovereign in this fashion was secure. The prerogative of mercy continued to lie with governors-in-council. Creech Jones defended the current position pointing out that if the Colonial Office were to take over these powers, the Secretary of State would be overwhelmed with petitions. This did not absolve him from intervention in the light of miscarriage of justice.

Creech Jones ended on an odd note given the entire and sorry history of his relationship with Burns. He said of Burns: 'he had to face not only the prolonged anxiety caused by repeated respites, but also considerable pressure and criticism from various quarters. Throughout all this difficult period his sole concern was the interests of justice in the Gold Coast and he had and has now the very fullest support and confidence of His Majesty's Government.' While this was palpably untrue, there is some reason to suppose that Creech Jones felt that he had misjudged Burns. Immediately after the final executions he had telegrammed: 'I want you to know how deeply I have felt for you during the past few days as in the earlier stages of this tragic affair. To me and to those in the Colonial Office who have been dealing with the case, its most distressing feature has been the burden which has fallen on you personally.'[70] In the same telegram Creech Jones claimed that he had been 'deeply moved' by Burns' statement on the final executions and commutations made to the Executive Council on 28 March 1947.

Burns was not so deeply moved by Creech Jones' hypocritical conversion. He remained outraged by the treatment he had received. This surfaced in two ways. First he sought the support of the Colonial Office in an attempt to bring Bryden and his supporters low. Burns also complained of the ways in which the BBC Overseas Service had reported the case.[71] He continued to persuade the Colonial Office that Bryden should at the very least be reported to the Law Society for professional impropriety. The Office's reluctance led Burns to suggest that he pursue Bryden in a personal capacity. By June of 1947, even some of Burns' most committed supporters were beginning to find his insistence tiresome and obsessive. Andrew Cohen, who had backed Burns, minuted to Sir Thomas Lloyd on 11 June 1947 that he had '... considerable doubts whether it is wise to pursue this any further ... Either Sir A. Burns must be asked not to pursue this or it ought to be pursued by the Colonial Office. I am doubtful about leaving it to the Governor ... to pursue it ... with the Society ... it ... would not ... lead to any useful purpose to take this matter any further'.[72]

70 Creech Jones to Burns, 'Personal', 30 March 1947, PRO CO 537/2099.
71 Ivor Thomas to the Lord Privy Seal, 22 May 1947, PRO CO 96/802/6.
72 On the same day Lloyd minuted below: 'I agree with Mr Cohen.' K.E. Robinson, a friend of Burns, was to send this kindly packaged advice: '... we ... all sympathise with you ... about Bryden ... the Law Society is not

The fourth and final appeal on behalf of Opoku Afwenee and Kwaku Amoaka Atta[73] was lodged with the Privy Council on 19 June and dismissed on 16 July 1947. Burns, the CO officials felt, had been vindicated and, if there were winners and losers in the whole beastly business, Burns had won. His wish for blood was, accordingly, undignified and unprofessional.[74] The advice he obtained from his friends in the Colonial Office was, it seems, unpersuasive. On 25 July 1947 he sent a letter to the Council of the Law Society and asked that the Colonial Office forward it for him.[75]

A long, resigned debate by minute took place in the Colonial Office as to the advisability of forwarding this letter of protest. It was pointed out that there was now no question of such a complaint being seen as an attempt to muzzle the defence as the last step in the legal process had ended before the Privy Council on 17 July. Robinson, on the basis of knowledge of Burns' rage, suggested compliance as although 'I don't think any good will come of it . . . Sir A. Burns may be very difficult to persuade – indeed only direct instructions from the S of S will . . . "persuade" him. . . .' The officials felt that it would be 'inappropriate' for the Secretary of State to intervene. The letter should be forwarded not least because, as Sir Thomas Lloyd argued, '. . . Sir A. Burns would take it badly amiss (and in my view that w'd be reasonable) any attempt to prevent him from having this letter sent'. The letter was sent on 11 August 1947.[76]

Burns continued to irritate Creech Jones. In the course of May and early June he constructed a vitriolic if accurate memorandum on the course of the case. He registered gratitude for the good things the Secretary of State had said about him in recent weeks and especially the comments made to the House on 3 April. But he insisted, and insisted in capital letters, that the entire and sequential mess was initiated on 3 December 1945 when he was instructed by telegram to delay executions once again. This, Burns said, 'was the first real delay and the beginning of the series of postponements, *against my advice* which caused all the later trouble . . . I was in no way responsible for the delays.'[77] This memorandum is angry but restrained; it is clearly closely

likely to produce anything effective [and] . . . it would . . . be better to let the matter drop . . .'. Robinson to Burns, 18 June 1947, PRO CO 96/803/1.

73 Whose principal ground was that Judge M'Carthy had misdirected himself and was wrong in fact and law in refusing to grant the petitioners' applications for writs of *habeas corpus. Times Law Report*, 17 July 1947.
74 Roberts-Wray minuted bluntly that 'If I were in the Governor's position, I should do nothing. . . .' *Minute*, 7 June 1947, PRO CO 96/803/1.
75 Burns to K.E. Robinson, 25 July 1947, PRO 96/803/1.
76 CO *Minute* sequence, 6–11 August 1947, PRO CO 96/803/1.
77 Sir Alan Burns, Memorandum . . . on the Apedwa Case, June 1947, PRO CO 96/802/6.

related to the much more agonised and indignant calendar he had constructed in Christiansborg Castle as his sense of indignity and frustration grew.[78] There is little doubt that anger haunted the drafting of his memoirs.[79]

After leaving the Gold Coast in August 1947, and *en route* for a holiday before taking up a new post as the Colonial Office's representative to the United Nations Trusteeship Council, Burns told Sir Thomas Lloyd about the forthcoming book. Lloyd wrote to Creech Jones' Personal Secretary saying that Burns had hoped to show the draft sections dealing with the Apedwa murder to the Secretary of State but Creech Jones had been unavailable at the time. Burns, he said, 'still hopes when he gets back here at the end of the year, to have the opportunity of sending this particular passage to Mr Creech Jones in proof form for comment...'.[80] Burns did submit his draft to Creech Jones on 24 December and, unseasonably, Creech Jones sought, successfully, for some significant watering-down of Burns' tone. One passage, Creech Jones claimed, 'appears unfair to me', whilst another 'implicates Ministers in a doubtful line of action'. Burns complied with six suggested changes in the draft. Further changes were suggested on the basis of checking the narrative through the official files in London by officials in the Colonial Office.[81] Even after such amendments, it still reads as an unusually forthright, boisterous and angry memoir for those more conservative and deferential days.

Burns had not finished with his pursuit of Bryden and his parliamentary allies. As late as October 1947 he was still actively considering a libel action against Sidney Silverman for uninformed and undoubtedly malicious comments in an article published in the *Tribune* well over a year previously.[82] In a letter to the Colonial Office he sought their support in getting counsel's opinion, as suggested by his personal solicitors, on the feasibility of such an action.[83] The Colonial Office

---

78   This can be inspected in the Alan Burns papers in Rhodes House Library, Oxford, Mss Afr S 1822. It is striking that this document, which runs to five pages, was virtually the only personal documentation he bequeathed to Rhodes House's Colonial Records Project. The Kyebi murder case and his vast sense of the unjust treatment he had received in the course of it from successive Secretaries of State never left him.

79   *Colonial Civil Servant* (London, 1949).

80   *Minute* by Lloyd to D.M. Smith, 5 November 1947, PRO CO 96/802/6.

81   *Minute* by J.K. Thompson to K.E. Robinson, 5 January 1948, PRO CO 96/802/6. This exchange suggests that Burns would be resistant to changes on grounds other than factual inaccuracy.

82   26 July 1946.

83   Burns Letter to J.K. Thompson (from the Athenaeum) on 26 October 1946: 'I am not disposed to put down 17 guineas for Counsel's opinion and to risk being heavily hit for costs if the libel action were lost, but at the same time I feel that

view was, surely correctly, that Burns' obsessional concern with self-vindication kept a matter which everyone else wished to forget on the boil. But refusing him this demanded tact. Lloyd replied wearily to Burns that

> In Parliament and in the country generally opinion is utterly with you . . . and the Secretary of State does not see that any good purpose could be served by bringing an action . . . a sorry business, now fortunately concluded, would thus be revived and there would almost certainly be that distortion which nowadays seems inevitable with some of our Press.

Creech Jones extended 'his sympathy and resentment at an attack of this kind' but said that he felt that it would be inexpedient for the Colonial Office to fund such an action.[84] This further rebuff was well argued and politically sound; Burns' reactions to it are unknown but predictable.

The whole matter simply refused to go away. It came to Burns' notice that in September 1949 Danquah had had printed a number of huge posters provocatively headed 'Sir Alan Burns, Governor of the Gold Coast versus Nana Ofori Atta II, Omanhene of Akim Abuakwa.' The text of the poster noted with favour that Robert Scott, as Acting Governor, had just paid an official visit to Kyebi. The poster correctly noted that this was the first such official visit since the murder and in Danquah's words this 'ended the six years "Cold War" between the head of the Administration and Kibi'. Since the murder 'the Governors had kept away from the Omanhene's capital. They might pass through, but not call on him as official and native custom demanded. Perhaps this was intended by the originator, Sir Alan Burns, as a rebuke to the State. . . . Mr Scott however who is a sympathetic and far-seeing administrator, thought it necessary to break the ice. . . .'[85] Burns was infuriated and demanded action. The view of the Colonial Office's West Africa desk, whose senior personnel had changed in the interim, was that Burns now 'exaggerates the importance of Danquah and the Kibi murders [sic] in the Gold Coast today. The case of the murderers may mean a great deal to Danquah personally but the murders [sic] are not . . . still the subject of political controversy, altho' they remain in the

Silverman should not be allowed to get away with it. It is time that people realised that they cannot rashly accuse a Colonial Government for the benefit of our enemies'; PRO CO 96/803/1.

84 Sir Thomas Lloyd to Burns, 2 November 1946, PRO CO 96/803/1.
85 The full text is given in an undated report in PRO CO 95/825/5.
86 *Minute* by Hanrott to Gorsuch on 9 January 1950, PRO 96/825/5. A day later

background of peoples' memories. Danquah too has lost a great deal of influence. . . .'[86]

This resurrection coincided with an anonymous review of Burns' memoirs in *The Times Literary Supplement*. Bryden whose cause and person were taken to task in the book put pen to paper and wrote a letter to the editor which was published on 2 December 1949. Burns demanded that the Colonial Office officially answer what he regarded as distortions and insults in Bryden's letter. In a polite reply Gorsuch told Burns that it was not the practice of the Office to engage in rough and tumbles in the press but that the Legal Advisers would help him draft a personal letter if he chose to write one. Burns was furious and wrote a stinging letter which received a bizarre reaction from Creech Jones. On the one hand the Secretary of State was quite reasonably angered by Burns' tone:

> I am sorry that Sir Alan Burns should wish to 'intimidate' us with the assertion that 'if I am compelled to write to the Press myself I shall have to say why – and I should prefer to avoid this'.[87] I dislike such language when there is a difference between himself and colleagues who respect him & are sympathetic to his approach to many questions. I dislike this constant theme of some retired Governors that their successors & the CO & Ministers should show more 'firmness' in colonial government. Such talk is just nonsense . . .[88]

But on the other hand Creech Jones supported the idea of an 'officially inspired reply' being sent to *The Times Literary Supplement*: 'I do not think that a grave criticism in a paper of repute & wide circulation should go unanswered. . . . It should be no more than a complete rebuttal of what Bryden says. . . .'[89] Circumspectly Creech Jones advised that the new Governor of the Gold Coast, Sir Charles Arden-Clarke, should be asked for his opinion. Arden-Clarke's reply was probably just what officials wanted. He had no objection to a letter being sent but 'thereafter it would be best from our point of view if correspondence

---

  Gorusch minuted: 'I think that from the Colonial Office point of view it is preferable to let this matter lie.'

87 That is, he would spell out the Colonial Office's reticence in taking up the assertions, which were generally agreed in Whitehall to be at least unfair assertions, in Bryden's letter.

88 This is surely a reference to Lord Milverton's performances in the House of Lords. Formally Sir Arthur Richards and Governor of Nigeria, Milverton was frequently on the offensive on the subject of communist leanings in the BBC, the British Council and the Colonial Office itself. A good example of this is analysed in my 'Political Intelligence and Policing in Ghana', in *Policing the Empire*, ed. D. Anderson and D. Killingray, p. 104.

89 *Ibid.*

ceased . . . At a Durbar on the 14th [January, 1950] at Kibi I was given a warm welcome and propose to continue my policy of rebuilding cordial relations with this state. I would ask that this old issue should be forgotten as soon as possible. Perhaps *The Times* would be prepared to help.'[90]

The letter was drafted, at considerable length, by Frank Gahan KC who appeared for the Crown at many of the appeals. On receipt of it the editor of the *Supplement*, Alan Pryce Jones, replied: 'I am afraid that we cannot carry any further controversy on the subject of Sir Alan Burns' book as many weeks have elapsed since the review appeared and both sides have now stated their case quite clearly. . . .'[91] Perhaps, in Arden-Clarke's words, the editor had not been 'prepared to help'. This was the last occasion on which Burns was to threaten exposure and litigation. But his indignation had irrevocably altered the Colonial Office's view of his judgement. He was to remain Britain's Permanent Representative on the Trusteeship Council of the United Nations until 1956. But his influence over colonial policy, influence that his long and distinguished career should have entitled him to, was to be marginal. He certainly perceived it as a grossly unfair ending to that career.

Arden-Clarke's comment about 'rebuilding cordial relations' is important. Danquah's perceived need to be once again on good terms with the colonial authorities owed a great deal to proximate politics in the Gold Coast. J.B. Danquah and some of the other older nationalist intelligentsia had been on a switchback ride so far as official perceptions of them went. This had all occurred in a very short period of time. The case had brought Danquah to a greater hostility towards the colonial regime than he had ever expressed before.

In the course of the case he had declared virtual war on Burns with whom he had been on reasonable terms beforehand. There is no record of Burns' dislike of Danquah or Danquah's distaste for Burns before the middle of 1945. Burns had consulted Danquah on many occasions. But only months after the executions Danquah had founded the United Gold Coast Convention, an organisation widely regarded as the Gold Coast's first 'real' political party. With his brother-in-law Edward Akuffo Addo and nephew William Ofori Atta, he served on the UGCC's Working Committee of six. The UGCC, demanding self-government 'in the shortest possible time', now denounced the reforming

90   Arden Clarke to the Secretary of State, 23 January 1950, PRO CO 96/825/5.
91   Quoted in Burchells to Kenneth Roberts-Wray, 17 February 1950, PRO CO 96/825/5.

Constitution of 1946 (which was usually called the Burns Constitution), in whose drafting Danquah had played a part.[92] At the inauguration of that constitution he had supported resolutions in the Legislative Council which, amongst other things, expressed 'the lively gratification felt by . . . the grant of this Constitution'.[93] By 1947 Danquah no longer felt any gratification. He and his colleagues sought to remove chiefs from the Legislative Council and to replace them with educated commoners;[94] this was an abrupt shift in his personal stance which, unlike that of many other members of the nationalist intelligentsia, had been consistently reverential about the role of 'natural rulers'. He and the rest of the UGCC now supported farmers' increasingly violent complaints about the government's policy of compulsorily cutting down cocoa trees infected with swollen shoot disease, an opposition regarded with no little insensitivity by the colonial regime as merely Luddite.

Understandably Danquah had constructed Burns and the colonial regime as an implacable enemy which had thwarted his best attempts to save his kinsmen from the rope and his family from notoriety. He sought every opportunity in his role as a journalist and prominent public figure to find fault, and there were many faults, with the colonial regime. While it would be foolish to pretend that there was no substance to his political case, there is no doubt that this was given a particular intensity by his personal feelings. In return, before and even after the return of Kwame Nkrumah to the Gold Coast in November 1947, Danquah was intensely disliked in Christiansborg Castle, the Secretariat and on the West African desk at the Colonial Office. He compounded this by authoring a telegram to the British Prime Minister at the height of the February riots of 1948 which declared that civil order had broken down and that he was prepared to head a caretaker government. The official antipathy such activities had aroused was obviously relevant to his illegal if short detention with the five other members of the UGCC during the State of Emergency following the disturbances of February and March 1948. In a relatively brief period the stock of this aristocratic scholar-lawyer, the doyen of Gold Coast constitutional nationalism, had fallen badly. He was, in short, regarded as a mischievous trouble-maker.

The Report of the Watson Commission of Inquiry into the 1948 riots had not entirely exonerated him from 'fishing in troubled waters' but it had certainly found that they were spontaneous riots rather than dem-

92 See Richard Rathbone, *Ghana*, vol. 1, 'British Documents on the End of Empire' series (London, 1992).
93 Leg. Co. *Debates*, 23 July 1946, NAG ADM 14/2/47.
94 Working Committee *Minutes*, 20 September 1947.

onstrations orchestrated by his evil hand. The emergence of Nkrumah on the left of the United Gold Coast Convention changed the rules of engagement for both Danquah and the colonial government. The latter, eager to keep moderate opinion on its side in turbulent times, had been obliged to appoint Danquah to the important Coussey Committee which designed the draft 1951 constitution.

Danquah might have been regarded as a trouble-maker, but he shared his half-brother, Nana Sir Ofori Atta's, profound distaste for radical political doctrines. While Danquah might have invoked the rights of 'the people' as a stump-speaker, there was little in his doctrinal development which suggested that he had much sympathy with the egalitarian and redistributive pretensions of the kind of populist socialism espoused by Nkrumah's Convention People's Party. His ideological position, undoubtedly influenced by his membership of one of the Gold Coast's great royal families and informed by his lofty position within the 'educated elite', was increasingly tenuous. In the Gold Coast, the postwar 'spirit of the age' was more radical than the mannered protest politics Danquah and other members of the professional elite had excelled at. The era of mass politics, a rougher time, had arrived.

Danquah and the leadership of the UGCC were threatened by these developments, developments that Kwame Nkrumah and his lieutenants understood so well. Both colonial government and the old professional elite felt that the appointment of the all-African Coussey Committee to draft a new constitution constituted an important opportunity to hold back this tide. A lawyer, a fine if wordy debater and a man with a great deal to lose if more radical politics were to come to dominate the Gold Coast, Danquah played a full, rich and partisan part in that Committee's deliberations. As the colonial government came increasingly to see more menace in Nkrumah and his Convention People's Party for its radicalism, Danquah and other representatives of what slowly came to be regarded as 'moderate opinion' by the colonial authorities were seen as preferable to the alternative. He was, in their terms, a moderate with a taste for patrician involvement in public affairs, an avowed anti-communist and an *aficionado* of legalism and parliamentary niceties. There is no doubt that Danquah's hatred of the CPP owed much to his seeing in them precisely the kinds of forces which had threatened his brother's and, since 1943, his nephew's stool. In the two short years since Sir Alan Burns' departure from the Gold Coast, Danquah had moved from being anathema to being at least the lesser of two evils. It was this that led the new Governor, Sir Charles Arden-Clarke, to resist Burns' attempts to stir the pot. Danquah was, moreover, well aware that he needed to court that government support if moderate, elite politicians were to overcome the threat to their past domination of the nationalist high ground which Nkrumah and the Convention People's Party now represented.[95]

But if some sort of *rapprochement* was possible between the colonial government and Danquah, and if the new Governor's administration sought to restore good relations with the Kyebi ruling family, there was no abiding peace in Akyem Abuakwa. The breach between the Amantoo Mmiensa and the stool was formally healed at a meeting on 30 May 1949, to the apparent satisfaction of the Okyenhene and the Governor.[96] But by July of that year petitions opposing that reconciliation were being generated in Amantoo Mmiensa towns.[97] While the Amantoo Mmiensa elders had backed away from their admitted intention to destool the Okyenhene and to secede from the authority of the Akyem Abuakwa Native Authority,[98] the ill feeling engendered by past events lingered on.

But that ill feeling, and other conflicts within the Akyem state, increasingly and perhaps inevitably took on the colouration of national politics. By the end of the 1940s, the Gold Coast's fundamental political fault-line divided the gradualist, constitutional and anti-socialist nationalism of the UGCC and the populist, socialist nationalism of Nkrumah's CPP. The royal family was more than merely identified with the United Gold Coast Convention. From the perspective of the palace, J.B. Danquah, Willie Ofori Atta and Edward Akuffo Addo[99] were not only leading figures in the UGCC Working Committee but were royal kinsmen. All three had, with others, been detained without charge by the colonial government in the immediate aftermath of the disturbances in Accra on February 28th 1948,[100] adding another group of the royal family who had found themselves behind bars. Largely because of this intimacy and in a break with his predecessor's caution in such matters, the Okyenhene identified himself and the Kyebi stool very directly with the UGCC. Nana Sir Ofori Atta I had, it is true, given some support to the Youth Conference, the loosely organised protest movement of the late 1930s, but had agreed only to become one of its many 'patrons', despite the leading role played in its organisation by his half-brother J.B. Danquah.[101]

---

95 Nkrumah split from the UGCC in June 1949 to form the CPP. It was to take much of the mass membership of the UGCC with it.

96 See Okyenhene to DC (St Muir Gerrard), 9 July 1949, and DC to Okyenhene, 28 July 1949, AASA 3/297.

97 See e.g. petition of the Apedwa Elite Club of 20 July 1949 to the Okyenhene, AASA 3/297.

98 See e.g. Amantoo Mmiensa petition to the DC, 20 April 1948, AASA 3/297.

99 Nana Ofori Atta I's brother, son and son-in-law respectively.

100 They entered Ghanaian martyrology as 'The Big Six'.

101 See Okyenhene to J.B. Danquah, 16 January 1938, AASA 10/345.

Ofori Atta II was to go very much further than this. The UGCC boasted an active Kyebi branch under Willie Ofori Atta's leadership. In July 1948 he wrote asking for the Okyenhene's support for a rally to be held later that month at Kyebi. This was heartily endorsed by the palace. The State Council promised Willie Ofori Atta 'all possible active co-operation in making your Rally, which is the first of its kind in Kibi, a golden success'.[102] Later in the year the Okyenhene invited the Kyebi branch of the UGCC to hold a rally within the confines of the palace in the open courtyard in front of the Tribunal buildings. The Okyenhene went even further when he published a strongly pro-UGCC letter in its recently established newspaper *The Evening News* in February 1949.[103] In addition he allowed his town house in Accra to be used for meetings of the UGCC Working Committee.

The motivation behind such open advocacy of a political party is obvious enough. The UGCC opposed the colonial regime and the royal family was alienated from that regime. Nana Ofori Atta II was also supporting his kinsmen who were active and prominent members of the UGCC's Working Committee. But that is only a partial explanation. There were also strong, local imperatives which impelled him. Above all he was covering his considerably exposed back. The rising tide of discontent amongst farmers over the colonial government's policy to contain swollen shoot disease is apparent from the *District Record Books*. The most offensive aspect of that policy was the attempt to contain the virus by 'cutting out' infected trees and by 'cutting out' uninfected trees in an attempt to create 'fire belts' to prevent the infection spreading. The crucial points were that this was being carried out whilst the cocoa price was rising steadily and that farmers were not, initially at least, compensated for lost acreage.[104] The *District Record Books* suggest that agitation amongst farmers included denunciation of the Okyenhene as being 'soft' on that unpopular cocoa policy. Chiefly support in the prosecution of that policy was demanded by government and, in the case of Akyem Abuakwa, grudgingly given. Okyenhene Ofori Atta II, whose person and state had suffered greatly since the death of his predecessor, was obviously in no position to challenge colonial government at this point of his troubled reign.

Some of the farming interest's agitation came to be skilfully articulated by J.B. Danquah and Willie Ofori Atta, who needed to maintain a posture of radical opposition after their detention in March 1948 even if

102   See W. Ofori Atta to Okyenhene, 16 July 1948, and K.T.A. Danquah to W. Ofori Atta of 23 July 1948, ASSA 10/345.
103   8 February 1949.
104   NAG ADM 32/4/100.

it embarrassed the king.[105] The Okyenhene's kinsmen, backed by the Akyem Abuakwa members of the UGCC and the protesting Akim Abuakwa Farmers' Union, were active in pressing the Okyenhene to express his support openly and actively. In terms of local politics, the Okyenhene could ill afford to alienate further elements in the Akyem Abuakwa population at a time when the rift with the Amantoo Mmiensa remained wide and divisive. His back was against the wall in early 1948, and there were suggestions that if formal destoolment charges were pressed, some of the Okyeman Council would have supported his removal.[106]

Oral evidence further suggests, logically enough, that the bruising relationship between palace and colonial government had made the anti-colonialism of the UGCC a much more attractive set of ideas to the State Council in Kyebi than such ideology would ever have been under the late king. No one in the palace had much love for the colonial administration for obvious reasons. None of this would have mattered greatly had the UGCC not split in June 1949. At this juncture, as is well known, the UGCC's General Secretary, Kwame Nkrumah, left the UGCC and established his Convention People's Party to the left of the UGCC.[107] Thus the royal family and the Kyebi State Council were to be very openly identified with a political party whose fortunes were declining rapidly whilst many in Kyebi and in Akyem Abuakwa more generally began to flirt with the new, more radical party.

CPP branches began to emerge in Akyem Abuakwa. They appear to have had their first and firmest roots in areas or amongst groups with older grievances against royal authority and against Kyebi. There is, for example, clear evidence of CPP success in Asamankese, Akwatia, Adeiso and especially in the Dwaben towns of Akyem Abuakwa's north-east. The *District Record Books* also suggest strong support for the CPP in the Amantoo Mmiensa towns. In Osiem, the unsuccessful faction in a recent election of a new Osiemhene declared themselves for the CPP.

Aaron Ofori Atta, a son of Nana Ofori Atta I, was amongst the most important of the CPP's stalwarts in Akyem Abuakwa. What is crucial to an understanding of why an aristocrat should appear to break ranks with the royal family is a recognition that his mother and hence his lineage came from Tafo, a Dwaben town. The UGCC versus CPP conflict was, thus, never a simple matter of royal versus non-royal. Older antagonisms and probably more profound ones translated themselves into inter-party disputes.

---

105 The Okyenhene was accused by some of having made no serious protest about their detention; *District Record Book*, 31 March 1948, *ibid.*
106 *Ibid.*
107 See Dennis Austin, *Politics in Ghana*, (London, 1964) pp. 78–85.

The Okyeman Council threw itself into the campaign against the CPP with great energy. Again and again they prevented the formation of a CPP branch in Kyebi. Native Authority Police were instructed to pull down CPP flags when these were raised. Even after the general election of February 1951 which returned the CPP to dyarchic power, the harrassment of the CPP continued. The Native Authority Police arrested CPP sympathisers on the thin grounds that they were disseminating 'malicious propaganda'. The Native Authority Police were, very publicly, collecting the names of CPP sympathisers in the Akyem Abuakwa state for the palace authorities.[108] The CPP were not, of course, beneath laying on their own provocations. Their propaganda denounced the royal family as 'feudal', resurrected the old horrors of the murder case and in June 1949 Nkrumah underlined that hostility by a distinctly provocative personal visit to Banso, the royal burial site.[109]

This was the beginning of a long struggle between the Kyebi royal family and the CPP, a struggle which begins to go some way towards an explanation of the neglect which Akyem Abuakwa has endured at the hands of governments ever since. Although in 1951 the UGCC was to win the two-member Akyem Abuakwa constituency, the CPP had split the constituency. This rural election, like all the non-municipal elections in 1951, was a collegiate rather than a direct election. Willie Ofori Atta polled 87 electors' votes and J.B. Danquah 95. But it was a close-run thing. The CPP's candidates, Ashie Nikoi and J.E. Turkson, both long-term antagonists of the Okyenhene, polled 85 and 83 votes respectively. Very publicly Akyem Abuakwa was now a house divided.

The Gold Coast's next general election, that of 1954, was fought within newly delimited constituencies, and this time polling was directly through the ballot box. In these contests, it was clear that the CPP had gained the upper hand. J.B. Danquah was to lose his seat to his nephew Aaron Ofori Atta of the CPP. Aaron Ofori Atta polled 4,958 votes, Danquah only 3,622. William Ofori Atta was also ousted by the CPP candidate, S.W. Owusu Afari, when Willie Ofori Atta polled 3,652 to his opponent's 4,963 votes. So far as the CPP, the country's governing party until February 1966, was concerned, Akyem Abuakwa was enemy territory. As Sir Frederick Bourne, the constitutional adviser brought in by the Colonial Office to try to resolve the constitutional impasse between the CPP and the National Liberation Movement, was to notice: 'Akim Abuakwa ... have for some reason or other got into the bad books of Government ... there has been considerable friction between

108   This can be seen in correspondence in AASA 10/345.
109   So far as I can see this was his first formal visit to Akyem Abuakwa. He compounded the insult by gradually adopting the title '*Osagyefo*', the most important of the Okyenhene's praise titles.

them ...'.[110] The Kyebi royal family were also regarded as enemies. A Colonial Office memorandum noted that '... Dr Danquah is regarded with intense suspicion not unmixed with contempt by Gold Coast Ministers... he now commands no political following and cannot be taken in any way as representative of the Gold Coast'.[111] Hyperbole apart, Danquah, one of the founding fathers of Gold Coast nationalism, had undoubtedly reached the nadir of a long career.

What had gone wrong? At the national level the UGCC was to all intents and purposes dead by the time of the 1954 election; Danquah and Ofori Atta actually campaigned under the banner of the Ghana Congress Party in that election. The profound failure of the GCP at that election left it with only one member in the Assembly, Kofi Busia, who had narrowly taken the Wenchi West constituency.[112] 'Moderate' nationalism had been obviously outgunned by the appeal of CPP's radical nationalism.

In November 1954 the National Liberation Movement, an Asante-led coalition which eventually advocated a federal solution to the Gold Coast's communal and ideological pluralism, emerged from the ashes of the opposition after the 1954 election. Amongst other thrusts, its complex and sometimes internally contradictory ideology sought to repair some of the damage done to chieftaincy by electoral reform and other legislation since 1951. It was within the NLM that the lingering tradition of the UGCC in Akyem Abuakwa led by J.B. Danquah, Willie Ofori Atta and the Okyenhene was to find a new if temporary home. In the last colonial general election, that of 1956, the interests of the royal family and the broader anti-CPP tradition were still strong. Although they were to win no seats in the five Akyem Abuakwa constituencies contested at that election, the NLM managed to poll 13,419 votes as against the CPP's 19,932. Interestingly this was a better showing than the NLM managed anywhere else in the other 39 seats in southern Ghana where they secured only 19,647 votes as against the CPP's 159,092 votes. But neither Danquah nor Willie Ofori Atta were to be members of the Legislative Assembly which took Ghana into Independence.

After March 1957 and in an independent Ghana, Danquah and Willie Ofori Atta were to be stalwarts of the new incarnation of the UGCC/NLM – the United Party. Post-independence legislation[113] outlawed parties which espoused regional or ethnic organising prin-

---

110   Bourne to Arden-Clarke, 19 December 1955, PRO CO 554/806.
111   CO memorandum to British delegation to the UN, 26 August 1954, PRO 554/1058.
112   By 3,765 to the 3,754 votes polled by his CPP adversary.
113   The Avoidance of Discrimination Act of December 1957.

ciples, a move designed to hobble the NLM. Danquah was to be the UP's candidate against Nkrumah in the presidential election of 1960. In that controversial contest[114] Danquah secured only 10.9 percent of the votes against Nkrumah's 89.1 percent. Worse was to follow so far as the Ofori Panin stool was concerned: Danquah along with over fifty members of the United Party were detained in October 1961 to be released only in June 1962. By the end of 1963 Danquah was again detained and he was tragically to die, still in detention, in Nsawam jail in 1964.[115] Danquah's failure in the presidential contest of 1960 was to be echoed in 1979 when 'Paa' Willie Ofori Atta stood as unsuccessfully as his uncle had done in the presidential election.

Akyem Abuakwa seemed destined to be on the losing side in Ghanaian politics. Its rulers in particular were cast as dissident and were never to recapture the dominant position enjoyed by Nana Ofori Atta I. Nana Ofori Atta II was removed from office by the CPP in 1958. This followed the setting up of a Commission of Inquiry[116] into the affairs of the Akyem Abuakwa State Council between 1954 and 1957. This fate was shared by a large number of anti-CPP rulers, especially in Asante. In Ofori Atta II's stead a more compliant candidate, who ruled under the stool name of Amoako Atta IV, was installed with, it must be said, some local support. The fall of Nkrumah and his CPP government in February 1966 saw the reinstallation of Ofori Atta II.[117]

But despite the re-emergence of the now ageing if always ebullient Willie Ofori Atta in the hectic politics of the late 1970s, Akyem Abuakwa had suffered greatly from its role in oppositional politics.[118] The Con-

---

114   The poll was extremely low – 54 percent; only 1,140,699 voted in the presidential contest. Austin concluded that 'the CPP almost certainly manipulated the voting'; *Politics in Ghana*, pp. 394–5.

115   In terrible circumstances. In an interview in August 1991 Ako Adjei, who was imprisoned on the same corridor, recalled Danquah's acute breathing difficulties before his death and the prison officials' reluctance to summon medical help for the dying man.

116   On 16 October 1957.

117   Who was to reign until his death in 1973.

118   In the Presidential elections of November 1992, Akyem Abuakwa appeared to repeat what had become by then a local tradition. It voted against the national trend but in a way which suggested that Akyemfo continued to inhabit a house divided. In these elections the man who had in effect ruled Ghana for over a decade, J.J. Rawlings, received 2,305,966 (58%) votes whilst his opponents netted 1,669, 931 votes and 42% of the poll. J.J. Rawlings took 151 constituencies, his opponents only 48. Amongst those constituencies was Abuakwa where Rawlings received just over 42% of the vote and his major opponent, Professor A. Adu Boahen just over 54%. See *Report of the Commonwealth Observer Group. Interim Statement on Ghana Presidential Election.* Commonwealth Secretariat News Release no 92/41. 4th November, 1992.

vention People's Party government was the last of the Ghanaian big spenders. Its generosity to its friends and clients, based increasingly on borrowed money, did not extend to Akyem Abuakwa for obvious reasons. By the time the CPP fell, Ghana was well advanced on its economic decline and less and less patrimony was available in the form of development funding for its regions. Akyem Abuakwa had definitively missed out on the good times and these seem unlikely to reappear.

But Akyem Abuakwa has not buckled under the strain. In 1991 the Head of State, Flight Lieutenant J.J. Rawlings, formally visited Kyebi. The occasion was the celebration, from 5 to 13 January 1991, of the Odwira festival by the present Okyenhene, Osagyefo Kuntunkununku II. It was the first celebration of Odwira for a decade.[119] It recaptured the great days of Kyebi, for not only did the State President arrive by helicopter, but he was also accompanied by the Zimbabwean Head of State, Robert Mugabe. Kyebi was again in the public eye. Akyem Abuakwa and other Ghanaians were reminded of the state's great history; and Akyemfo enjoyed that. But it also reminded Akyemfo of grimmer elements of that history. During that festival the Okyenhene leaves the palace and, on his way to the sacred rites at the River Birim, he is symbolically reminded of his humanity by the populace lightly striking him with sticks.[120] On this occasion many Akyemfo felt that the youngmen of the Amantoo Mmiensa towns went 'too far' by lashing out quite violently at their king. More importantly perhaps, most Akyemfo had no doubt about why the Amantoo Mmiensa youngmen got out of hand in this way. Nearly fifty years after the Odikro's disappearance, memories linger on.

While the decline of Kyebi and its great ruling house was, like most great tragedies, the result of many other, smaller intersecting tragedies, the death of Nana Sir Ofori Atta and the murder of Akyea Mensah are central events in an understanding of this painful decline and fall. But the impact of all this was not confined to central southern Ghana. The tragic backwash of tragic events shook the trees in Accra and London and played no small part in the more intimate history of nationalism in Ghana.

Historians take risks when they pose 'What if . . . ?' questions. But

---

119   The cost of this elaborate and wonderful festival and the relative penury of the stool had been responsible for this entirely untraditional gap in what is supposed to be a yearly celebration. CPP legislation which has never been repealed effectively confiscates all but a minute proportion of what had constituted stool revenue.

120   On his return, his kingship reasserted, he strikes the populace.

it is probable that had the sequence of events which this book has examined not happened, the political history of the Gold Coast in the 1940s and early 1950s might have been very different. Had Danquah and his Kinsmen not been so thoroughly alienated by this affair, would they have formed the United Gold Coast Convention? If that had not occurred, when and under what circumstances would Kwame Nkrumah have returned to the Gold Coast? But such speculation is idle. We can more safely say that these events are a period piece. The interwoven quality of the international, national and local owed much to the transforming and transformed nature of colonial rule during and after the Second World War. Nana Sir Ofori Atta's death coincided with, and possibly made more simple, the gradual discarding of the alliance with 'natural rulers' by a colonial authority increasingly more interested in economic development than the more limited project of law and order. That created some of the space for the generation of what has been called 'mass nationalism'; accordingly royalty and royal families were to be subjected to the growing indifference of the colonial power and the hostility of the *menu peuple*, a not insignificant element of radical nationalism in the Gold Coast.

The murder served to underline both of these hostile positions. At a time when they were beginning to despair of indirect rule, the British were satisfied that the events showed in stark relief the volatile fragility of 'traditional rule' and its inherently unprogressive qualities. For ordinary people in Ghana, their ears ringing with the modernising rhetoric of the CPP, the Kyebi murder seemed to confirm that party's insistence on the 'feudalism' of chieftaincy. It is no coincidence that these events straddle the transition from the 'old' Gold Coast, dominated by a governmental preference for 'indirect rule', to the 'new' democratic Ghana based upon economic development, centralisation and popular participation. The murder both contributed to that change and, at the same time, was emblematic of it.

Select Bibliography

As will be clear from the footnotes, I have tried wherever possible to rely on contemporary records. The most important archival collections proved to be the holdings in the British Public Record Office (PRO) at Kew, the National Archives of Ghana (NAG) in Accra and the Akyem Abuakwa State Archives (AASA) in the Ofori Panin Fie, Kyebi, Ghana. The following list refers only to secondary works consulted and found useful during my research and does not pretend to be a bibliography on Ghana or even southern Ghana in this period.

Addo-Fening, R. 'Asante Refugees in Akyem Abuakwa 1875–1912', *Transactions of the Historical Society of Ghana*, xiv, 1973.
Addo-Fening, R. 'The Pax Brittanica and Akyem Abuakwa *c*.1874–1904', *Universitas*, 3.3, 1974.
Addo-Fening, R. 'The Deportation of Kwabena Atwere: An Episode in Abuakwa-Kotoku Relations', *Journal of the Faculty of Social Sciences (Legon)*, 4.1, 1974.
Addo-Fening, R. 'The Asamankese Dispute, 1919–1934', in P. Jenkins (ed.), *Akyem Abuakwa and the Politics of the Inter-War Period in Ghana* (Basel, 1975).
Addo-Fening, R. 'The Gyadam Episode, 1824–1870', *Universitas*, 6.1, 1977.
Addo-Fening, R. 'The "Akim" or "Achim" in 17th and 18th Century Historical Contexts; Who Were They?', in *Research Review (NS)*, 4.2, 1988.
Aidoo, K.O. *Of Men and Ghosts* (Tema, 1991).
Akuffo, S.B. *Ahenfie Adesua*, Accra, n.d.
Akyem Abuakwa, *Programme: Final Funeral Rites of the Late Osagyefo Ofori Atta III* (Accra, 1978).
Akyem Abuakwa (Presbyterian Church), *Mfee ohe afahye kwaebibirem, 1861–1961* [*The Akyem Abuakwa Presbyterian Church's Centenary History*] (Accra, n.d.).
Arhin, K. *West African Traders in Ghana in the Nineteenth and Twentieth Centuries* (London, 1979).
Arhin, K. *Traditional Rule in Ghana* (Accra, 1985).
Ariès, P. *Western Attitudes Toward Death* (Baltimore, 1974).
Attobrah, K. *The Kings of Akyem Abuakwa and the Ninety Nine Years Was Against Asante* (Tema, 1976).
Austin, D. *Politics in Ghana* (London, 1964).
Bing, G. *Reap the Whirlwind* (London, 1968).
Black, J. *The Aesthetics of Murder* (Baltimore, 1991).
Bloch, M. and Parry, J. (eds.), *Death and the Regeneration of Life* (Cambridge, 1982).
Bohannen, P. (ed.), *African Homicide and Suicide*. (New York, 1967).
Burns, A. *Colonial Civil Servant* (London, 1949).
Chin, S.-P. 'Gold Coast Delegations in Britain in 1934', in *National Chengchi University Studies in African Affairs*, no. 2, 1970.
Christaller, J.G. *A Dictionary of the Asante and Fanti Language called Tschi* (Basel, 1881).
Crakye Denteh, A. 'Ancient Burial Rituals of the Akan', *Sankofa* I, 1975.
Danquah, J.B. *Gold Coast Akan Laws and Customs* (London, 1928).

Danquah, J.B. *An Objectified History of Akyem Abuakwa* (Accra, n.d.).

Danquah, J.B. *Okanni bai* (Kyebi, n.d.).

Danquah, J.B. *The Akan Doctrine of God* (London, 1944).

Danquah, J.B. *Akim Abuakwa Handbook* (London, 1928).

Dolphyne, F.A. *The Akan (Twi-Fante) Language* (Accra, 1988).

de Heusch, L. *Sacrifice in Africa* (Manchester, 1985).

Edsman, B. *Lawyers in Gold Coast Politics: c.1900–1945* (Uppsala, 1979).

Fiddes, G.V. *The Dominions and Colonial Offices* (London, 1926).

Field, M.J. *Akim Kotoku: an Oman of the Gold Coast* (London, 1948).

Ginzburg, C. *Clues, Myths and the Historical Method* (Baltimore, 1989).

Goody, J. *Death, Property and the Ancestors: a Study of the Mortuary Customs of the LoDagaa of West Africa* (London, 1962).

Gyekye, K. *An Essay on African Philosophical Thought, the Asante Conceptual Scheme* (Cambridge, 1987).

Hagan, K. *Okyeame 1970* (Accra, 1970).

Hill, P. *The Gold Coast Cocoa Farmer* (London, 1956).

Hill, P. *Migrant Cocoa Farmers of Southern Ghana* (Cambridge, 1963).

Holmes, A.B. 'Economic and Political Organizations in the Gold Coast, 1920–1945' Unpublished Ph.D thesis (University of Chicago, 1972).

Huntington, R. and Metcalf P. *Celebrations of death: The Anthropology of Mortuary Rituals* (Cambridge, 1979).

Hsia, R.P-C. *The Myth of Ritual Murder* (New Haven, 1988).

Jeary, J.H. 'Trial by jury and trial with the aid of assessors in the superior courts of West Africa', in *Journal of African Law*, IV, 1960 and V, 1961.

Jenkins, P. (ed.), *Akyem Abuakwa and the politics of the inter-war period in Ghana* (Basel, 1975).

Jenkins, P. (ed.), 'Abstracts of the Basel Mission's Gold Coast Correspondence'; in progress.

Kullas, H. and Ayer, G.A. *What the Elders of Ashanti say* (Kumasi, 1967).

McCaskie, T. 'Anti-witchcraft Cults in Asante: An Essay in the Social History of an African People', in *History in Africa*, VIII, 1981.

McCaskie, T. 'State and Society, Marriage and Adultery: Some Considerations towards a Social History of Pre-colonial Asante', in *Journal of African History*, XIII, 1981.

McCaskie, T. 'Accumulation, Wealth and Belief in Asante History, i. To the Close of the Nineteenth Century', *Africa*, LII, 1982.

McCaskie, T. 'Accumulation, Wealth and Belief in Asante History, ii. The Twentieth Century', *Africa*, LVI, 1986.

McCaskie, T. 'R.S. Rattray and the Construction of Asante History; an Appraisal', *History in Africa*, X, 1983.

McCaskie, T. 'Death and the Asantehene: a Historical Meditation', *Journal of African History*, 30, 1989.

Macleod, M.D. *The Asante* (London, 1981).

Nkrumah, K. *Ghana: the Autobiography of Kwame Nkrumah* (London, 1957).

Nuamah, A. *An Account of the Kibi Ritual Murder Case*, Accra, 1985.

Nana Ofori Atta II, *Odwira Festival* (Accra, 1949).

Ofori Atta, F. 'The Amantoo Mmiensa in the Political and Administrative Set-up of Akyem Abuakwa', unpublished BA dissertation (University of Ghana, Legon, 1978).

Ofori Atta, W. *Ghana; a Nation in Crisis* (Accra, 1988).

Opoku, A.A. *Mpanyinsen* (Accra, 1969).

Perbi, A. 'The Abolition of Domestic Slavery by Britain; Asante's Dilemma, *The Legon Journal of the Humanities*, 6, 1992.

Rathbone, R. 'Parties' Socio-economic Bases and Regional Differentiation in the Rate of Change in Ghana', in *Transfer and Transformation in the New Commonwealth* (Leicester, 1983).

Rathbone, R. 'A Murder in the Colonial Gold Coast; Law and Politics in the 1940s', in *Journal of African History*, 30, 1989.

Rathbone, R. *Ghana*, 2 vols., 'British Documents on the End of Empire' series (London, 1992).

Rathbone, R. 'Political Intelligence and Policing in Ghana in the Late 1940s and 1950s', in *Policing and Decolonisation: Nationalism, Politics and the Police, 1917–65* (Manchester, 1992).

Rathbone, R. 'Politics and Murder; a West African Case', *Boston University African Studies Center Working Papers*, no. 164 (Boston, 1992).

Rattray, R.S. *Ashanti* (Oxford, 1923).

Rattray, R.S. *Religion and Art in Ashanti* (London, 1927).

Rhodie, S. 'The Gold Coast Aborigines Abroad', in *Journal of African History*, VI. 3, 1965.

Sarpei, J. 'A Note on Coastal Elite Contact with Rural Discontent before the First World War: the "Good templars" in Akyem Abuakwa', in P. Jenkins (ed.), *Akyem Abuakwa and the Politics of the Inter-war Period in Ghana* (Basel, 1975).

Sarpong, P.K. *The Sacred Stools of the Akan* (Accra, 1971).

Sarpong, P.K. *Ghana in Restrospect* (Accra, 1974).

Sarpong, P.K. *The Ceremonial Horns of the Ashanti* (Accra, 1990).

Schildkrout, E. (ed.), *The Golden Stool: Studies of the Asante Center and Periphery* (New York, 1987).

Schleifer, R. *Rhetoric and Death* (Urbana, 1990).

Shaw, J.K. 'Akim Abuakwa', *Gold Coast Review*, 1, 1925 and 2, 1926.

Simensen, J. 'Rural Mass Action in the Context of Anti-colonial Protest: the Asafo Movement of Akyem Abuakwa, Ghana', *Canadian Journal of African Studies*, 1, 1974.

Simensen, J. 'Commoners, Chiefs and Colonial Government. British Policy and Local Politics in Akim Abuakwa, Ghana, under Colonial Rule, unpublished Ph.D thesis (University of Trondheim, 1975).

Simensen, J. 'Nationalism from Below – the Akyem Abuakwa Example', in P. Jenkins (ed.), *Akyem Abuakwa and the Politics of the Inter-war Period in Ghana* (Basel, 1975).

Simensen, J. 'Crisis in Akyem Abuakwa: the Native Administration Revenue Measure of 1932', in P. Jenkins (ed.), *Akyem Abuakwa and the Politics of the Inter-war Period in Ghana* (Basel, 1975).

Simpson, K. *Forensic Medicine* (London, 1988; 9th edition).

Swinfen, D.B. *Imperial Appeal: the debate on the appeal to the Privy Council, 1833–1986* (Manchester, 1987).

Swithenbank, M. *Ashanti Fetish Houses* (Accra, 1969).

Warren, D. *The Akan of Ghana* (Accra, 1986).

Wilks, I. *Asante in the 19th Century* (Cambridge, 1975).

Wilks, I. 'The State of the Akan and the Akan States; a discursion', *Cahiers d'Études Africaines*, XIII. 3 and 4, 1982.

Wilks, I. 'Human Sacrifice or Capital Punishment? A Rejoinder', in *International Journal of African Historical studies*, XXI, 1988.

Williams, C. 'Asante: Human Sacrifice or Capital Punishment? An assessment of the period 1807–1874', in *International Journal of African Historical Studies*, XXI, 1988.

Index